W9-AAA-710

BRETT FOR MVP!

Last season George Brett appeared in left field in a game against the Milwaukee Brewers. It was the first time he had played in the outfield since 1983. After the game, he had this to say (as reported in USA Today, July 21, 1989):

"That's for all the Rotisserie League guys," the Royals first baseman said. "Now if they have another first baseman, they can get him in the lineup and use me in left. My goal is to get behind the plate for one inning so they can get points out of me as a catcher, too. I was a catcher until I was a sophomore in high school."

ROTISSERIE LEAGUE BASEBALL®

1990 Edition

Edited by
Glen Waggoner and Robert Sklar
Introduction by Daniel Okrent

The Rotisserie League
Lee Eisenberg • Rob Fleder • Peter Gethers
Daniel Okrent • Michael Pollet • Cary Schneider
Robert Sklar • Cork Smith • Harry Stein
Glen Waggoner • Steve Wulf

A
BANTAM
TRADE
PAPERBACK

BANTAM BOOKS
NEW YORK • TORONTO • LONDON • SYDNEY • AUCKLAND

ROTISSERIE LEAGUE BASEBALL®

A Bantam Book / March 1984
Bantam Second Edition / April 1987
Bantam Third Edition / March 1989
Bantam Fourth Edition / March 1990

Produced by Ink Projects.

Rotisserie League Baseball is a registered trademark of The Rotisserie League
Baseball Association, Inc. Registered in the U.S. Patent and Trademark Office
and elsewhere.
All rights reserved.
Copyright © 1984, 1987, 1989, 1990 by The Rotisserie League.
Official Constitution of The Rotisserie League © 1980, 1984 by The Rotisserie League.
Cover design copyright © 1990 by Rich Rossiter.
No part of this book may be reproduced or transmitted in any form or by
any means, electronic or mechanical, including photocopying, recording, or
by any information storage and retrieval system, without permission in writing
from the publisher.
For information address: Bantam Books.

Library of Congress Cataloging-in-Publication Data
Rotisserie League baseball.

   1. Rotisserie League Baseball (Game)   I. Waggoner,
Glen.   II. Sklar, Robert.   III. Eisenberg, Lee, 1946–
IV. Rotisserie League.
GV867.3.R67   1987   794   86-47880
ISBN 0-553-34825-6

Published simultaneously in the United States and Canada

Bantam Books are published by Bantam Books, a division of Bantam Doubleday
Dell Publishing Group, Inc. Its trademark, consisting of the words "Bantam
Books" and the portrayal of a rooster, is Registered in U.S. Patent and Trade-
mark Office and in other countries. Marca Registrada. Bantam Books, 666 Fifth
Avenue, New York, New York 10103.

PRINTED IN THE UNITED STATES OF AMERICA

CW   0 9 8 7 6 5 4 3 2 1

ROTISSERIE
LEAGUE
BASEBALL®

Contents

Introduction

===

A ROTISSERIE
DECADE

The Year George Foster Wasn't Worth $36

(In honor of the tenth anniversary of Rotisserie Baseball, an annotated version of our Declaration of the Rights of Rotisserians) by Daniel Okrent

Ten years ago this April, the first-ever Rotisserie League auction draft was held in the plush Park Avenue dining room of our present commissioner, Corlies M. Smith. A year later, the following description of our first season appeared in Inside Sports *magazine. When the first edition of this book was published in 1984, a slightly updated version of that epochal piece was included as the volume's introduction. This year, we called on Beloved Founder and Former Commissioner-for-Life, Daniel Okrent, and asked him to annotate that introduction from the perspective of this jubilee year. The original essay appears in regular type; Okrent's 1990 comments are in boldface.*

Was George Foster worth bags of money? He'd bashed the horsehide so hard for so long that you knew he wasn't coming cheap. He'd been an MVP, he'd nabbed homer and ribby crowns, he'd won pennants for the Reds. And it was 1980; he hadn't yet become a Met. (**This opening paragraph reveals the infantile fantasy that can overcome a Rotisserie League owner. The very fact that I asked the question—that I wondered whether Foster might be worth the money—demonstrated my loosening grip on reality. Of course Foster wouldn't be worth the money: as a**

Fenokee, he was ipso facto doomed to failure. As Fenokees, Babe Ruth would've decided to hit singles, Lou Gehrig would have become Chris Brown, George Bush would have lost to Pee Wee Dukakis.)

But, I asked myself, sitting alone in the dark night of the soul that only my fellow general managers could recognize, could Foster do it for the Okrent Fenokees? Could George's hefty Louisville Slugger carry our team—we already had Garry Templeton shining bright at short, Burt Hooton on the mound, Bruce Sutter on call in the Fenokee pen—over the top? Pennants are not won by the faint of heart or the tight of pocket, so I opened the vault and bought George. A championship was in reach. (**Here we have a virtual clinical case study of Rotisserie delusion. Every Rotisserie owner believes a championship is in reach. Even Cork Smith, back when he ran the woeful Smith Coronas, believed a championship was in reach. What we now know is that Rotisserie delusion is induced by alpha rays emitted from an AT&T-owned transmitter located in Hopatcong, New Jersey. The rays, which are picked up in dental fillings, produce a benign sense of optimism, which in turn translates into enthusiasm, which finally manifests itself in the urge to call 900-226-STAT seven or eight times a day to find out if Curtis Wilkerson got an RBI.**

(**There's also the matter of Garry Templeton. Garry Templeton! Should anyone who thought Garry Templeton would remain an offensive force be allowed to show his face in public?**)

If only, that is. Looking back on that dismaying 1980 season, I remember most vividly the June evening when George's thigh gave way and how he limped through the long summer. Who could have known this would happen? Or that Dennis Bleeping Lamp would throw more gopher balls than strikes? Or that no amount of relief pitching could help my club, bereft of power, leaden on the bases, suspect in the rotation? (**Lemme tell you about "suspect in the rotation." Here are the names of those men who once ascended the mound in Fenokee mauve-and-fuchsia, and who also showed up for last winter's Fenokee Alumni Association Reunion and Mah Jongg Tournament: Silvio Martinez, Steve Fireovid, Marty Decker, Dickie Noles, Roy Thomas, Mike Madden, Eddie Buddy Joe King Solomon, John Urrea and Chris Seaman were invited, but had to decline because of a demonstration they were doing for the American Urological Society.**)

Yeah, I know a GM can't be held responsible for injuries, or sudden reversals of form, or the unpredictable flowering of the other guy's rookies. But when I finally admitted no flag would flutter over Fenokee Park in October, my excuses were as rain checks in my mouth. Worse, we finished behind the sorry Fleder Mice, the woeful Pollet Burros, even the ragtag Smith Coronas, who passed us in August, smirking with glee. It was a dreadful season, eighth in the ten-team Rotisserie League. (Who knew from dreadful? In 1985, fresh off a fabulously successful sixth place finish the year before, the Fenokees came home last, with 20.5 points. Rotisserie points in a ten-team league are sort of like the SAT—the best you can do is 80 points, the worst 10. A 20.5-point season is the precise equivalent of 290 on the SATs, which is why such a performance is called "pulling a Chris Washburn." Except Rotisserians are not well enough placed to get Jim Valvano to take our tests for us.)

The origins of the Rotisserie League, chronicled in the official league archives in my desk drawer, were inauspicious enough: Six of us gathered on a dreary January day at La Rotisserie Francaise, a restaurant on Manhattan's East Side, now defunct. Later there would be eleven—a few editors, a few writers, a lawyer, a college professor, a university administrator, and a couple of people out of the advertising business. All of us had a firm belief that we could do what Al Campanis could do—or John McHale, or Paul Owens. Hadn't we been appraising talent all of our lives? I mean, being a GM was easy. (There are three matters worth commenting upon in this paragraph. First, our choice of restaurants. What if we had gone instead to The Quilted Giraffe? Can you imagine asking a friend, "How's your Quilted team doing?" Or to Peter Luger's: "Are you still playing with your Peter lineup?" Or Twenty-One: "Have you drafted your Twenty-One Twenty-Three?"

(Second, occupations. The university administrator Glen Waggoner saw his life degenerate to the point that he became an unemployed hack writer, and one of the ad biz types (Valerie Salembier) was appointed publisher of *TV Guide* and fired seventeen minutes later. The lawyer, Michael Pollet, had better luck— the New York State Board of Bar Examiners still hasn't caught on to the fact that he got his law degree from the same school that gave Al Sharpton his divinity degree.

(Finally, the GMs I cited as our models, particularly Al Campanis. "All of us had a firm belief that we could do what Al Campanis could do." Indeed, many of us have, making public fools of ourselves at every opportunity.)

One could say we merely wanted to raise the ineluctable movements of generations enthralled by baseball to another, higher plateau. Assembling a collection of baseball cards, playing two-man stoopball while doing an eight-year-old's version of a play-by-play, proposing trades to hypercritical radio talk-show hosts—what were all of these preadolescent endeavors but preparation for the Rotisserie League? It wasn't enough to watch baseball, or to study it in the box scores and leaders lists: we all wished, in some way, to possess it, to control it. Lacking twenty million bucks, membership in the right country clubs, and a pair of plaid pants, I was clearly never going to own a major league club unless I invented my own major league. **(A critical thought, that last one. Imagine saying, "I was clearly never going to own a Ford Escort unless I invented the assembly line." I mean, am I weird, or what?)**

It was film historian and critic Bob Sklar, now a tenured professor at a bona fide institution of higher learning, who, with a couple of other eggheads, had laid the groundwork for the Rotisserie League years before, in Ann Arbor, Michigan. Using "imaginary" money (whatever the hell *that* is), Sklar and a few sociologists and historians selected various major league players at the beginning of each season, and their performance—batting average for hitters, ERA for pitchers—determined the winner, who got a blue ribbon, or something. **(Little to comment upon here—the pathetic nature of Sklar's endeavor was apparent even then in 1981.)**

With tedious stories of these wonderful times repeated to me over the years (Sklar had been a teacher of mine at the University of Michigan, my parents actually paying hard-earned tuition dollars so that I could receive Official Wisdom from some nut who picked players for a nonbetting contest), I had long sought a way to improve on the Assistant Professors League, or whatever it was called. Last year, I found the answer. True, Sklar had laid the seed, but his game was to the Rotisserie League as rounders is to the 1927 Yankees. **(Let's pause a moment to get a sense of time. In 1981, as these words were written, Sklar's league was already in the distant past. If I was an adult (chronologically, at least) when I recalled those Ann Arbor days, and if Sklar was old enough to have been a teacher of mine in the '60s, what does that make him two decades later? A miracle of modern science, that's what! The Dorian Gray of Rotisserie! A man old enough to be dead already for years! But Bob Sklar has found the secret to eternal life—Italian clothes. The guy's underpants are Italian, fer chrissakes. He thinks Sir Francis Drake defeated the Spanish Armani! On February 14 he celebrates St. Valentino's Day! His favorite manager was Joe Altobelli! He used to think the Reds' catcher was named Gianni Bench!)**

Our idea was that each of us would assemble a team of 23

National League players—nine pitchers, five outfielders, two catchers, seven infielders. By trading, waiving, and even creatively juggling players on the disabled list, we'd all try for a championship. The pennant would go to the team whose players collected—in real-life baseball—the most home runs, stolen bases, wins, saves, and the like, all solid indices of baseball performance. The prize turned out to be a seedy trophy and a check for $1,662. (**I still think the trophy is seedy, but never having won it I guess I could be accused of sour grapes. An outfit in California is now selling a bronze bust of "Trader Jack" McKeon to be given to league champions, but this seems inappropriate. A more apt choice for league-champion statuary might be Charlie Starkweather, Richard Speck, or some other figure whose sense of proportion matches that of the usual Rotisserie winner.**)

The auction was held in April, on a pleasant Sunday morning. And afternoon. And evening. There being no Marvin Miller to look over our shoulders, we had agreed to a form of price-fixing, prohibiting any one GM/owner from spending more than $260 to assemble a team. That was, we thought, very ownerlike. Bowie would have been proud. But then the Rennie Stennett phenomenon set in. We each had slightly more than $11 to spend, on the average, per player, but the sound of chops being licked filled the room at every drop of a ho-hum name. Would $38 buy enough Gravy Train for Dave Kingman? How about $33 for Bobby Bonds? The wiser among us waited for the fever to subside, and the Sklar Gazers picked up Mike Schmidt for $26. In the waning moments, Bob Welch was acquired for $3. The Getherswag Goners, owned by editor and novelist Peter Gethers and university administrator Glen Waggoner, got Neil Allen, whose 22 saves would win them the pennant, for a lousy two bucks. And to think I spent $36 for George Foster. (**Many have asked who the most expensive players in our league's history have been. Vince Coleman once went for $51, Dale Murphy for $50, and Eric Davis for $48. But spending is relative. Valerie Salembier once owned Ruppert Jones for $16, and then signed him to a four-year contract extension that brought his annual salary to $36. The total outlay due him for those years was $144, and the penalty she paid to release him after one year was $216. And what happened to Valerie, you ask? Amazingly, she and Ruppert were married just last year.**)

Trades? The talk never stopped. The Eisenberg Furriers swapped like rug merchants, dealing a sorry collection of nobodies into a team that led for four months. The conservative Salembier Flambes made not a single deal and nabbed fourth-place money. I

7

took the middle path, nudging my beloved Fenokees this way and that, trading delicately, moderately—and abysmally. On the way to my dismal finish, I even contemplated firing myself. Bruce McCall, of the Collects, did even worse, dealing Omar Moreno to the Goners for Dave Goltz and Elliott Maddox. (You wonder how Goltz got his millions from the Dodgers? Ask my friend Bruce.) When McCall asked to be suspended from making further trades, I, as Commissioner, obliged, announcing the proscription by citing the best interests of baseball and the integrity of the game. (**Consumed by self-loathing, McCall quit the league after that first summer. Salembier, whose loathing was directed at me, hung on for five seasons. Omar Moreno, who merely loathed catching a major league fly ball, retired from baseball and went into the tent-making business with his sister Rita.**)

The game—The Rotisserie League—occupied the lives of all of us that first summer as no mere job or family ever could. "I am possessed by Mike Ivie," said one original Rotisserian, who called the San Francisco Giants' publicity office daily to get the latest on the reluctant slugger's physical and mental health. When Bill Madlock was suspended for duking an umpire, Lee Eisenberg of the Furriers contemplated filing a friend-of-the-court brief with the National League. McCall issued a weekly newspaper about his warriors, spicing it with a Rotisserie gossip column by "C. Nile Hack III" and dotting it with pictures cribbed from sports pages, each airbrushed so Steve Garvey, Johnny Bench, and their teammates appeared to be wearing Collects uniforms. (**The Giants' publicity office, like that of every major league team, was soon flooded by calls from Rotisserians nationwide: Is Atlee Hammaker's shoulder still sore? Will Scott Garrelts return to the rotation next week? Is Matt Williams going to make the team? Where did Roger Craig get his nose? At one of baseball's annual winter meetings, the 26 publicists got together to discuss the Rotisserie calls that were tying up their phone lines. Feeling sorry for them—feeling, in fact, the guilt of the ages—we began to investigate ways to ease their pain. Unable to locate James Earl Jones and Kevin Costner, we instead instituted the first, the genuine, the one and only national Rotisserie Stat Phone and Injury Report. At press time, the number for this extremely convenient, not-too-costly, absolutely essential public service was 900-226-STAT. That's 900-226-STAT. Have it tattooed on your wrist. Call it early, call it often. If you don't want to pay the perfectly reasonable 85 cents for the first minute and 50 cents for each minute thereafter, we offer two simple alternatives: call it from your** employer's phone, or call it from the headquarters of the Republican National Committee.)

As Commissioner and owner, I probably put more energy into this glorious nonsense than any other Rotisserian, although Glen Waggoner repeatedly said, "This is the best thing that ever happened to me," and spent the summer sending away for glossies from big league teams and memorizing Rick Auerbach's birthdate and Johnnie LeMaster's hat size. It was not hard to make rulings on various disputes, even though my interests as owner and Commissioner were in conflict. Invariably, I ruled in my favor. Did Walter O'Malley abstain when the National League voted to transfer the Dodgers westward? And, after all, I was the one who had to put in endless hours each week, compiling and computing our stats from the pages of *The Sporting News*. Of course, until I dropped out of the race and into the Three-Eye League, this was a task of such compelling interest that I didn't wait for the regular Friday mail delivery of the good ol' Bible. Instead, I'd drive twenty miles each week to a newsstand that got the paper on Thursday. (**Lest you think the comment on the paragraph before this one was an unseemly and atypical advertisement, I'll offer another one. Who wants to rely on antiquated stats from *TSN*? Who wants to punch a calculator all day long after *USA Today* publishes the weekly numbers? Who wants to patronize one of our unlicensed competitors, who never invented the game that has changed your life? The one, the only, the official Rotisserie League Baseball Association still conducts the best stat service in the business; for information, call Marketing Director and Official Batboy John Hassan at 212-691-7846. Or, for leagues that pay the measly, $50 annual membership fee to belong to the RLBA, we provide impartial Commissioner service—dispute settlement, rules interpretations, Yoo-Hoo locator service. Batboy Hassan, whose adoration of Glen Waggoner is so extreme he has given up a promising career in spinach maintenance to devote himself to the great man, now staffs league headquarters full-time. If you have a question and he's not around, he'll get back to you quicker than a Rick Reuschel fastball. Can 6,000 satisfied leagues be wrong? Call now, and we'll name a tree after you in the Rotisserie League National Shrine and Forest in Worthington, Massachusetts!**)

We had a good pennant race in 1980. When Ellis Valentine's jaw was shattered by a rising fastball, so were the Furriers' hopes for a championship. The Gazers never quite recovered from Ivie's walkabout, the Flambes from J.R. Richard's tragedy. The Goners, who played the waiver wire like a harp, who assembled a Tekulve-Allen-

Sambito bullpen, who purloined Moreno from the Collects, grabbed the flag, the trophy, and fifty percent of the kitty. (**Ivie, Richard, Tekulve, Sambito, Moreno. O tempora, o tzuris!**)

It was not until after the World Series in "other" baseball— we stopped calling it "real" baseball about an hour and a half into the total absorption of Rotisserie life—that we gathered to pour the ceremonial bottle of Yoo-Hoo over the heads of the victorious Waggoner and Gethers. It was a solemn moment, a consecration of our summer of fellowship. Then we started to argue over rules changes, to propose obscene trades to our competitors, and, finally, to divide up the prize money—owners to the core. (**If you're wondering what happened to the Waggoner-Gethers partnership, it met its end during an extraordinary and unprecedented piece of surgery conducted at St. Luke's Hospital in New York in the 1983-84 off-season. Previously joined to each other for the full length of their bodies, they were separated by the extraordinary surgical skill of Dr. Bobby Brown, assisted by Dr. George Medich, Dr. Ron Taylor, and Doc Gooden. However, miscalculation led to Waggoner being left with both torsos, and Gethers with the two noses.**)

So it has been for three summers since. We have sharpened our baseball wits, expanded rosters, developed farm systems, welcomed new leagues to Rotisserie baseball, fine-tuned our rules, and seen new management come to three franchises. The charm of baseball, though, is its slowness to change. Before the 1983 season I signed George Foster to another contract, this one just shy of the maximum twenty percent cut allowed under major league rules. Perhaps if he's hungry, I reasoned, he'll respond to the challenge. He didn't, but his teammates did. The Fenokees finished third. (**Obviously, ten seasons have now passed, and every year I keep re-signing George Foster. Call me crazy, but I'm a loyal guy.**)

George may not be back with the Swampmen this year, but I will—this time, armed with a pennant-winning strategy named Darryl Strawberry. The way I read the scouting reports, there'll be plenty of power in the draft, and I can trade for speed. The bullpen's okay, but I'm going to need three starters. The Brenners are loaded again, and the Goners and Furriers are always tough. (**To see how the 1984 Fenokees finished, turn to page 78. To learn how they felt about it, read the collected works of Celine.**)

Play ball! (**And call 900-226-STAT!**)

1

GROUND RULES

How to Play the Game

It happens every spring. Someone buys the new edition of this book. Talks to a friend. And before you can say Razor Shines, ten to twelve apparently normal, reasonably intelligent, generally responsible people voluntarily lock themselves in a stuffy room on a pleasant April morning—only to emerge, six hours later, groggy but eyes ablaze, cheeks flushed with passion, all babbling at once, loudly, about needing more speed and being ready to trade relief for power and when do we get the first stats and how did I wind up with Ken Caminiti and Gerald Perry at the corners and. . . .

We know. We've been there. It comes with the (natural) turf of owning a Rotisserie League Baseball team.

A decade has passed since the first band of innocents went blithely into the first draft auction of the first season of what they—we—all thought would be a diverting little game. Poor babies. Little did we know that we were crossing an invisible boundary line, a one-way checkpoint Charlie (Leibrandt? Hayes?), a point of no return into a brave new world filled with clichés that knew no end. And from which no one would ever return.

Would we have done it if we had known then what we know now? That old maxims would be dashed to the ground and lifelong loyalties rent asunder? That Rotisserie League Baseball would rattle our brains, shake our booties, tiddle our winks? That Harry Stein would win three pennants?

No way! What do you think we are, nuts or something? But we *didn't* know what we were doing, so we *did* bid $9 for Gene Richards even though we didn't know his first name, and we *did* embark on a ten-year odyssey into a peculiar world inhabited by Fenokees and Furriers, Burros and Fish, Nations and Gazers and Goners, Fledermice, a Wulfgang, and far, far too many Brenners.

And you know what's even crazier? Upwards of a million people have followed suit. (That's what *USA Today* says, and who are we to argue with so important a scouting tool?)

Chances are, you're one of them—of *us*—already. If so, welcome to the fourth edition of "The Official Rulebook and Complete Guide to Player Values." (Funny—we never noticed before how stiff and starchy collared that sounds. Oh, well. . . .) Resist your temptation to jump straight into the Scouting Report, and spend some time with the Constitution. Yeah, yeah, you're an old veteran and you already know how to play the game. But we did spend some time clearing up ambiguities and resolving contradictions, and there are a few new refinements—so indulge us: have a fresh look at the Constitution and the rules for Rotisserie Ultra. After that, you're on your own.

If you have never played Rotisserie League Baseball before, consider this: you can stop right here, burn this book, and save yourself a lifetime of aggravation—not to mention a small fortune spent calling 900-226-STAT. Understand? This is a warning. We cannot be held responsible if you go beyond this period.

But as you have, here's what you do, rookies and second-year players afraid of the sophomore jinx: Read, then reread, "The Rules, Simplified" that follow; then go back to the "Introduction" by Beloved Founder and Former Commissioner-for-Life of Rotisserie League Baseball, Dan Okrent; now jump ahead (skipping "Have an Ultra Good Day") to the Scouting Report and dip into your favorite league. Now it's time to read the Constitution—slowly. After that, "Ask Dr. Rotisserie" will answer some questions before you ask them; sudden Pete Gethers ("Sacre du Printemps de Choo-Choo") will tell you what you've missed by not learning about Rotisserie League Baseball before now; and the "Media Guide" will bring you up to date on recent Rotissehistory.

Then, after finishing the book any damn way you please (you bought it, you can use it to start a fire in the grill), read the Constitution *one more time*. Now you're ready to join the Rotisserie League Baseball Association (see page 285) . . .

. . . and PLAY BALL!

The Rules, Simplified

Rotisserie League Baseball is complicated. We know. That's what we like about it. You want simple, go flip baseball cards with a ten-year-old. But if you're looking for a baseball experience that's elegantly complex, subtly detailed, and loaded with nuance, then you've come to the right game.

And, hey—the *basics* are as simple as one-two-three strikes, yer OUT!

1. Teams are made up of real, live major league baseball players who are selected at an auction draft that takes place at the beginning of the season (typically on the first weekend following Opening Day).

2. Each team is composed of 23 players taken from the active rosters of National or American League teams. A Rotisserie League drawn from National League players should have ten teams; a Rotisserie League using American League players should have twelve teams. You can, however, have fewer teams.

3. A team consists of five outfielders, two catchers, one second baseman, one shortstop, one middle infielder (either 2b or ss), one first baseman, one third baseman, one corner man (1b or 3b), one utility man (NL) or designated hitter (AL), and nine pitchers.

4. Players are purchased at an open auction. Spending is limited to $260 per team. (If you don't want to use money, call them units or pocorobas or whatever. The point is resource allocation.) Teams may spend less. The first bidder opens the auction with a minimum bid of $1 for any player he chooses. The bidding then proceeds around the room (at minimum increments of $1) until only one bidder is left. The process is repeated, with successive owners introducing players to be bid on, until every team has a complement of 23 players.

5. A player is eligible to be drafted for any position at which he appeared in 20 or more games the preceding year. If he did not appear in 20 games at any one position, he is eligible for the position at which he appeared the most times. Once the season commences, a player qualifies for a position by playing it at least once. Multiple eligibility is okay.

6. Trading is permissible from Auction Draft Day until the last out of the All-Star Game. After every trade, both teams must be whole—that is, they must have the same number of active players at each position that they had before the trade. The transaction fee for trades is $10, payable to the prize pool, regardless of the number of players involved.

7. If a major league player is put on the disabled list, sent to the minors, traded to the other league, or released, he may be replaced by a player selected from the Rotisserie League's free agent pool of unowned talent. The price for calling up such a replacement is $20 until the All-Star break, $40 thereafter. Replacement must be made by position: you cannot replace a disabled catcher with an outfielder, even if the free agent pickings at catcher are slim, unless you have another player on your team who can be moved to the catcher slot. The original player may either be released or placed on his Rotisserie League team's reserve list (for an additional fee of $10). When he is activated by his major league team, a reserved player may be activated by his Rotisserie League team, at which time the replacement player called up in his slot must either be waived or moved to another position where a natural opening exists (and for which he qualifies). A team may not release, reserve, or waive a player without replacing him with another active player.

8. Cumulative team performance is tabulated in four offensive and four pitching categories:

  • Composite batting average (BA)
  • Total home runs (HR)
  • Total runs batted in (RBI)
  • Total stolen bases (SB)
  • Composite earned run average (ERA)
  • Total wins (W)
  • Total saves (S)
  • Composite ratio: bases on balls (BB) + hits (H) ÷ innings pitched (IP)

9. Teams are ranked from first to last in each of the eight categories. For example, in a ten-team league, the first-place team receives ten points, the second-place team nine points, on down to one point for last place. The team with the most points wins the pennant.

10. Prize money is distributed as follows: 50% for first place, 25% for second, 15% for third, and 10% for fourth. Even more important, the owner of the winning team receives a bottle of Yoo-Hoo—poured over his/her head. (See Chapter 9, *Postgame Wrap-Up,* pages 283–289).

Okay, you've got a lot of questions, and two of them get answered right now:

"Do I have to play for money?" No. *We* do, but unlike the big league version, Rotisserie League Baseball can be played for very little money, or none at all. Our stakes require a $350–$450 investment per team, depending on the number of trades and call-ups over the course of a season, but you can play for pennies, Cracker Jacks, or nothing at all and still have fun. Just be sure to keep the ratio of "acquisition units" to players at 260:23 for each team on Auction Draft Day.

"What do I do if it's May 15 and I've just gotten around to reading this book? Wait till next year?" Absolutely not! That's second-division thinking! Put your league together, hold your auction draft, and deduct all stats that accrue prior to that glorious day. Next year, start from scratch.

The rest of your questions are dealt with in the pages that follow. We hope. If not, write us *c/o* **Rotisserie League Baseball Association, 41 Union Square West, Suite 936, New York, NY 10003.** Or call at **(212) 691-7846.** We'll do our best to get you playing what we still modestly call The Greatest Game for Baseball Fans Since Baseball.

Stop!

Complacent veterans of Rotisserie League Baseball may be tempted to skip over a Constitution they think they already know a darned sight better than the one written 200 years ago. Big mistake. Take a look at some mighty important changes made since the Rotisserie League Constitution was ratified in 1984:

- New farm system draft order! (**Article IV**)
- New minimum innings-pitched requirement! (**Article IX**)
- New, definitive tiebreaker! (**Article IX**)
- New anti-dumping rule! (**Article XI**)
- New clarification of reserve list trades! (**Article XII**)
- New waiver regulations! (**Article XIV**)

OFFICIAL CONSTITUTION OF ROTISSERIE LEAGUE BASEBALL

PREAMBLE

We, the People of the Rotisserie League, in order to spin a more perfect Game, drive Justice home, kiss domestic Tranquility good-bye, promote the general Welfare in Tidewater—where it's been tearing up the International League—and secure the Blessings of Puberty to ourselves and those we've left on Base, do ordain and establish this Constitution for Rotisserie League Baseball, and also finish this run-on sentence.

I. OBJECT

To assemble a lineup of 23 National League or American League baseball players whose cumulative statistics during the regular season, compiled and measured by the methods described in these rules, exceed those of all other teams in the League.

II. TEAMS

There are ten teams in a duly constituted Rotisserie League composed of National League players, twelve if composed of American League players.

> **NOTE:** If you choose to play with fewer teams, be sure to make necessary adjustments so that you acquire approximately 80% of all available players at your auction draft. You could have a six-team league using American League players, for example, and draft only from the AL East or AL West (or your seven favorite teams, whatever their division). Unless you reduce the available player pool proportionately to reflect a reduced number of teams, you'll never learn to appreciate the value of a good bench.

> **NOTE:** Do *not* mix the two leagues. Bryant Gumbel does, and he's got a job that requires him to get up at 4:30 in the morning, for Jane Pauley's sake! It's unrealistic and silly, it's

not the way the big leagues do it, it means you end up using only All-Stars and established regulars, and it's fattening.

III. ROSTER

A team's active roster consists of the following players:

1. **NATIONAL LEAGUE PLAYERS**

   Five outfielders, two catchers, one second baseman, one short-stop, one middle infielder (either second baseman or short-stop), one first baseman, one third baseman, one corner man (either first baseman or third baseman), one utility player (who may play any nonpitching position), and nine pitchers.

2. **AMERICAN LEAGUE PLAYERS**

   The same, except that the utility player is replaced by a player who qualifies as a designated hitter. (See **Article V** for rules governing position eligibility.)

IV. AUCTION DRAFT DAY

A **Major League Player Auction** is conducted on the first weekend after Opening Day of the baseball season. Each team must acquire 23 players at a total cost not to exceed $260. A team need not spend the maximum. The League by general agreement determines the order in which teams may nominate players for acquisition. The team bidding first opens with a minimum salary bid of $1 for any eligible player, and the bidding proceeds around the room at minimum increments of $1 until only one bidder is left. That team acquires the player for that amount and announces the roster position the player will fill. The process is repeated, with successive team owners introducing players to be bid on, until every team has a squad of 23 players, by requisite position.

- Don't get hung up on the bidding order; it's irrelevant. Do allow plenty of time; your first draft will take all day.
- Players eligible at more than one position may be shifted during the course of the draft.
- No team may make a bid for a player it cannot afford. For example, a team with $3 left and two openings on its roster is limited to a maximum bid of $2 for one player.
- No team may bid for a player who qualifies only at a position that the team has already filled. For example, a team that has acquired two catchers, and whose utility or

designated hitter slot is occupied, may not enter the bidding for any player who qualifies *only* at catcher.

- Players who commence the season on a major-league team's disabled list *are* eligible to be drafted. If selected, they may be replaced upon completion of the auction draft (see below, **Article XII**, for details).

NOTE: Final 24-man Opening Day rosters for all twelve National League or all fourteen American League teams will be needed on Auction Draft Day. Getting them from the newspapers is a pain, as teams often don't make their final roster moves until the last minute. Even *USA Today*'s rosters, published on Opening Day, have holes. The best way to get the most complete, updated rosters is with membership in the Rotisserie League Baseball Association. (See page 285 for details.)

A Minor League Player Draft is conducted immediately following the major league auction, in which each Rotisserie League team may acquire players who:

(a) are not on any National/American League team's active roster and

(b) still have official rookie status, as defined by major league baseball.

NOTE: The major league rule reads: "A player shall be considered a rookie unless, during a previous season or seasons, he has (a) exceeded 130 at-bats or 50 innings pitched in the major leagues; or (b) accumulated more than 45 days on the active roster of a major league club or clubs during the period of a 24-player limit (excluding time in the military service)."

- Selection takes place in two rounds of a simple draft, not an auction.
- In the first season, the selection order shall be determined by drawing paired numbers from a hat (that is, positions 1 and 20, 2 and 19, and so on in a ten-team league).
- In subsequent years, the selection order is determined by the order in which the teams finished in the previous season. In the National League version, the order of selection is 5th place team, 6th, 7th, 8th, 9th, 10th, 4th, 3rd, 2nd, 1st. In an American League version, the 6th place team selects first, proceeding in descending order to the 12th

place team, which is in turn followed by the 5th, 4th, 3rd, 2nd, and 1st place teams.
- The price and subsequent salary upon activation of each farm-system player drafted is $10.
- See **Article XIII** for operational rules governing farm systems.

NOTE: The order of selection stated above represents a change from previous years, when teams selected in reverse order of the final standings of the preceding season's pennant race. By awarding the first selection to the highest finisher among second-division teams instead of the last place team, we seek to offer an incentive to teams to keep plugging and a disincentive to finish last (i.e., in the past, a last place finish would be "rewarded" with the first farm system draft pick).

V. POSITION ELIGIBILITY

A player may be assigned to any position at which he appeared in 20 or more games in the preceding season. If a player did not appear in 20 games at a single position, he may be drafted only at the position at which he appeared most frequently. The 20-games/most games measure is used only to determine the position(s) at which a player may be drafted. Once the season is under way (but after Auction Draft Day), a player becomes eligible for assignment to any position at which he appears at least once. In American League versions, players selected as DHs must qualify according to these rules. In National League versions, players selected for the utility slot may qualify at any position except pitcher.

NOTE: The best sources for determining player eligibility are the National League's *Green Book* and the American League's *Red Book*. Both list appearances by position under fielding averages. The *Red Book* lists all players who appeared as designated hitters the preceding season. Circulating an eligibility list by position before Auction Draft Day saves a lot of time. Prepare one yourself in March, when the *Green Book* and *Red Book* are published. Or obtain it with membership in the Rotisserie League Baseball Association—our list is available at least three months earlier, so you'll be able to spend the winter doing something worthwhile (see pages 285–286 for details). Spend a few minutes before your auction to settle eligibility questions and assign eligibility to rookies. When in doubt, use common sense—it's one of the Seven Pillars of Rotisserie League Wisdom.

VI. FEES

The Rotisserie League has a schedule of fees covering all player personnel moves. No money passes directly from team to team. No bets are made on the outcome of any game. All fees are payable into the prize pool and are subsequently distributed to the top four (NL) or five (AL) teams in the final standings (see below, **Articles VIII** and **IX**).

1. **BASIC:** The cumulative total of salaries paid for acquisition of a 23-man roster on Auction Draft Day may not exceed $260.

2. **TRANSACTIONS:** $10 per trade (no matter how many players are involved) or player activation (from reserve list or farm system). In a trade, the team that pays the fee is subject to negotiation.

3. **CALL-UP FROM FREE AGENT POOL:** $20 until the All-Star Game, $40 thereafter until season's end.

4. **RESERVE:** $10 for each player placed on a team's reserve list (see **Article XII**).

5. **FARM SYSTEM:** $10 for each player in a team's farm system (see **Article XIII**).

6. **ACTIVATION:** $10 for each player activated from the reserve list or farm system.

7. **WAIVERS:** $10 for each player claimed on waivers (see **Article XIV**).

8. **SEPTEMBER ROSTER EXPANSION:** $50 (see **Article XV**).

VII. PLAYER SALARIES

The salary of a player is determined by the time and means of his acquisition and does not change unless the player becomes a free agent or is signed to a guaranteed long-term contract (see below, **Article XVI**).

- The salary of a player acquired in the major league draft is his auction price.
- The salary of a player called up from the free agent pool during the season is $10 (regardless of his call-up fee).
- The salary of a player activated from a team's farm system during the season is $10.
- The salary of a player claimed on waivers is $10.

• The salary of a player called up during September Roster Expansion as an extra (24th player) is $25 if he is drawn from the free agent pool (see below, **Article XIV**).

NOTE: Because you can commit only $260 for salaries on Auction Draft Day, and because you will keep some of your players from one season to the next, salaries are *very* important, particularly after the first season ends and winter trading begins. Would you trade Jose Canseco for Ellis Burks? Sandy Alderson wouldn't, not even if the Red Sox threw in Fenway Park. But a smart Rotisserie League owner just might make the deal. Jose's salary in Tony's Italian Kitchen League, an officially authorized Rotisserie League using AL players, is a whopping $50, not enough to fix even one speeding ticket but still among the highest in the game. Burks only makes $15, and the $35 difference is enough to buy a Roger Clemens *and* a Dave Valle to catch him.

Maintaining accurate, centralized player-personnel records (i.e., salary and contract status) is *the most important* task of the League Secretary, who deserves hosannas from the other owners for all the work he does.

VIII. PRIZE MONEY

All fees shall be promptly collected and wisely invested by the League Treasurer, who is empowered to subject owners to public humiliation and assess fines as needed to ensure that payments are made to the League in a timely fashion. The interest income from this investment can be used to defray the cost of a gala postseason awards-ceremony and banquet. The principal shall be divided among the first four teams in the final standings as follows:

• First place—50%
• Second place—25%
• Third place—15%
• Fourth place—10%

IX. STANDINGS

The following criteria are used to determine team performance:

• Composite batting average (BA)
• Total home runs (HR)
• Total runs batted in (RBI)

- Total stolen bases (SB)
- Composite earned run average (ERA)
- Total wins (W)
- Total saves (S)
- Composite ratio: bases on balls (BB) + hits (H) ÷ innings pitched (IP)

Teams are ranked from first to last in each of the eight categories and given points for each place. For example, in a ten-team league, the first-place team in a category receives ten points, the second-place team nine, and so on down to one point for last place. The team with the most total points wins the pennant.

> **NOTE:** A team that fails to pitch a total of 1000 innings cannot be ranked ahead of any team that does pitch 1000 innings, in either ERA or Ratio. (This is a new rule, passed in 1988, to prevent an "all-relief" strategy attempted by the Okrent Fenokees in 1987. The strategy was not successful, because Swampmaster Dan Okrent abandoned it after six weeks or so. But it might have worked, in more disciplined hands. Hence the new rule.)

> **NOTE:** Pitchers' offensive stats are *not* counted, mainly because they don't appear weekly in *USA Today* or *The Sporting News*. Nor are the pitching stats of the occasional position player called in to pitch when the score is 16–1 after five innings and the relief corps is hiding under the stands.

- In cases of ties in an individual category, the tied teams are assigned points by totaling points for the rankings at issue and dividing the total by the number of teams tied.
- In cases of ties in total points, final places in the standings are determined by comparing placement of teams in individual categories. Respective performances are calculated and a point given to each team for bettering the other. Should one team total more points than the other, that team is declared the winner.
- Should the point totals still be equal, the tie is broken by adding each team's *total at-bats* at season's end, plus *triple the number of its innings pitched*. The team that scores a higher total by this measure wins the pennant.

> **NOTE:** In the early days of Rotissehistory (1980), the Sklar Gazers and the Eisenberg Furriers finished in a flat-footed tie

for second with fifty-two points each. Only seven categories were employed at that time. (Wins were added in 1981.) The Gazers were ahead in four categories, the Furriers in three, so the Gazers got second place and the bigger check, while the Furriers got heartburn.

X. STATS

The weekly player-performance summaries published in *USA Today* beginning in late April constitute the official data base for the computation of standings in Rotisserie League Baseball.

NOTE: Box scores in daily newspapers are riddled with errors, and official scorers occasionally change rulings. *USA Today* is the final word. When we first started out, we used *The Sporting News.* That was when *TSN* cared more about baseball than about all the Stanley Cup skate-offs, NBA playoffs, and NFL summer camping rolled into one (which, by the way, is how the Rotisserie League's Founding Fathers view them). Not for nothing was the Holy Bible known to baseball people as *The Sporting News* of religion. But that was then, and this is now. *The Sporting News* has passed from the last Spink to new owners who seem intent on taking the "Sporting" part seriously—that is, covering other sports at the expense of baseball. A pity.

• The effective date of any transaction for purposes of statistical calculation is the Monday (AL) or Tuesday (NL) *immediately after* the deadline for reporting transactions to the League Secretary.

NOTE: This is because cumulative weekly stats appear in *USA Today* on Tuesday for AL games through the preceding Sunday and on Wednesday for NL games through the preceding Monday. Reporting deadlines should be established as close to these breaks as possible but not later than the start of any game at the beginning of a new week. We use noon on Monday (Tony's Italian Kitchen/AL players) and 2:00 P.M. on Tuesday (Rotisserie League/NL players). Why the difference? Might as well ask why the strike zones in the two leagues are different.

• Transactions recorded *on* Auction Draft Day, including trades and call-ups to replace disabled players, are effective retroactive to Opening Day. Transactions occurring *after* Auction Draft Day but *before* the closing date of the first cumulative summaries to appear in *USA Today* in April are effective the Monday (AL) or Tuesday (NL) immediately after the first closing date.

- Performance stats of a player shall be assigned to a Rotisserie League team *only* when he is on the active 23-man roster of that team.

NOTE: It is common for a player to appear on the roster of more than one Rotisserie League team during the season because of trades and waiver-list moves. Even a player who is not traded may spend time on a team's reserve list, during which period any numbers he might compile for his major league team do not count for his Rotisserie League team.

- Standings shall be tabulated and issued in a regular and timely fashion, as determined by the League owners.

NOTE: Keeping score (see pages 267–281) is the only part of Rotisserie League Baseball that isn't any fun. It's eight or nine hours of number-crunching for each standings report if you're not computerized, a couple of hours of data entry if you are. It's especially important to have weekly standings during the April-May-June trading period, however, and teams still in the race will want weekly standings as the season draws to an end. So divvy up the workload (if some poor innocent won't volunteer), hire someone to do it for you, or become a member of the Rotisserie League Baseball Association and subscribe to its statistical service (see page 281).

XI. TRADES

From the completion of the auction draft until the final out of the All-Star Game, Rotisserie League teams are free to make trades of any kind without limit, except as stipulated below, *so long as the active rosters of both teams involved in a trade reflect the required position distribution upon completion of the transaction, and so long as the anti-dumping rules outlined below are adhered to*. From the All-Star Game through August 31, trades may take place *only* between teams contiguous in the preceding week's standings. No trades are permitted from September 1 through the end of the season. Trades made from the day after the season ends until rosters are frozen on April 2 prior to Auction Draft Day are *not* bound by the position distribution requirement.

> **NOTE:** This means that if Team A wants to swap Darryl Strawberry to Team B for Orel Hershiser anytime between Auction Draft Day and the trade deadline, Team A will have to throw in a bum pitcher and Team B a duff outfielder to make the deal. During the off-season, the Strawman could be dealt for the Big O even-up.

> - Trades do not affect the salaries or contract status of players.
> - Each trade is subject to the $10 transaction fee. The fee is not affected by the number of players involved in the trade.
> - Unless you want knife fights to break out among owners, prohibit all trades involving cash, "players to be named later," or "future considerations." Trust us.

Anti-Dumping. Players in the last year of a guaranteed contract, or playing out their option year, and players with a salary of $25 or more, are considered "asterisk" players. Such players may be traded only under the following conditions:

> - One team may trade asterisk players to another team provided that for each asterisk player traded, one is received in the same deal.
> - The above notwithstanding, a team may trade *one* asterisk player to another team without an asterisk player coming in return, but may only make *one* such trade in the course of the season. (In the 1989 edition of this book, we permitted one such trade *with each team* in the course of the season. This year, after consulting with veteran leagues, we're tightening the restriction on asterisk trades even further.)
> - Between the end of the season and Roster Freeze Day, asterisk players may be traded without restriction whatsoever.

> **NOTE:** "Dumping" is the inelegant but scientifically precise term used to describe what happens when a team out of contention gives up on the season and trades to a contending team its most expensive talent and its players who will be lost to free agency at the end of the year, typically for inexpensive players who can be kept the following season. A "dumping" trade is always unbalanced, sometimes egregiously so, with the contending team giving up far less than it gets, and the noncontending team giving up much more in order to acquire

a nucleus for the following season. While this strategy makes sense for both clubs, extreme cases can undermine the results of the auction draft, which should always be the primary indicator of an owner's ability to put together a successful team. What the new anti-dumping rule outlined above is intended to accomplish is to restrict the most extreme forms of dumping, while at the same time permitting a noncontending team to rebuild for the future.

XII. THE RESERVE LIST

A team may replace any player on its 23-man roster who is

- placed on the **disabled list**,
- **released**,
- **traded** to the other league, or
- **sent down** to the minors by his major league team.

To replace such a player, a Rotisserie League team must first release him outright or place him on its reserve list. A team reserves a player by notifying the League Secretary and paying the $10 transaction fee. A reserved player is removed from a team's active roster at the end of the stat week (on Monday or Tuesday) —when formal notification is given—and placed on the team's reserve list. There is no limit to the number of players a team may have on its reserve list. Reserving a player protects a team's rights to that player.

A team has two weeks to take action once a player is placed on the disabled list, released, traded to the other league, or sent to the minors by his major league team. If no action is taken, the position is frozen open until the original player's return, and no replacement may be made.

- *A suspended player may not be reserved, released, or replaced.*

NOTE: When we first wrote that, we were thinking about the old-fashioned things players might do to get themselves suspended—Bill Madlock hitting an umpire (1980), say, or Gaylord Perry throwing a spitter (1962 to 1983), although he was suspended for doing it only once (1982). Then came the drug suspensions of 1984 and afterwards. We have decided to consider players suspended for substance abuse as if they were on the disabled list, and allow teams to replace them.

- Once a specific action has been taken to remove a player from its 23-man roster (via release or placing him on the reserve list), a team is then free to select any eligible player from the free agent pool of players not already owned by another Rotisserie League team. The salary assigned to a player so selected from the free agent pool is $10; the call-up fee is determined by the time of the season in which the call-up is made (see above, **Article VI**).
- If the same player is claimed by more than one team in a given week, he goes to the team ranking lowest in the most recent standings.
- Every reserve move must be accompanied by a concomitant replacement move (i.e., a team may not reserve a player without replacing him).
- Placing a player *on* the reserve list and activating a player *from* the reserve list are *each* subject to a $10 transaction fee.
- The call-up takes effect as soon as it is recorded by the League Secretary, although the player's stats do not begin to accrue to his new team until Monday (AL) or Tuesday (NL) of the week the League Secretary records the call-up.
- A player on a Rotisserie League reserve list may not be traded *unless* the replacement player linked to him is also traded. Thus, a team might trade Andre Dawson (on reserve) and Curt Ford (called up to replace him) for Brett Butler.
- A replacement player may be traded or otherwise replaced (e.g., in case of injury, he could be reserved and a free agent called up to fill his slot). In such a case, the newly acquired player becomes linked to the original reserved player.
- When a player on a reserve list returns to active major league duty, he must be **reinstated** to the active 23-man roster of his Rotisserie League team *two weeks* after his activation or be **waived**. Failure to notify the League Secretary shall be considered a waiver of the player on the reserve list. A player may not be **reinstated** or **waived** until he has been activated by his major league team.

NOTE: Intended to prevent stockpiling of players, this rule is tricky to monitor. Daily newspaper transaction columns and telephone sports-information lines are unreliable about reporting major-league roster moves. The clock starts ticking when the League Secretary *is made aware of* a player being reactivated. By the way, "two weeks" means two full reporting periods and may actually be as much as two weeks plus six days (as in the case of a player being reactivated the day after a reporting deadline). In fairness, and because this is not full-contact karate but a game played among friends, an owner should be given warning by the league secretary that time is up and he will lose a player if he doesn't make a move. Especially if there are extenuating circumstances (i.e., anything from being away on vacation in Australia to just plain laziness.)

- When a player is reinstated to the active 23-man Rotisserie League roster from a team's reserve list, the player originally called up to replace him must be waived, unless the replacement player *or* the original player can be shifted to another natural opening on the roster for which he qualifies.
- If the replacement player has himself been replaced (e.g., he is injured, put on reserve, and a free agent is called up), then *his* replacement becomes linked to the original player on the reserve list.
- A player reinstated from the reserve list may not displace any active player on the Rotisserie League team's 23-man roster *other than* his original replacement (or his successor).

NOTE: The intent of all this is to minimize the benefit a team might derive from an injury. Say Wally Joyner is injured and you call up Terry Francona to replace him. Joyner comes back. What you'd like to do is activate Joyner, keep Francona, and waive your other corner man, Bill Pecota, who hasn't had an at-bat in six weeks. Our rules say you can't, on the premise that *a team is not ordinarily helped by an injury to a key player*. We know the big leagues don't handle it this way, but art doesn't always imitate life. Without some restriction, an owner might never have to pay the price for his bad judgment in drafting Veal Pecota in the first place.

XIII. FARM SYSTEM

If a farm system player is promoted to the active roster of a major league team at any time during the regular season *prior to* September 1 (when major league rosters may expand to 40), his Rotisserie League team has *two weeks* after his promotion to **activate** him (at any position for which he qualifies) *or* **waive** him.

- The fee for activating a player from a team's farm system is $10.
- If a farm system player is activated, the player displaced from the 23-man roster to make room for him must be placed on waivers, *unless* the farm system player can be activated into a natural opening, in which case no waiver is required. **Example:** One of your pitchers is placed on a major league disabled list; you reserve him and activate a pitcher from your farm system who has been called up by his major league team.
- Once brought up from its farm system by a Rotisserie League team, a player may not be returned to it, although he may be placed on a team's reserve list in the event he is returned to the minor leagues by his major league club.
- A farm system player not brought up to a team's 23-man roster during the season of his initial selection may be kept within the farm system in subsequent seasons upon payment of an additional $10 per year, so long as he retains official rookie status and the League Secretary is duly notified on April 1 each year, when rosters are frozen (see also **Article XVII**).
- At no time may a team have more than three players in its farm system.
- A farm system player may be traded during authorized trading periods, subject to prevailing rules governing transactions, as may a team's selection rights in the minor league draft.

NOTE: This means that a team could acquire and exercise as many as three farm system draft picks, providing that it does not exceed the maximum of three players in its farm system at a given time.

XIV. WAIVERS

Under certain conditions, a Rotisserie League player may be placed on waivers.

- When a player on a Rotisserie League team's reserve list is activated by his major league team, either he or the player called up earlier to replace him *must* be placed on waivers (see **Article XII**).
- When a team activates a player from its farm system, except into a natural opening (see **Article XIII**), the player dropped

from the 23-man roster to make room for him *must* be placed on waivers.

- A player no longer on the active roster of his major league team and whose Rotisserie League position is taken by a player activated from the reserve list or farm system may not be placed on waivers but *must* be released outright.

NOTE: This is to prevent a team from picking up a player on waivers merely for the purpose of releasing him and replacing him with a player of higher quality from the free agent pool.

- The waiver period begins at noon on the Monday (AL) or Tuesday (NL) after the League Secretary has been notified that a player has been waived and lasts one week, at the end of which time the player shall become the property of the lowest-ranked team to have claimed him. To make room on its roster, the team acquiring a player on waivers must assign the player to a natural opening or waive a player at the same position played by the newly acquired player.
- Waiver claims take precedence over the replacement of an injured, released, or demoted player. That is, a player on waivers in a given week may be signed by a team with a roster opening at his position only if no other team lower in the standings claims the player on waivers.
- A team may acquire on waivers *no more* than one player in a given week, but there is no limit to the number of players a team may acquire on waivers during the season.
- A player who clears waivers—that is, is not claimed by any team—returns to the free agent pool.
- The fee for acquiring a player on waivers is $10. The salary of a player acquired on waivers shall be $10.
- A player with a guaranteed long-term contract may not be waived during the season. However, he may be released and replaced if he is traded to the "other" league.
- A player may be given his outright release *only* if he is
  (a) unconditionally released,
  (b) placed on the "designated for assignment" list,
  (c) sent to the minors,
  (d) placed on the "disqualified" list,
  (e) traded to the "other" major league, or
  (f) placed on the disabled list

XV. SEPTEMBER ROSTER EXPANSION

If it chooses, a team may expand its roster for the pennant drive by calling up one additional player after September 1 from the free agent pool, its own reserve list, or its own farm system.

- The order of selection for September Roster Expansion is determined by the most recent standings, with the last-place team having first selection, and so on. During this 24-hour period, September Roster Expansion claims take precedence over waiver claims and routine call-ups to replace players who are disabled, released, or traded to the other league by their major league teams. This selection order pertains until midnight, September 2 *only*, after which time a team forfeits its order in the selection process, though *not* its right to make a selection. Selection after midnight, September 2, is on a first-come, first-served basis. Also, after midnight, September 2, waiver claims and routine call-ups to fill natural openings take precedence over September roster expansion claims.
- The performance stats of a player called up during September Roster Expansion start to accrue on the Monday (AL) or Tuesday (NL) after the League Secretary has been notified of the player's selection.
- The fee for expanding the roster in September is $50.
- The salary assigned to a September call-up from the free agent pool is $25. The salary of a September call-up from a team's reserve list or farm system is the salary established at the time he was previously acquired (on Auction Draft Day, or subsequently from the free agent pool, or via waivers).

NOTE: A device for heightening the excitement for contending teams and for sweetening the kitty at their expense, September Roster Expansion will generally not appeal to second-division clubs (who should, however, continue to watch the waiver wire in the hope of acquiring "keepers" for next season at a $10 salary).

XVI. THE OPTION YEAR AND GUARANTEED LONG-TERM CONTRACTS

A player who has been under contract at the same salary during two consecutive seasons and whose service has been uninterrupted (that is, he has not been waived or released, although he may have been traded) must, prior to the freezing of rosters in his third season, be released; signed at the same salary for his option year; or signed to a guaranteed long-term contract.

If **released**, the player returns to the free agent pool and becomes available to the highest bidder at the next auction draft. If signed at the same salary for an **option year**, the player must be released back into the free-agent pool at the end of that season. If signed to a **guaranteed long-term contract**, the player's salary in each year covered by the new contract (which commences with the option year) shall be the sum of his current salary plus $5 for each additional year beyond the option year. In addition, a signing bonus, equal to one half the total value of the long-term contract, but not less than $5, shall also be paid.

> **NOTE:** This rule is intended to prevent blue-chippers, low-priced rookies who blossom into superstars, and undervalued players from being tied up for the duration of their careers by the teams who originally drafted them. It guarantees periodic transfusions of topflight talent for Auction Draft Day and provides rebuilding teams something to rebuild with. And it makes for some interesting decisions at roster-freeze time two years down the pike.

Here's how it works. Let's say you drafted Mark McGwire of the Oakland Athletics for $4 in 1987, a fair price then for an unproven talent who wasn't even in the Opening Day lineup. It's now the spring of 1989 and McGwire, who has become the next Babe Ruth, is entering his option year. Only a Charlie Finley would let him play out his option; only a Calvin Griffith would trade him. You compare McGwire's stats with those of other players at various salary levels, assess your needs, project what's likely to be available in the upcoming draft, cross your fingers against injury—and sign him to a five-year guaranteed contract. McGwire's salary zooms to $24 ($4 plus $5 plus $5 plus $5 plus $5), but he's yours through the 1993 season. His signing bonus, which does not count against your $260 Auction Draft Day limit, is $60 (one half of 5 × $24). If he really *is* the next Babe Ruth, you've got a bargain.

• In determining a player's status, "season" is understood to be a full season or any fraction thereof. Thus, a player called up from the free agent pool in the middle of the 1988 season and subsequently retained at the same salary without being released in 1989 (even though he may have been traded) enters his option year in 1990 and must be released, signed at the same salary for an option year, or signed to a long-term contract.

- A team may sign a player to only one long-term contract, at the end of which he becomes a free agent.
- Option-year and long-term contracts are entirely transferable, both in rights and obligations; the trade of a player in no way affects his contract status.
- If, during the course of a long-term contract, a player is traded from the National League to the American League (or vice versa), the contract is rendered null and void. The team that loses the player's services shall be under no further financial obligations.
- In all other cases—specifically *including* sudden loss of effectiveness—a team must honor the terms of a long-term contract, as follows: A player with such a contract *may* be released back into the free agent pool (that is, not protected on a team's roster prior to Auction Draft Day), but a team that chooses to do so must pay into the prize pool, above the $260 Auction Draft Day limit, a sum equal to **twice** the remaining value of the player's contract.

NOTE: This is an escape hatch for the owner who buys a dog but can't stand fleas. It's costly, but it's fair.

XVII. ROSTER PROTECTION

For the first three seasons of the League's existence, each team must retain, from one season to the next, *no fewer than* 7 but *no more than* 15 of the players on its 23-man roster. After three seasons, this minimum requirement is eliminated, the maximum retained. The minimum is removed because, after three seasons, a team might find it impossible to retain a specific minimum because too many players had played out their option.

- The names of players being retained must be recorded with the League Secretary by midnight, April 1. Specific notice must also be made at that time of any guaranteed long-term contract signings and farm system renewals.
- The cumulative salaries of players protected prior to Auction Draft Day are deducted from a team's $260 expenditure limit, and the balance is available for acquisition of the remaining players needed to complete the team's 23-man roster.

- The League Secretary should promptly notify all teams in the league of each team's protected roster, including player salaries, contract status, and amount available to spend on Auction Draft Day.
- Failure to give notice of a guaranteed long-term contract for a player in his option year will result in his being continued for one season at his prior year's salary and then released into the free agent pool. Failure to renew a farm system player's minor league contract will result in his becoming available to all other teams in the subsequent minor league draft.
- A farm system player whose minor league contract is renewed on April 1 and who subsequently makes his major league team's active roster may, at his Rotisserie League owner's option, be added to the protected list of players on Auction Draft Day (and another player dropped, if necessary, to meet the 15-player limit), or he may be dropped and made available in the auction draft. He may not be retained in his Rotisserie League team's farm system.

NOTE: The April 1 roster-protection deadline was originally set to correspond with the end of the major leagues' spring interleague trading period, a rite of spring that no longer exists. We've stuck to April 1 anyway, because it gives us a couple of weeks to fine-tune draft strategies. Until you know whom the other teams are going to keep, you won't know for sure who's going to be available. And until you know how much they will have to spend on Auction Draft Day, you won't be able to complete your own pre-draft budget. So April 1 it is; don't fool with it.

XVIII. SUBSTANCE ABUSE

After one year from the ratification of this article, the manufacture, sale, or transportation of intoxicating liquors within, the importation thereof into, or the exportation thereof from the United States and all territory subject to the jurisdiction thereof for beverage purposes is hereby prohibited.

NOTE: The Rotisserie League is convinced that you have to take a stand somewhere, even if it didn't work so well the first time.

XIX. GOVERNANCE

The Rotisserie League is governed by a Committee of the Whole consisting of all team owners. The Committee of the Whole may designate as many League officials as from time to time it deems appropriate, although only two—the League Secretary and the League Treasurer—ever do any work. The Committee of the Whole also designates annually an Executive Committee composed of three team owners in good standing. The Executive Committee has the authority to interpret playing rules and to handle all necessary and routine League business. All decisions, rulings, and interpretations by the Executive Committee are subject to veto by the Committee of the Whole. Rule changes, pronouncements, and acts of whimsy are determined by majority vote of the Committee of the Whole. The Rotisserie League has three official meetings each year: Auction Draft Day (the first weekend after Opening Day), the Trade Deadline Meeting (at the All-Star break), and the Gala Postseason Banquet and Awards Ceremony. Failure to attend at least two official meetings is punishable by trade to the Detroit Tigers.

XX. YOO-HOO

To consecrate the bond of friendship that unites all Rotisserie League owners in their pursuit of the pennant, to symbolize the eternal verities and values of the Greatest Game for Baseball Fans Since Baseball, and to soak the head of the League champion with a sticky brown substance before colleagues and friends duly assembled, the **Yoo-Hoo Ceremony** is hereby ordained as the culminating event of the baseball season. Each year, at the awards ceremony and banquet, the owner of the championship team shall have a bottle of Yoo-Hoo poured over his or her head by the preceding year's pennant winner. The Yoo-Hoo Ceremony shall be performed with the dignity and solemnity appropriate to the occasion.

> **NOTE:** If Yoo-Hoo, the chocolate-flavored beverage once endorsed by soft-drink connoisseur Yogi Berra, is not available in your part of the country, move.

ON DECK

Okay, so now you have the blueprint for the rest of your life. But before you run out to recruit other owners for your new league, have a gander at the practical tips in the next chapter. Even veteran leagues will find there many helpful suggestions on a variety of nuts-and-bolts matters. Indeed, this brief compendium of concrete, useful information should put to rest forever the commonly held belief that the founders of Rotisserie League baseball are just a bunch of dazzling theoretical geniuses. That's a base canard—and not to be confused, etymologically speaking, with the term "ducks on the pond."

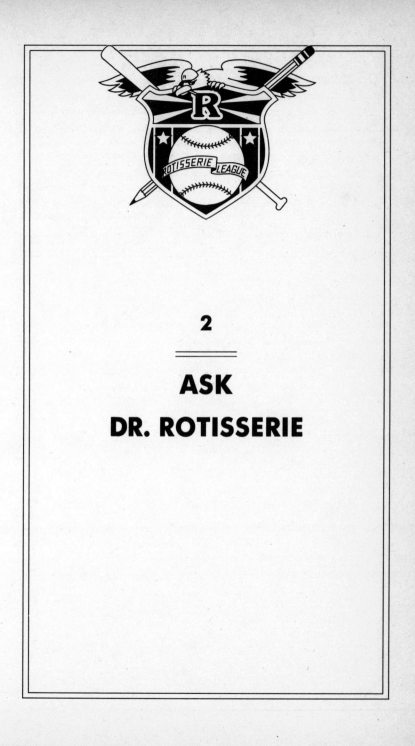

2

ASK
DR. ROTISSERIE

A Little Q and A

with Glen "Iron Horse" Waggoner

People are always running up to me on the street and saying things like, "Hey, you. . . ." Normally, being a New Yorker by adoption, and streetwise to the bottom of my cold, cold heart, I stare straight ahead and keep on walking, my fingers tightening on the sawed-off Louisville Slugger I always carry in a special shoulder holster under my jacket.

But at this time of year I figure to myself, hey, maybe they have a Rotisserie League question. So I lighten up a bit and answer.

Did you guys really invent this thing in a greasy-spoon diner?

No. We invented it in a classy bistro called La Rotisserie Francaise, then located on Manhattan's fashionable East Side. The fact that it closed shortly thereafter is utterly irrelevant.

And never, ever refer to the Greatest Game for Baseball Fans since Baseball as "this thing," or we'll send Harry Stein of the Stein Brenners over to tell you his life story. Halfway through you'll be begging him to break your kneecaps.

Who is Dan Okrent?

He is our Moses, our Muhammad, our Confucius. He is Ben Franklin, James Madison, and Thomas Jefferson all rolled into one. He is the Captain of our Pinafore, the Philosopher-King of our Republic, the olive in our martini. He is Being and Nothingness. He is our Prime Mover, our Uncaused Cause, our pal. He is the Beloved Founder and Former Commissioner-for-Life of Rotisserie League Baseball.

Which means he's the one who'll have to answer if this thing ruins baseball.

Ruin baseball? What are you talking about?

Tell me, Pilgrim, when was the last time you root-root-rooted for the home team? Just as we thought: It was before you started playing Rotisserie League Baseball.

Now the only team you care about is your own, the one you put together so brilliantly with your clever auction draft strategy and your wily trades. Some kind of home team fan you've become. Oh, sure, you're a much more knowledgeable student of the game than you used to be—you follow baseball more closely than you ever could have imagined—you appreciate the game's beauty, subtlety, and soul far more than ever before. You call that being a fan? What's that? You do? Yeah, well, maybe you're right.

What about using players from both major leagues? I hear some people do.

Right, and some people paint their faces blue and go out and howl at the full moon. The problem with mixing leagues is that you end up with only regulars and all-stars on your team. A league of ten 23-man teams drawn from all 624 major leaguers would tap only the top 33% of the available player pool. That's too easy. How would you ever experience the ecstasy of Mark Parent's 5-6 home runs in only 120 or so at-bats if you never had to draft him? Or the agony of seeing Carmen Castillo not turn into the $1 steal you were sure he'd become? In an AL league of 12 teams, you use 276 of 336 available players, or 82%. In a 10-team NL league, you use 230 of 288, or 80%. The result, if you stick to one league, is that you have to scrounge up a decent second-string catcher, decide which utility infielder will get you a few stolen bases, figure out which fourth and fifth outfielders will get more playing time, and pick a middle-inning reliever or two who won't jack up your ERA and Ratio. In other words, you have to dig and sweat and do your homework to put together a solid bench—just like the GMs in the other two big leagues do.

What should I do if I don't know enough baseball fanatics to form a 10-team NL or a 12-team AL Rotisserie League?

Make some new friends. But until you do, scale back the number of major league teams you use to approximate the same team/player pool relationship in a full-sized league. Thus, a six-team AL

Rotisserie League might restrict its draft auction to players on the seven teams in, say, the American League West. So long as you're using up 75-80% of available players in your draft auction, you're on target for the full Rotissexperience.

What is Harry Stein really like?

Harry who? Harry "Three-Time Winner of the Rotisserie League Pennant" Stein? Guy with Groucho Marx eyebrows and Karl Marx *joie de vivre*? Named his son Vince Coleman Stein? Oh, *that* Harry Stein.
    Never heard of him.

What about defense? How come you guys don't use defensive stats?

Because the most revealing defensive stats aren't readily accessible in morning box scores, and the readily accessible ones aren't all that revealing. Anyhow, we *do* take defense into account. We just do it indirectly. Consider: In our scoring categories, we assign stolen bases equal weight to home runs, not because we're loopy enough to think they are that important as an offensive stat, but because they reflect overall team speed. And what does team speed, particularly in the outfield, usually produce? You guessed it: good defense.

How many lawyers can you have in a league?

Never few enough. We have one, although Michael Pollet, General Secretary of the Pollet Burros, could be disbarred any minute. (It's really just a matter of picking up the phone and calling the Bar Association, but who has the time?)
    The Philadelphia Lawyers League, based predictably enough in the tonier suburbs west of Philly, has yet to have its first auction draft, although it was founded in 1984. First one owner gets a temporary restraining order, then another asks for a continuance, and pretty soon it's World Series time. They do have a pretty impressive constitution, though. Long, too.

Our league is expanding from eight teams to ten. We figure we'll just let the two expansion teams start from scratch at the auction draft. What do you think?

Nice, very nice. Not only will you have a huge advantage in experience. You also want Kevin Mitchell at $22 and John Smoltz at $1. Please. Look into your hearts and try to be a little more generous than your major league peers are when *they* expand.

Each holdover team protects seven players. The rest are exposed to an expansion draft. Each expansion team, picking in order determined by lot, may select up to seven players, whose salaries and contract status are carried over to their new teams. No holdover team may lose more than two players. In addition, each expansion team shall receive one additional first-round farm system draft pick, such supplementary picks coming at the end of the first round (order determined by lot).

It's also a good idea to prevent expansion teams from trading for a month or so after they are enfranchised. Lambs were born to be fleeced, but you ought to at least wait until they're haired over.

Can you trade a player who is on your Reserve List?

Next to "What is Harry Stein really like?" this is the question we get asked most frequently. Here's the answer: You may trade a reserved player *and* his replacement for another active player at the same position; you may trade a replacement player for another player, who then becomes linked to the reserved player; but you may *not* trade a reserve list player alone.

Got that? Good.

You guys cost me the pennant. I drafted Mark Langston in my AL Rotisserie League. He was going to win 25 games with a 2.00 ERA—and then he was traded to the NL. Because you don't provide compensation for teams that lose star players, I had to replace him with the best available stiff from the free agent pool, which was Dale Mohorcic. He killed my ERA and Ratio, and I finished seventh. Who's your lawyer? I'm going to sue you.

We don't have a lawyer—only Michael Pollet. So sue us already. You ever draw blood from a turnip?

Look: The reason we don't have a "Compensation Rule" covering players lost to the "other" league is that we've never been able to come up with one that was totally satisfactory. Even worse than losing a player to the other league is the effect of a team's *acquiring* a player like Langston with the call-up salary of $10. But doing anything about *that* is dicey, too. To say that a player so acquired must be released back into the free agent pool the following season removes any incentive to second division teams to fill empty positions with call-ups, *i.e.*, to keep on playing. So we still don't have a Compensation Rule, after all these years.

Some leagues, though, have rushed in where we have feared to tread. One, the River City League (based in Florida, but with members as far away as Chicago), sent us their "Inter-League Trade Rule." We've sent it to our Rules Committee (aka Okrent) for evaluation. As soon as we secure FDA approval, we'll have another announcement to make. Until then, we offer it for your perusal as a public service. As River City Commissioner Sam Northrop says, "It ain't perfect, but it's the best we could come up with."

RIVER CITY INTER-LEAGUE TRADE RULE

A. *One-for-One Trades*. The owner of the player traded away has the option to pick up the player coming into the league at the salary of the player traded away.

B. *One-for-Two Trades*. The owner of the player traded away has the option to pick up either player coming into the league at the salary of the player traded away.

C. *Two-for-One Trades*. The owner of the higher salaried player traded away has the option to pick up the player coming into the league at the salary of *his* player traded away. Second option goes to the owner of the lower salaried player traded away, at that player's salary.

D. All players not acquired under options A, B, and C above are handled under the waiver rule, except that no owner may acquire more than one player in any single trade under the waiver rule.

E. Trades involving more than 3 players, as above, not including minor league players, will be handled under the waiver rule as modified in D above.

F. The salary of any player acquired under D and E above, shall be $10.

G. Integrity by roster position must be maintained.

In September, major league teams stop using the disabled list, even when players are clearly out for the season. Is there a way for a Rotisserie League team to replace an injured player then?

Yes. Appoint a September Review Committee to handle—on a case-by-case basis—all requests to replace an injured player who is not put on the DL in the last month of play. The burden of proof is on the owner, who must present sufficient evidence to convince the committee that his player is definitely out for the season. If, after he is reserved and replaced by this process, a player should by some miracle recover and play again, then the stats of his replacement are thrown out and the original player's are reinstated as if he had never been replaced. Note: Even a single appearance, not necessarily involving a single at-bat, is sufficient to invoke the reinstatement provision.

All this—as you may have surmised—is little more than the application of common sense to address a problem. We're not above that, from time to time.

We're forming a new league and some of the guys think we should do a simple player draft, like football. How come you guys insist on a player auction?

The key words there are "like football." Rotisserie League Baseball is no more like football than poetry is like cold porridge. 'Nuff said.

We insist on a player auction because it's the best possible way to test your ability to evaluate players and assemble a team. It's one thing to say that Don Mattingly is a valuable player; you don't need to be a baseball genius to figure that one right. But how valuable is he if you have $260 to spend and 23 players to buy? $33? $35? $39? Going, going . . . do you bid $40? You get the picture.

If this is your first year, take this on faith: Auction Draft Day is the most exciting day of the year. And it's because of the auction format.

What's the best way to prepare for Auction Draft Day?

Subscribe to *Baseball America* (call 800-845-2726 for information). Start buying *USA Today* as soon as pitchers and catchers report. Move to a town that sells *The National*. Renew *Sports Illustrated*. Pick up *Bill Mazeroski's Baseball* the minute it hits the newsstands. (While you're at it, you might as well get all the other baseball annuals as well, although all of them went to press last fall and none of them contains any fresh news.) Get *Baseball America's* annual *Almanac* (complete player stats for all major and minor leaguers for 1989), the newest *Baseball Register*, the American League's *Red Book*, and the National League's *Green Book*. Order a gross of yellow writing pads for making lists (Sphinx is the brand of preference).

Then quit your job, tell the wife and kids you're going on a little trip, and enter the Federal Witness Protection Program for a minimum of three months, preferably six. (Those with a religious bent may prefer a Trappist monastery, although it may compromise your ability to call 900-226-STAT for daily updates.)

Sound a bit extreme? Maybe, but it worked last season for the Cary Nations.

This is our first auction draft. Can you guys give us some tips on how to run it?

You betcha. Got your pencils ready? Here goes.

1. Persuade someone who is *not* a team owner to run the auction. This is a lot more important than you might think. A team owner has his hands full trying to decide how high to go for Andre Dawson; running the auction on top of that would be a crippling burden. In the Rotisserie League, we depend on the good humor (and even better dining room) of the venerable Cork Smith; in Tony's Italian Kitchen League, the redoubtable Kit Molone runs things with an iron gavel and a velvet manner. Neither, as a consequence, will be available for your auction draft. But you really should get someone.

2. Food is important, because owners get so nervous that they might otherwise start eating their lists. (Plenty of time for that after the auction draft.) Nothing requiring forks and knives, however—you don't want anything around that might be used as a weapon.

3. Figure a first auction draft to last six hours or more. Veteran leagues should be able to get through in four. In either case, allow 3-6 months for convalescence.

4. Settle all dangling eligibility questions before the auction draft commences; once underway, the absolute letter of the law prevails.

5. The auction starts when an owner puts a player up for auction with a minimum bid of $1. In veteran leagues, last season's cellar dweller has the honors. In new leagues, flip a coin. After the first player is bought by the highest bidder, continue around the table in clockwise direction (unless you live south of the equator, in which case it's counter-clockwise). As this is an auction, not a simple draft, the order doesn't really matter.

6. An owner may not "pass" when it comes his turn to put a player up for auction. You'll understand the reason for this when you reach the end game of the auction draft, *i.e.*, when you only have a few positions to fill but not many dollars to spend. Often the only way to get a player you want at that time, when the most you can spend on him may be $2 or even $1, is to bring up some

other player's name—and hope another owner will be sucked into buying him. It's at this stage that you feel your hair turning gray.

7. Stop periodically at the end of a complete round for a money and player check. As a single dollar more or less can mean the difference between getting Junior Felix or settling for Felix Jose, you don't want any mathematical mistakes cropping up. (This is particularly important if you have owners like Sudden Pete Gethers of the Smoked Fish, who has as much affinity for math as he does for roadmaps; see pages 246–247.) In 10 years of play, we've only had one serious foulup. One year the Sklar Gazers spent $10 above the $260 limit because somebody forgot to carry a one. Go figure: Bob Sklar only has a Ph.D. from Harvard!

8. Players who begin the season on a major league disabled list may be bought at the auction draft, at the conclusion of which they may be reserved and replaced. If more than one team wishes to call up a replacement player at the same position from the free agent pool, the order is determined by lot.

9. If you hold your auction draft on the first weekend after Opening Day, as we do, be prepared to call in sick on Monday. Just in case.

10. Be prepared for some wild price variations your first year. The first batch of stars to go in the early rounds will be at startling prices—all in the high $30s and $40s. But at the very end, a lot of very good players will go for $1 or $2 because teams don't have any money left. Knowing this, you'll tell yourself that you'll hold back, conserve your money, and scoop up bargains. You'll tell yourself that, but you won't be able to do it. Nobody is. Might as well tell a bluefish to eat light at the feeding frenzy and save room for dessert.

What is 900-226-STAT?

A magic formula that will answer your every prayer, bring peace and prosperity to the world, and grow hair on a billiard ball.

See page 239 for details.

Where does Rotisserie League Baseball go from here?

That's easy: We take two and hit to right. Hey, who knows. When we first started playing in 1980, we had no idea—**NO** idea—what would happen. Ten years, four books, and upwards of a million Rotisserians later, the game is sweeping the country.

Not even the tiniest hamlet is safe from the Greatest Baseball Game Since Baseball. Clearly it has tapped into something basic shared by all baseball fans: the feeling that, so help me Frank Cashen, if I were running this team, I could do a better job than Lou Gorman. Rotisserie League Baseball lets baseball fans try to do just that—without having to put up $75 million for the privilege.

ILLIGITIMATE MOVES (SIC)

The guys in the Genesee Valley League in Michigan are weird. For one thing, they don't know how to spell "illegitimate"— amazing, as illegitimacy is the keystone of their erratic behavior. But understandable, perhaps, because of a Rotisselifetime spent outside the rule of law. Here's league founder, commissioner, and clubhouse attendant Terry Abernathy.

As you are well aware of from doing our stats, our league probably has more transactions than most. Not fully understanding the intent of the rules, we started out by allowing player movements consistent with those of major league baseball, *i.e.*, if your player isn't performing up to your expectations, ship his ass to the free agent pool. After you explained in more depth to us the intent of your rules, we decided we like it our way better. It was at that moment that the "Illigitimate Move" was born. Initially, we allowed only three such moves per season, but now we have made it a combination of six waiver and illigitimate moves, but no more than four of either. We placed a limit on the "illigitimates" so one team could not Steinbrenner the others and buy a pennant. Our average number of transactions are about 225 per year, which gives us a substantial amount of cash in the pot at the end of the season. When an owner uses up his last "illigitimate" move, the saying in our league is that he has "smoked his last cigarette."

3

HAVE AN *ULTRA*
GOOD DAY!

The Other Game in Town

A year ago the good folks who brought you the Wheel introduced you to Fire. Yep, we're talking about Rotisserie Ultra, now recognized from sea to shining sea as the Greatest Game for Baseball Fans since the Greatest Game for Baseball Fans Since . . . uhh, Baseball.

(Sort of like spelling "banana," isn't it? You don't know for sure when to quit.)

Rotisserie Ultra is not intended for the faint of heart, the weary of spirit, or for Rotisserie Leagues in the first years of their existence. Why, the Sturgeon General himself—Peter Gethers, owner of Peter's Famous Smoked Fish—has warned that playing Rotisserie Ultra too soon can lead to sensory overload, stress-related insomnia, pattern baldness, and premature ejaculation.

But if you've been around the basepaths a few times . . . if you're ready to devote the rest of your waking hours to Rotisseresearch and Player Development . . . and if you're willing to see family and friends only on alternate weekends in months without an "R" (except September) . . . well then, Bucky, Rotisserie Ultra just may be your dream come true.

Inasmuch as many of the rules set forth in the official Constitution (see Chapter 1, *Ground Rules*) also apply to Rotisserie Ultra, we decided not to repeat every footnote, binding rider, and line of fine print that applies to both—unless repeating passages seemed necessary for clarity. Thus, the "Rules of Play" that follow for Rotisserie Ultra should be read together with the original Constitution. If that means buying a second book, go for it. Collectively, they will lead you to Rotisserie Valhalla.*

*Not to be confused with a vacation condo development of the same name we recently opened in downtown Newark. Offering by prospectus only.

ROTISSERIE ULTRA: THE RULES OF PLAY

ULTRA I. THE ROTATION DRAFT

After the conclusion of the auction draft, in which teams acquire their 23-man active rosters for a sum not to exceed $260, owners successively draft up to 17 additional players in 17 separate rounds of selection. Initially, players acquired in this fashion comprise a team's reserve roster.

- Any baseball player is eligible for this draft. *Exception:* In National League versions, no player on the roster or in the minor league organization of an American League team may be selected; and, in American League versions, the opposite is true. Eligible players include (in the NL version, by way of example) previously undrafted NL players, NL-owned minor leaguers, unsigned players, Japanese players, high-school or college players, and the kid down the block with the great arm.

- In the rotation draft, owners are not required to select players by position. They may select all pitchers, all position players, or a mix.

- The order of selection for each of the 17 rounds is determined by the order in which the teams finished in the previous season. In the National League version, the order of selection is 5th place team, 6th, 7th, 8th, 9th, 10th, 4th, 3rd, 2nd, 1st. In the American League version, the 6th place team selects first, proceeding in descending order to the 12th-place team, and is in turn followed by the 5th, 4th, 3rd, 2nd, and 1st-place teams.

NOTE: For leagues switching over from Rotisserie League rules to Rotisserie League Ultra rules, the first two rounds of the rotation draft shall follow the order of the former farm system draft effective at the conclusion of the winter trading period, on Roster Freeze Day. Only players who have rookie status and are not on a major league 24-man roster or disabled list may be selected in these two rounds. This protects the property rights of teams that may have acquired additional farm system draft picks or improved their draft position via trades prior to the shift from Rotisserie League to Rotisserie League Ultra.

ULTRA II. THE RESERVE ROSTER

A team's reserve roster consists of those players acquired through the rotation draft, through trades, through demotions from the active roster, or through waiver claims. Any transaction (e.g., trade, demotion, waiver claim) that increases the size of the reserve roster beyond 17 players must be accompanied by a concomitant transaction (e.g., trade, promotion, waiver) that simultaneously returns the reserve roster to its maximum 17.

ULTRA III. FEES

1. **Basic:** The cumulative total of salaries paid for acquisition of a 23-man active roster on Auction Draft Day may not exceed $260.
2. **Reserve Roster:** There are no fees payable for the acquisition of players for the 17-man reserve roster.
3. **Transactions:** $10 per trade (no matter how many players are involved), per player activation (*from* the reserve roster), and per player demotion (*to* the reserve roster). In a trade, which team pays the fee is open to negotiation between the trading teams.
4. **Waivers:** $10 for each player claimed on waivers.
5. **September Roster Expansion:** $50 for each player added to a team's active roster after September 1.

ULTRA IV. PLAYER SALARIES

The salary of a player is determined by the time and means of his acquisition and does not change unless the player becomes a free agent by means of release or is signed to a guaranteed long-term contract.

- The salary of a player acquired in the auction draft is his auction price.
- The salary of a player acquired in the rotation draft is determined as follows: if the player was selected in the first round, $15; rounds 2–10, $10; rounds 11–15, $5; rounds 16–17, $2.
- The salary of a player claimed on waivers is $10.

ULTRA V. TRADES

From the completion of the rotation draft until noon on the Monday (AL) or Tuesday (NL) on or following August 1, teams are free to make trades of any kind without limit (except as indicated in **ULTRA VI. ANTI-DUMPING**, below). However, at no time can any team have on its active roster more players at a particular position than allowed under the rules of the auction draft (see **Article III** of the Official Constitution of Rotisserie League Baseball, p. 19). A team may, however, be underrepresented at a position. So long as these strictures are adhered to in the immediate wake of a trade, teams may trade any number of players, at any position, irrespective of the number or position of players being received in such trade (except, again, as indicated in **ULTRA VI. ANTI-DUMPING**).

- At no point may a team have more than 17 players on its reserve roster or more than 40 players on its active and reserve rosters combined.
- At no point may a team have more than 23 players on its active roster, except during the September roster-expansion period (see below, **ULTRA X. SEPTEMBER ROSTER EXPANSION**).
- Between August 1 and September 1, trades may only be made between teams that are adjacent to each other in the most recent standings.
- No trades of any kind may be made between September 1 and October 15, nor between April 2 (Roster Freeze Day) and the conclusion of the rotation draft on Auction Draft Day.

ULTRA VI. ANTI-DUMPING

Players in the last year of a guaranteed contract or playing out their option year and players with a salary of $25 or more are considered "asterisk" players. Such players may be traded only under the following conditions:

- One team may trade asterisk players to another team provided that for each asterisk player traded, one is received in the same deal.
- The above notwithstanding, a team may trade *one* asterisk player to another team without an asterisk player coming in return, but may only make *one* such trade with each team in the course of the season.

- Between October 15 and Roster Freeze Day, asterisk players on winter rosters may be traded without restrictions whatsoever.

ULTRA VII. MOVEMENT BETWEEN ACTIVE ROSTER AND RESERVE ROSTER

An owner may demote a player from the active roster to the reserve roster, or promote a player in the reverse direction, at any time and for any reason, such promotions to take effect with the subsequent stat deadline (Monday noon for AL leagues, Tuesday for NL leagues). However, no player may be demoted without being replaced on the active roster by an eligible player—that is, a player who fulfills position eligibility requirements (which may include shifting another active player into the demoted player's position and the promoted player into the shifted player's position) *and* who is currently on a major league roster and not on a major league disabled list.

- **Exception:** If the acquisition of an active player in a trade places the acquiring team's active roster above the positional limit (e.g., more than two catchers), a player at that position may be sent down without the need for the recall of another player.
- Fees for such moves are paid per player: $10 per promotion or demotion.
- A player acquired by trade from another team's active roster is considered active with the acquiring team on the effective date of the trade, unless the acquiring team chooses (or is compelled by roster restrictions) to demote him and pay the appropriate fee. Similarly, a player acquired in trade from another team's reserve roster is considered to be reserved with the acquiring team, unless the acquiring team chooses to promote him and pay the appropriate fee.

ULTRA VIII. SIGNING FREE AGENTS

Active major league players not on any Rotisserie League team's active roster or reserve roster at the conclusion of the auction draft become free agents. During the course of the season the pool of free agents may also include minor league players not on any Rotisserie League team's reserve roster who are promoted to an active major league roster; players traded from the "other" major league; and waived players who are not claimed. Beginning one week after the first standings report, and continuing through the season until the last weekly transaction deadline before September 1, such free agents may be signed, without limit, in the following manner:

- Each team shall have, for the purpose of acquiring free agents during the course of the season, a supplementary budget of $100.
- At the deadline established by each Rotisserie League for recording weekly transactions, a Rotisserie League team may submit a *sealed* bid for one or more free agents.
- The minimum bid shall be $1; the maximum shall be the amount remaining in a team's Free Agent Acquisition Budget ("FAAB").
- A free agent so selected goes to the highest bidder. If more than one team bids the same amount on a player, and if that amount is the highest bid, the player goes to the team that is lowest in the most recently compiled standings.
- The salary of a free agent signed in this manner is his acquisition price. His contract status is that of a first-year player.
- For each free agent that it signs, a team *must* at the same time waive a player at the same position from its *active* roster. (The waived player must also be on an active major league roster at the time; a player on a major league disabled list may not be waived, even if he is on the active roster of his Rotisserie League team.)
- A newly acquired free agent must spend at least one week on his Rotisserie League team's active roster before he is eligible for reassignment to its reserve roster.
- A free agent signed for a salary of $25 or more is deemed to have a limited no-trade clause in his contract, and may not be traded, waived, or released during the current season.

NOTE: The reason for the pre-September 1 deadline is to prevent a Rotisserie League team from completely restocking with $1 players when the major leagues expand their rosters to 40 in September.

NOTE: The mechanics of the "sealed bid" process will vary from league to league. Where practicable, as in leagues that have weekly meetings, the sealed bid should be just that—a bid sealed in an envelope that is opened at the meeting. In other cases, it may be more efficient to recruit a disinterested party to record all bids and report them to the League Secretary for action. Whatever mechanism you devise, keep matters in perspective. These aren't the secrets to nuclear fusion, for Einstein's sake! So try to balance the gee of security with the haw of mutual trust. (And if you don't know what *that* means, ask Catfish Hunter.)

ULTRA IX. WAIVERS

Players are placed on waivers (a) when they cannot be accommodated on a team's active or reserve roster, because of space and/or positional limitations; and (b) under the rules governing the winter roster (see below, **ULTRA XI. WINTER ROSTER**).

- The waiver period commences at noon on the Monday (AL) or Tuesday (NL) immediately following the team's notification of waiver to the league secretary and extends for one full reporting period (i.e., one week). At the conclusion of that week, if the player is unclaimed, he goes into the free agent pool, and may be acquired by a team only as outlined above (see **ULTRA VIII. SIGNING FREE AGENTS**).
- Waiver claims are honored according to the inverse order of the standings effective the week before the close of the waiver period.
- A team may reclaim a player it has waived only if all other teams in the league decline to claim him.
- The fee for acquiring a player on waivers is $10, payable to the league treasurer; that player's prior contract is voided and he is considered to be in his first contract season.
- Only a player currently on a 24-man major league roster (i.e., not on a disabled list) may be claimed on waivers.
- A player traded to the "other" league may not be claimed on waivers.
- A player on a guaranteed long-term contract may not be placed on waivers, even in the final year of his contract.

ULTRA X. SEPTEMBER ROSTER EXPANSION

If it chooses, a team may expand its roster for the pennant drive by promoting from its reserve roster an *unlimited* number of players, as the post-September 1 active-roster size expands to a maximum of 40 players. Such players may play any position.

- September expansions can be effective no earlier than noon on the Monday (AL) or Tuesday (NL) immediately following August 31. Expansions made later in September become effective the subsequent Monday or Tuesday at noon.
- A fee of $50 must be paid for every promotion that increases the active-roster size beyond 23. Player salaries are not affected by such promotions.

ULTRA XI. WINTER ROSTER

Effective October 15, each owner is required to submit to the League Secretary a list of 23 players, irrespective of position, taken from its combined active and reserve rosters, but one not including any players who have concluded their option year or the last year of a guaranteed long-term contract. This group of players becomes the winter roster.

- Immediately after the submission of winter rosters, a waiver period concluding at noon, November 1, begins. By inverse order of the final standings in the season just ended, teams may select no more than one player from that group of players not protected on a winter roster, again with the exception of players who have concluded their option year or the final year of a guaranteed long-term contract. On the claiming of such a player, the claiming team must, in turn, waive a player from its own winter roster. Players thus waived become eligible for a second round of waiver claims, for a period of one week, that are conducted in the same fashion. (Unclaimed players from the first waiver period are no longer eligible.) The winter-waiver process continues until there is a week in which no one is claimed.
- All winter-waiver claims cost the claiming team $10, to be paid into the league treasury for the coming season.
- The salary of a player claimed on winter waivers is $10, and he shall be deemed to be commencing the first year of his new contract with the coming season.
- After October 23, winter rosters may exceed or fall below 23 players through trading action. Whatever size the roster, however, any successful claim of a player on waivers must be accompanied by the placing of another player from the claiming team on waivers.

IT'S FAAB!

Two years ago, in our first, experimental season playing Ultra, we watched in frustration as Tom Brunansky, crossing over from the American League, banged out 22 home runs, knocked in 79 runs, and stole 16 bases. Under original Ultra rules none of us got those numbers. At the time BFFCL Okrent promised to scratch our itch by developing a "midsummer supplementary draft" of unowned players. He didn't, but we came up with something better. It's called the "Free Agent Acquisition Budget," or FAAB; and it works like a charm. Spelled out in detail above (in **ULTRA VIII**), FAAB is a fiendishly clever device for acquiring players traded into one major league from the other or for picking up useful minor leaguers who are promoted after the season starts. And, if you are as crafty as the GM of the Eisenberg Furriers, for rebuilding rather than languishing idly in the second division. Last season the Furriers picked up John Wetteland ($1), José Gonzalez ($1), Terry Mulholland ($3), and Charlie Hayes ($6) via crafty use of FAAB. None is a Mark Langston—he went for $100 to the Fleder Mice—but all could be keepers. Indeed, bottom feeding paid off so handsomely that the club's nomenclature consultant has recommended renaming the team the Eisenberg Carp.

ULTRA XII. ROSTER PROTECTION

Roster protection in Rotisserie League and Rotisserie League Ultra is identical (see **Article XVII** in the Official Constitution), except as follows:

- Players frozen may include players who have spent the entire previous season on a reserve roster—typically because they played only in the minor leagues. Even so, such players who are subsequently frozen are deemed to be in the *second* year of their contract with their Rotisserie League Ultra team.
- The cumulative salaries of frozen players are deducted from a team's $260 expenditure limit in the auction draft, and the balance is available for the acquisition of the remainder of a team's active roster. However, salaries of players frozen on

April 2 who are not on 24-man major league rosters on draft day do not count against the $260 limit. For penalty fines concerning players with guaranteed long-term contracts who are not on 24-man major league rosters (or who are not frozen on April 2), see Constitution **Article XVI**, pages 33–35.

• Frozen players not on 24-man major league rosters count against the limit of 17 players on draft day reserve rosters, and the salaries they carry must be paid into the league treasury on draft day.

4

MEDIA GUIDE

How I (Almost) Finished First in Two Leagues: A Story Gene Mauch Could Have Told
by Robert Sklar

The dream started on a night in June. I walk into a bar. "What'll it be?" says the bartender. "Gimme a Yoo-Hoo," I say. "Make it a double."

That's it. The dream ended there. Night after night, the same. I kept waiting for something more to happen. That I *drink* it? Feh, are you crazy? *For someone to pour it on my head.* That might have meant it was more than a dream, it was an omen. For two weeks in June, both my teams—the Sklar Gazers in the Rotisserie League (National) and the Robert Barons of Tony's Italian Kitchen League (American)—were in first place at the same time.

Among the original Rotisserians with teams in both leagues, no one had ever reached this summit before. Not the Big Shooter, Glen Waggoner. Not Peter "Sudden Pete" Gethers. Not Steve Wulf and Rob Fleder, who shared a Tony's team. There I was, top of the standings. Head of the pack. Yoo-Hoo, my pate awaited!

Well, if I couldn't win both crowns, there was a backstory that was almost as good. Who was my arch-rival in both races? None other than the Shooter himself, mastermind of those sometime juggernauts, the Glenwag Goners in Rotisserie and the Waggoner Wheels in Tony's Italian Kitchen. All through June we were toe-to-toe. One week, I was ahead of him by two points in one league, he led me by three in the other.

Maybe this could be an even better story: The co-editors of *Rotisserie League Baseball* with the best teams in both leagues. I

could imagine the cover blurb for this book: THE GREATEST
BOOK ABOUT THE GREATEST GAME SINCE THE GREAT-
EST GAME, EDITED BY ITS GREATEST PLAYERS. I wanted
Roger Kahn to ghost my autobiography. Waggoner could have
Pete Golenbock.

You can see the Draft Day rosters for my teams and the
Shooter's. Look them over carefully. They make excellent pre-
draft case studies, like at Harvard Business School. Do they look
like potential championship clubs? You're right, they sure as hell
don't. So how did these four teams, the Gazers and the Goners,
the Barons and the Wheels, manage among them to hold down
first place 13 of the first 14 stat report weeks *in both leagues?*

CO-EDITOR CONTENDERS
1989 ROTISSERIE LEAGUE DRAFT DAY ROSTERS

Sklar Gazers	Position	*Glenwag Goners*
Dwight Gooden 21A	p	Tim Belcher 4C
John Franco 43A	p	Jose DeLeon 6C
Craig Lefferts 3A	p	Bryn Smith 1C
Juan Agosto 3D	p	Ed Whitson 1C
Cris Carpenter 3D	p	Joe Boever 27D
Gene Harris 1D	p	Mitch Williams 29D
Tim Crews 1D	p	Derek Lilliquist 1D
Danny Darwin 1D	p	G.W. Harris 1D
Terry Leach 2D	p	Paul Kilgus 3D
Jeff Reed 2D	c	Jody Davis 11D
Barry Lyons 1D	c	Joe Girardi 3D
Eddie Murray 33D	1b	Gerald Perry 14C
Ron Oester 2D	2b	Juan Samuel 25D
Howard Johnson 13A	ss	Andres Thomas 14D
Barry Larkin 17A	3b	Mike Schmidt 24D
Spike Owen 2D	mif	Tim Jones 1D
Darrell Evans 1D	cor	Andres Galarraga 43D
Kevin McReynolds 31A	of	Geronimo Berroa 1D
Barry Bonds 39D	of	Gary Redus 7D
Kevin Mitchell 31D	of	Mike Davis 3D
Luis Salazar 7D	of	Von Hayes 24D
Mickey Hatcher 1D	of	Chris James 14C
Domingo Ramos 5D	util	Tim Teufel 2D

Well, one answer—for the Rotisserie League at least—is that we've finally managed, like the NFL, to legislate parity (you might think that's a synonym for mediocrity, but I didn't say it). By gum, we put some teeth into our anti-dumping rule. In 1988 you could make an unbalanced trade (involving players in their final contract year or with salaries of $25 or more) with *every other team*; in 1989 you could make only one such trade all year.

Since we play by Ultra rules (see Chapter Three), we also plugged a loophole in our first Ultra year that prevented us from picking up free agents, rookie call-ups, and cross-overs from the American League. We established a $100 fund for mid-season

CO-EDITOR CONTENDERS, PART II
1989 TONY'S ITALIAN KITCHEN LEAGUE
DRAFT DAY ROSTERS

Robert Barons	Position	Waggoner Wheels
Bobby Thigpen 26A	p	Dennis Eckersley 11BB
Greg Swindell 16C	p	Jeff Musselman 1A
Jeff Russell 1C	p	Mark Gubicza 12A
Jim Abbott 4D	p	Mike Moore 2A
Tom Gordon 11D	p	Charlie Leibrandt 15C
Eric Plunk 15D	p	Dave LaPoint 5D
Todd Burns 8D	p	Jeff Montgomery 4D
German Gonzalez 1D	p	Juan Berenguer 4D
Tony Castillo 2D	p	Kenny Rogers 1D
Ron Hassey 2D	c	Dave Valle 5A
Mickey Tettleton 6D	c	Mike Stanley 1D
Torey Lovullo 12D	1b	George Brett 31A
Al Newman 1A	2b	Marty Barrett 9C
Walt Weiss 11D	ss	Greg Gagne 7A
Jim Presley 11D	3b	Edgar Martinez 5D
Felix Fermin 4D	mif	Cal Ripken, Jr. 26C
Jim Traber 8D	cor	Gary Gaetti 35C
Mike Greenwell 15A	of	Chet Lemon 5A
Dan Gladden 12A	of	Ellis Burks 15B
George Bell 37A	of	Glenn Braggs 10B
Joe Carter 43D	of	Henry Cotto 1C
Steve Finley 7D	of	Oddibe McDowell 25D
Steve Balboni 7D	dh	Harold Baines 30D

pick-ups, with a bidding system that's explained in the Ultra rules. The Fleder Mice shot the whole $100 on Mark Langston and the Pollet Burros blew their C-note on Sweet Music Viola. These rule adjustments kept all ten teams alert and playing all season long. But I'm getting ahead of my story.

Tony's Italian Kitchen League, under the old Rotisserie rules, still rewards poor judgment. Did I think that German Gonzalez and Tony Castillo were future Guillermo Hernandezes? No, but I couldn't afford better. This league over-prices pitchers. I threw back Allan Anderson, the 1988 ERA leader, because I thought he was too pricey at $15, and he went for $22. So did Don August. Cursed with too much money in the draft, the Charlie Horses spent $29 each on Bob Welch and Charlie Hough.

But Castillo was sent down and Gonzalez went on the DL, and I turned them into Kevin Brown and Jay Tibbs. (I will take credit for having the guts to draft Jim Abbott. Only one other team bid on him.)

Over in the Rotisserie League, there was one other new rule that shaped the fate of the Gazers. Ever since he failed with his masterplan to draft only relief pitchers, Dan Okrent wanted to make sure that no superbrain like Harry Stein could make it succeed. At Okie's behest we passed a rule that your pitchers had to total 1,000 innings for the season; if not, your team fell to last place in both ERA and ratio.

I didn't like the prices pitchers were fetching in the Rotisserie Draft either. With Dwight Gooden, John Franco, and Craig Lefferts as holdovers, I went for the big bang on offense—Kevin Mitchell $31, Eddie Murray $33, Barry Bonds yeeks-$39—until all that was left were bullpen hardtimers like Tim Crews and Terry Leach (I did get Danny Darwin for a buck). Check it out: There I was with one starter, two stoppers, and six moppers. Not a championship staff, and guaranteed to fail the thousand-inning test.

So what did I do? I dealt. With whom? The Big Shooter, of course. You probably heard about it on 900-226-STAT. He waxed so poetic about our trade that it cost me $2.71 to listen to his "analysis." I couldn't even talk back. I needed innings. I gave him—who else?—Kevin Mitchell and change for Ed Whitson and Paul Kilgus. Some may think the Gazers were dragged down by the Okie Fenokee swamp. I prefer to say I got kilgused.

The All-Star Breakdown

"What does the guy do?" moans the Shooter. "Arrives late, makes a trade that guarantees the pennant, and leaves early." We were sitting in Dan Farley's concrete backyard—yes, indeed, a privileged few do have backyards in Manhattan, and his was, in fact, bricked. Ronald Reagan was goofing on the All-Star game telecast, and it was the trading deadline for Tony's Italian Kitchen League. I wish it was all as easy as the Shooter said.

At the end of June the Robert Barons had a 16-point lead over the second place team (no longer the Wheels, who had begun to fade). But it was soft, soft, soft. Though I led in all four pitching categories, for 48 points, ERA and ratio can be volatile, and I was far down in BA and stolen bases. Other contenders were improving rapidly—there was no bar to dumping in this league, and the lower teams were bailing out.

The Kaplan Kangaroos had offered Mike Boddicker and Dwight Evans for Bobby Thigpen and Dan Gladden. It didn't make sense and I turned them down. Then Boddicker pitched five great games in a row and Gladden tore up his hamstring. On Farley's *terrazzo* I was primed to deal. Peter Gethers, whose Rosebuds were fading, made the proverbial offer I couldn't refuse. Gregg Olson 25D, Frank Tanana 10D, Terry Steinbach 1A, and Paul Molitor 12A—for Jeff Russell 1C, Jim Abbott 4D, Mickey Tettleton 6D, Jim Traber 8D. Three great keepers for him, batting average plus speed plus no loss in pitching numbers for my all-or-nothing bid for the crown.

Guaranteed, huh? Steinbach and Molitor went into mid-summer swoons. So did the Orioles, costing Olson his save opportunities, and Tanana couldn't get a win for the Tigers if he pitched a shutout. Then Jay Tibbs went on the DL, followed by Greg Swindell. The Barons had peaked, and the race was tightening.

Over on the Rotisserie side, the story was arms and the men. While I was supposedly locking up a Tony's League pennant, Barry Larkin let my Rotisserie flag escape out the barn door when he hurt his elbow during All-Star warm-ups. This followed by a few days Dwight Gooden's armpit pain that effectively ended his season. No Mitchell, no Larkin, no Gooden. The only thing between the Gazers and the second division was HoJo, HoJo, HoJo.

Dog Days

For the record, the last hurrah of the Double Yoo-Hoo dream came in the last week of July, when the Gazers and the Barons both sat atop the standings together (or separately) for the last time. The lead was a mere half-point over the Goners in Rotisserie, four points in Tony's Kitchen. By the first of August new teams had emerged as front-runners.

In Rotisserie, it was the Cary Nations edging ahead of the Goners and the Gazers. If the Starman has sometimes been called a quiet type, I'm a loudmouth in comparison to League Secretary Cary Schneider. He's crafty rather than showy, unlike his former partner, Harry Stein; and because he's employed, he changes his shirts. He's the kind of guy who dies for the St. Louis Cardinals, but stocks his team with Expos (well, there's a Cardinal or six).

The 1989 Nations were built like their owner, unspectacular but quietly productive. The only Nation having any kind of a major year was Lonnie Smith, the comeback kid. But every day there were Bobby Bonilla, Tim Wallach, Tim Raines, Jose Oquendo, and the likes of Bip Roberts, putting up the numbers for the best all-around offense in the league—first in BA, RBI, and stolen bases. In this balanced season, where even the contenders had major weaknesses (the Goners were running last in BA, the Gazers on the bottom in wins), a bit of excellence seemed enough to tip the balance.

In Tony's League, it was the Blood Brothers who slipped past the Barons into first. Where owners Dave and Terry Bromberg got their team name is a little hard to figure. They have a penchant for obscure names: In another league they called their team the Falkland Islanders, perhaps to honor Margaret Thatcher. Maybe the Blood Brothers name is to honor their distant cousin, Count Dracula of Transylvania. Or it may come from the pact they signed in blood, never to make a trade of equal value with another team.

Harry Stein likes the Brothers because in any popularity contest where they were entered, Harry would never come in last. But you can't fault them for being anything less than serious about the Rotissegame. They start strong, prey on the weak, and get even stronger. Their holdovers from a 1988 third place team included Chris Bosio and Jerry Browne at a buck apiece, and Fred McGriff, Carney Lansford, and Ruben Sierra all at $25 or under. Then they drafted Nick Esasky for, as it turned out, the bargain price of $25.

Nothing like a bunch of career years from your regulars to make your scouting staff look good. Still, they were contenders but not a serious challenge to the leaders until that All-Star evening in Dan Farley's brickyard. That night they picked up Dave Stieb from the ninth-place Solly Manders, and a middle of the pack pitching staff suddenly zoomed forward in wins, ERA, and ratio. For the Manders, the key to the trade was acquiring Dave Clark, whom someone in the Manders front office regards as the next Joey Meyer.

What, you ask, happened to the maestro's Waggoner Wheels? In a word, injuries. Dennis Eckersley went on the DL, George Brett went on the DL, but the loss that made the difference was of Ellis Burks, a potential four-category player. The Wheels dropped almost 20 points from their early season peak. It was this kind of season for the Big Shooter: He took a flyer on Wilson Alvarez, who, you may remember, faced five batters in his single 1989 major league appearance, giving up three hits, two walks, and three earned runs in 0 innings pitched.

September Swan Song

After Labor Day, the Barons threw in the towel. No Yoo-Hoo in Tony's Italian Kitchen. Paul Molitor and George Bell began the equivalent of September salary drives, but Greg Swindell, back from the DL, was ineffective, and Tom (Flash) Gordon, after 16 wins and a shot at Rookie of the Year, came up with a tired arm and terrible numbers. No more a perfect 48 in pitching, I could at least look forward to a solid third-place finish.

The big news in Tony's was the O'Henrys. In mid-September they were just a point behind the Blood Brothers. Where had Henry Horenstein's club come from? Like the Brothers, they had been contenders all along, but out of striking distance from the top. Still, ever since their big trade with the Farley Grangers in mid-June, everyone knew it was only a matter of time before the O'Henrys made their move.

When Dan Farley decided to dump, he laid a brick. Farley had a legitimate first division shot, but he couldn't see himself keeping up with the Barons, Wheels, Blood Brothers, and O'Henrys. (Unlike Steve Wulf of the Wulfmice, who believes baseball seasons last 162 games, and it's best to be patient.) Farley laid on the O'Henrys Bret Saberhagen 23A, Dan Plesac 30C, and Robin Yount 14A, among others, for the likes of Andy Hawkins 4D, Dale Mohorcic 7A, and Ken Griffey, Jr. 10D (a "future"). It took the

O'Henrys a long time, but at least in September the other clubs had someone to root for against the Blood Brothers.

In Rotisserie, it was shaping up as another of those races that would be decided on the last day of the season (as when the Gazers won in 1984 and the Fleder Mice in 1987). Most of the cumulative stat categories were set, but in ratio the Nations, Goners, and Gazers were among five teams bunched between 1.2600 and 1.2787. Swings of three or four points could occur with one good or bad outing. It looked like either the Nations or Goners could take the crown, with the Gazers trying to hold on to third against the late-season surge of that ol' debil Harry Stein, whose Brenners were about to finish in the top four in a "rebuilding" season.

The dream started on a night in September. I walk into a greengrocer's. "What'll it be?" says the greengrocer. "Gimme sour grapes," I say. "Two pounds will do."

All Right Already, Who Won?

You've probably figured out that everything up till now in this chapter was written—because of deadlines—before the season ended. For those who've skipped to the end, to find how the story turns out, I've half a mind to bury the results somewhere in the Scouting report ("Joker defeats Batman," right in the middle of Darryl Strawberry's stats). But since the Final Standings are right next door, I'll tell you how it happened.

With a week to go, the Rotisserace suddenly tightened. Heading into the final weekend, the Cary Nations had 54 points, the Sklar Gazers 52, the Glenwag Goners 51. Then the Nations got great pitching from Dennis Cook, Ken Howell, and, of all people, Dennis Rasmussen (who had gifted the Schneidermen with a 5.75 ERA and a 1.657 ratio up till then), and it was all over. The Nations picked up points in wins and ratio and won going away with 57 points. The Goners also got great pitching (from Tim Belcher, Doug Drabek, and Ron Robinson) and slipped into second.

Let me tell you what happened to the Gazers. The Giants were trailing 2–0 in the ninth inning of the season's last game when Roger Craig decided to give Craig Lefferts a little pre-playoff action. Rusty Lefferts surrendered two hits and the Gazers' chance at second place. Those two hits cost me a point in ratio, by the infinitesimal margin of .00005 (1.26486 to the Nations' 1.26481). That point would have created a tie with the Goners at 52, and I would have won the tie-breaker with a 5–3 lead in categories. Hmmm Babe.

In becoming the second team owner (after, of course, Harry Stein) to win more than one Rotisserie League title, modest Cary Schneider grew emboldened enough to recall that he owned 49 per cent of the 1983 Stein Brenners' juggernaut. Though Schneider may never become a media darling like Stein, let the Rotisserecord show: Stein has 2.51 championships, Schneider 2.49, and the others (except, of course, Dan Okrent and Michael Pollet) have one apiece.

The Tony's Italian Kitchen race turned out even more of a throat-grabber. With a week remaining, the O'Henrys pulled in front by half a point. Then the Blood Brothers passed them in RBIs, reversing the half-point lead. It also came down to the last day. Up in Boston, the O'Henrys' Luis Rivera was standing on first when Dwight Evans stepped to the plate. Dewey had 99 runs batted in and the Sox wanted to give him a shot at 100, so they flashed Rivera (who had had one stolen base all year) the steal sign. He made it. The stolen base gave the O'Henrys the half-point they needed to tie the Blood Brothers for first with 84 points. It also deadlocked the two teams in head-to-head competition in categories, the League's only tie-breaking procedure. For the Blood Brothers, the tie was like biting your sister's neck.

The Robert Barons trailed in third with 72.5 points, comfortably ahead of a close race for fourth. That ended with the Kaplan Kangaroos surging to tie the Wulf Mice at 59 points (they also tied in categories). The once-mighty Waggoner Wheels limped home out of the money with 57 points.

Now, if you *really* want to know the no-holds-barred, down and dirty truth about this astounding season, turn to Chapter Twenty-Seven, "How I finished Third in Two Leagues."

FINAL 1989 ROTISSERIE LEAGUE STANDINGS

1. CARY NATIONS	57.0		6. FLEDER MICE	41.0
2. GLENWAG GONERS	52.0		7. EISENBERG FURRIERS	39.0
3. SKLAR GAZERS	51.0		8. POLLET BURROS	38.0
4. STEIN BRENNERS	49.0		9. WULFGANG	35.0
5. OKRENT FENOKEES	44.0		10. SMOKED FISH	34.0

PITCHING RECORDS

WINS			SAVES		
STEIN BRENNERS	108	10.0	GLENWAG GONERS	67	10.0
FLEDER MICE	91	9.0	SKLAR GAZERS	64	9.0
CARY NATIONS	89	8.0	OKRENT FENOKEES	59	8.0
GLENWAG GONERS	87	7.0	SMOKED FISH	57	7.0
EISENBERG FURRIERS	86	6.0	EISENBERG FURRIERS	54	6.0
POLLET BURROS	83	5.0	POLLET BURROS	43	5.0
OKRENT FENOKEES	76	4.0	CARY NATIONS	35	4.0
WULFGANG	70	3.0	FLEDER MICE	29	3.0
SMOKED FISH	62	2.0	WULFGANG	26	2.0
SKLAR GAZERS	54	1.0	STEIN BRENNERS	14	1.0

ERA			RATIO		
SMOKED FISH	3.1192	10.0	STEIN BRENNERS	1.1804	10.0
STEIN BRENNERS	3.1215	9.0	SMOKED FISH	1.2065	9.0
SKLAR GAZERS	3.2762	8.0	FLEDER MICE	1.2390	8.0
GLENWAG GONERS	3.2911	7.0	CARY NATIONS	1.2648	7.0
OKRENT FENOKEES	3.3266	6.0	SKLAR GAZERS	1.2648	6.0
FLEDER MICE	3.3287	5.0	GLENWAG GONERS	1.2670	5.0
EISENBERG FURRIERS	3.5709	4.0	EISENBERG FURRIERS	1.2724	4.0
CARY NATIONS	3.6304	3.0	OKRENT FENOKEES	1.2807	3.0
POLLET BURROS	3.6670	2.0	WULFGANG	1.3048	2.0
WULFGANG	3.8591	1.0	POLLET BURROS	1.3311	1.0

BATTING RECORDS

BA			HOME RUNS		
CARY NATIONS	.27411	10.0	POLLET BURROS	171	10.0
STEIN BRENNERS	.26508	9.0	SKLAR GAZERS	156	9.0
EISENBERG FURRIERS	.26259	8.0	GLENWAG GONERS	147	8.0
WULFGANG	.26182	7.0	OKRENT FENOKEES	129	7.0
SKLAR GAZERS	.25883	6.0	FLEDER MICE	118	6.0
OKRENT FENOKEES	.25334	5.0	CARY NATIONS	114	5.0
FLEDER MICE	.24982	4.0	EISENBERG FURRIERS	110	4.0
POLLET BURROS	.24820	3.0	WULFGANG	106	3.0
SMOKED FISH	.24483	2.0	SMOKED FISH	91	2.0
GLENWAG GONERS	.24026	1.0	STEIN BRENNERS	79	1.0

RBI			STOLEN BASES		
CARY NATIONS	725	10.0	CARY NATIONS	190	10.0
WULFGANG	709	9.0	GLENWAG GONERS	184	9.0
OKRENT FENOKEES	671	8.0	WULFGANG	165	8.0
SKLAR GAZERS	669	7.0	STEIN BRENNERS	162	7.0
POLLET BURROS	656	6.0	POLLET BURROS	159	6.0
GLENWAG GONERS	621	5.0	SKLAR GAZERS	134	5.0
FLEDER MICE	614	4.0	EISENBERG FURRIERS	125	4.0
EISENBERG FURRIERS	608	3.0	OKRENT FENOKEES	111	3.0
STEIN BRENNERS	494	2.0	FLEDER MICE	109	2.0
SMOKED FISH	437	1.0	SMOKED FISH	81	1.0

FINAL 1989 TONY'S ITALIAN KITCHEN LEAGUE STANDINGS

1. (Tie) BLOOD BROTHERS	84.0		7. NEU BILES	48.5
1. (Tie) O'HENRYS	84.0		8. SOLLY MANDERS	40.0
3. BARONS	72.5		9. FARLEY GRANGERS	39.5
4. (Tie) KAPLAN KANGAROOS	59.0		10. CHARLIE HORSES	27.5
4. (Tie) WULFMICE	59.0		11. GETHERS YE ROSEBUDS	27.0
6. WAGGONER WHEELS	57.0		12. ABEL BAKERS	26.0

PITCHING RECORDS

WINS			SAVES		
O'HENRYS	94	12.0	ROBERT BARONS	78	12.0
BLOOD BROTHERS	88	11.0	WAGGONER WHEELS	72	11.0
KAPLAN KANGAROOS	86	10.0	O'HENRYS	54	10.0
NEU BILES	84	9.0	NEU BILES	50	9.0
WULFMICE	83	8.0	WULFMICE	45	8.0
CHARLIE HORSES	80	6.5	CHARLIE HORSES	44	7.0
ROBERT BARONS	80	6.5	FARLEY GRANGERS	40	6.0
WAGGONER WHEELS	76	5.0	BLOOD BROTHERS	39	5.0
GETHERS YE ROSEBUDS	72	4.0	GETHERS YE ROSEBUDS	36	4.0
SOLLY MANDERS	63	3.0	ABEL BAKERS	31	3.0
FARLEY GRANGERS	59	2.0	KAPLAN KANGAROOS	29	2.0
ABEL BAKERS	57	1.0	SOLLY MANDERS	26	1.0

ERA			RATIO		
ROBERT BARONS	3.3249	12.0	BLOOD BROTHERS	1.2658	12.0
O'HENRYS	3.4117	11.0	ROBERT BARONS	1.2708	11.0
BLOOD BROTHERS	3.5179	10.0	O'HENRYS	1.2778	10.0
WAGGONER WHEELS	3.5828	9.0	WAGGONER WHEELS	1.2967	9.0
NEU BILES	3.6218	8.0	WULFMICE	1.3142	8.0
WULFMICE	3.6826	7.0	NEU BILES	1.3147	7.0
SOLLY MANDERS	3.8405	6.0	FARLEY GRANGERS	1.3289	6.0
KAPLAN KANGAROOS	3.8959	5.0	KAPLAN KANGAROOS	1.3309	5.0
CHARLIE HORSES	3.9158	4.0	SOLLY MANDERS	1.3581	4.0
GETHERS YE ROSEBUDS	4.0685	3.0	CHARLIE HORSES	1.3806	3.0
FARLEY GRANGERS	4.1653	2.0	GETHERS YE ROSEBUDS	1.4238	2.0
ABEL BAKERS	4.7783	1.0	ABEL BAKERS	1.4675	1.0

BATTING RECORDS

BA			HOME RUNS		
SOLLY MANDERS	.27911	12.0	O'HENRYS	182	12.0
BLOOD BROTHERS	.27499	11.0	BLOOD BROTHERS	168	11.0
KAPLAN KANGAROOS	.26954	10.0	ROBERT BARONS	157	10.0
O'HENRYS	.26805	9.0	KAPLAN KANGAROOS	147	9.0
FARLEY GRANGERS	.26760	8.0	WULFMICE	145	8.0
ABEL BAKERS	.26264	7.0	GETHERS YE ROSEBUDS	140	7.0
NEU BILES	.26098	6.0	WAGGONER WHEELS	138	6.0
ROBERT BARONS	.25856	5.0	FARLEY GRANGERS	132	4.5
WAGGONER WHEELS	.25844	4.0	NEU BILES	132	4.5
WULFMICE	.25552	3.0	ABEL BAKERS	112	3.0
GETHERS YE ROSEBUDS	.24841	2.0	CHARLIE HORSES	82	2.0
CHARLIE HORSES	.24675	1.0	SOLLY MANDERS	81	1.0

RBI			STOLEN BASES		
BLOOD BROTHERS	856	12.0	BLOOD BROTHERS	165	12.0
O'HENRYS	852	11.0	SOLLY MANDERS	149	11.0
KAPLAN KANGAROOS	775	10.0	WULFMICE	137	10.0
ROBERT BARONS	743	9.0	O'HENRYS	134	9.0
WAGGONER WHEELS	722	8.0	KAPLAN KANGAROOS	133	8.0
WULFMICE	717	7.0	ROBERT BARONS	132	7.0
ABEL BAKERS	683	6.0	FARLEY GRANGERS	129	6.0
FARLEY GRANGERS	661	5.0	WAGGONER WHEELS	124	5.0
NEU BILES	647	4.0	ABEL BAKERS	116	4.0
GETHERS YE ROSEBUDS	612	3.0	CHARLIE HORSES	97	3.0
SOLLY MANDERS	587	2.0	GETHERS YE ROSEBUDS	76	2.0
CHARLIE HORSES	480	1.0	NEU BILES	70	1.0

The Rotisserie Era
Ten Years That Shook the World

There are some short-sighted historians around who want to call the 1980s the era of some guy who used to broadcast re-creations of Cubs games out in Corn City. Speaking of inventing baseball games, we think we've created a game far beyond the imagination of even a dreamy fellow like young "Dutch." Anyway, his Presidency lasted only from 1981 to early 1989. Rotisserie League baseball launched the decade, and now that we're into 1990 it's bigger than ever. We think future historians will dub the 1980s the Age of Rotisserie.

We brought to the decade not Boeskian greed but a desire to improve the breed—the breed, that is, of baseball fans. We made the box scores and the transaction column more important than the stock tables. We stressed family values, home, and children. Tens of thousands became students of the game at a higher level than they ever thought possible. The 1960s had the sexual revolution, the 1980s the Rotisserie Revolution.

To commemorate our ten glorious years, we're printing a statistical overview of the Original Rotisserie League's first decade— the highs, the lows, the ups, the downs. Each of the ten current franchises (with, in four cases, their previous names and owners noted) is shown with its finishing place and points for every year from 1980 through 1989. As an added bonus for stat freaks, we've appended two cumulative rankings, one based on total points for the decade, the other calculated on the year-by-year standings.

On to the year 2000, and the dawn of the Rotisserie Century!

STEIN BRENNERS
Owner: Harry Stein

Place	Points	Place	Points
1980: Ninth	24*	1985: Sixth	43.5
1981: Seventh	42.5	1986: First	67
1982: Third	58	1987: Sixth	49
1983: First	77.5	1988: First	68
1984: Third	56	1989: Fourth	49

Note: In 1980, this storied franchise was the less storied McCall Collects.

EISENBERG FURRIERS
Owner: Lee Eisenberg

Place	Points	Place	Points
1980: Third(tie)	52	1985: Second(tie)	53
1981: Third	53	1986: Second	60.5
1982: First	63	1987: Fifth	50
1983: Fifth	50	1988: Third	58.5
1984: Eighth	32	1989: Seventh	39

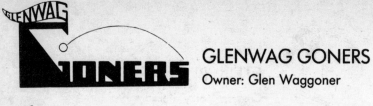

GLENWAG GONERS
Owner: Glen Waggoner

Place	Points		Place	Points
1980: First	55		1985: Fourth	49
1981: Second	57		1986: Eighth	28
1982: Second	58.5		1987: Second	65
1983: Second	57		1988: Ninth	26.5
1984: Second	57.5		1989: Second	52

FLEDER MICE
Owner: Rob Fleder

Place	Points		Place	Points
1980: Sixth	37		1985: Seventh	42
1981: Fourth	51		1986: Eighth(tie)	28
1982: Fourth	49.5		1987: First	66
1983: Fourth	52		1988: Sixth	35
1984: Fifth	46.5		1989: Sixth	41

SKLAR GAZERS
Owner: Robert Sklar

Place	Points	Place	Points
1980: Second(tie)	52	1985: Eighth	39.5
1981: Eighth	37.5	1986: Sixth	39.5
1982: Ninth	32.5	1987: Seventh	39
1983: Ninth	21	1988: Second	62
1984: First	61.5	1989: Third	51

OKRENT FENOKEES
Owner: Dan Okrent

Place	Points	Place	Points
1980: Eighth	27	1985: Tenth	20.5
1981: Fifth	46.5	1986: Fourth	55.5
1982: Fifth	44.5	1987: Third	57
1983: Third	53	1988: Seventh(tie)	27
1984: Sixth	40	1989: Fifth	44

CARY NATIONS
Owner: Cary Schneider

Place	Points	Place	Points
1980: Fourth	43	1985: First	58
1981: Ninth	30.5	1986: Tenth	26
1982: Sixth	43	1987: Eighth	25.5
1983: Sixth	44.5	1988: Fifth	56
1984: Tenth	30*	1989: First	57

Note: From 1980 to 1984, this franchise was owned by Valerie Salembier and known as the Flambés. Valerie now works at the New York Post where she often receives mail simply addressed "Publisher." Harry Stein gets no mail.

POLLET BURROS
Owner: Michael Pollet

Place	Points	Place	Points
1980: Fifth	38	1985: Ninth	33.5
1981: Sixth	43	1986: Fifth	50
1982: Eighth	34	1987: Fourth	54
1983: Eighth	32.5	1988: Tenth	22
1984: Fourth	51	1989: Eighth	38

WULFGANG
Owner: Steve Wulf

Place	Points	Place	Points
1980: Tenth	22*	1985: Fifth	48
1981: First	60	1986: Third	56.5
1982: Seventh	41	1987: Ninth	17
1983: Seventh	34.5	1988: Seventh(tie)	27
1984: Seventh	35	1989: Ninth	35

Note: For our inaugural season only, this team was owned by Tom Guinzburg and known as the Guinz Burghers. Steve's performance the very next year, compared to the next seven, proves an old Rotisserie adage: It's a lot easier to follow a Burgher than a Wulfgang.

SMOKED FISH
Owner: Peter Gethers

Place	Points	Place	Points
1980: Seventh	34	1985: Second	53
1981: Tenth	19	1986: Seventh	29
1982: Tenth	16	1987: Ninth(tie)	17
1983: Tenth	18*	1988: Fourth	58
1984: Ninth	30.5	1989: Tenth	34

Note: This franchise was founded in 1980 by Corlies M. "Cork" Smith and run by him for four years as the Smith Coronas. As everyone knows, Cork is the current Commissioner-for-Life of the Rotisserie League because he finished tenth a lot. Smith's move upstairs allowed Gethers to own his own team, after running what is now the Goners with Glen Waggoner for four years. Even as a child, Sudden Pete didn't like to share.

TOTAL POINTS: 1980–1989

Team Name	Points		Team Name	Points
1. Stein Brenners	534	6.	Okrent Fenokees	415
2. Eisenberg Furriers	511	7.	Cary Nations	413
3. Glenwag Goners	505.5	8.	Pollet Burros	396
4. Fleder Mice	448	9.	Wulfgang	376
5. Sklar Gazers	435	10.	Smoked Fish	308.5

We'd like to look at the last ten years in one other way; that is by assigning ten points for a first place finish down to one point for last, the same way you do for your weekly stat categories. Sort of Rotisserieing Rotisserie. It's an interesting way to look at the last ten years and it's a way for Waggoner to finish first in something.

RANKING BY ORDER OF FINISH: 1980–1989

Team Name	Points		Team Name	Points
1. Glenwag Goners	76	6.	Okrent Fenokees	54
2. Eisenberg Furriers	71	7.	Cary Nations	50
3. Stein Brenners	69	8.	Wulfgang	45
4. Fleder Mice	59	9.	Pollet Burros	40
5. Sklar Gazers	55	10.	Smoked Fish	32

GREAT IDEA!

JEFFREY C. METZGER
A L A W C O R P O R A T I O N

July 18, 1989

Mr. Glen Waggoner
c/o Rotisserie League Baseball Association
211 West 92nd Street
Box 9
New York, NY 10025

Dear Mr. Waggoner:

I am a member of the Orange County (Not So) Big Ten League, a
member of your association. I am writing to let you know of a
charitable act that our league is doing this year.

Before the season started, we read that Don Mattingly was donating
$1,000 to the homeless in New York City for every home run that
he hits this year. We are doing something similar in our league.
For every home run that Mattingly hits, we are donating $45 to
the local shelter for the homeless in Orange County.

We hope that you will publicize what we are doing in hopes that
other Rotisserie players will do something similar either this
year or next year. Since we all enjoy playing Rotisserie baseball,
and we have no hesitancy in paying a significant amount to do so,
we feel that it is only appropriate that we also contribute to
those less fortunate than us.

Very truly yours,

Jeffrey C. Metzger
For the Orange County (Not So) Big Ten League

23151 MOULTON PARKWAY, SUITE 102 • LAGUNA HILLS, CA 92653 • (714) 951-1323 • FAX (714) 588-7271

5

SCOUTING
REPORT

1989 Player Ratings

Rotisserians don't thrive on analytical brilliance and creative genius alone. We're driven by intuition and self-delusion as much as logic and reason. While we claim to operate our teams in the light of knowledge and wisdom, it's in the shadow world of hunches and rumors that our rosters are shaped for submission to the Fates.

We understand your quest for truth, justice, and the American way. That's why we've expanded the statistical information in this book to give you more than a single season snapshot of player performance. You now have information in-depth at your greedy fingertips. Go ahead, figure out the trend lines of careers in development, decline, or resurgence.

But we also know very well that numbers aren't enough to satisfy the darker angels of your nature. That's why we've included our own hunches and rumors to feed that essential craving. So before you begin your race to the pennant or march of folly, you must read this chapter.

A Note About Our Stats

This year our player ratings are preceded by the relevant statistics for the past four seasons. The numbers come from John Dewan, Bob Mecca, and all the gang at STATS, INC. (7250 N. Cicero, Lincolnwood, IL 60646; Telephone 312-676-3322). They handle baseball stats the way Orel Hershiser handles the outside corner. Thanks, STATS-people!

As a special treat, we provide you with an additional line that summarizes those four seasons in "Seasonal Notation." This device, invented by the great Bill James, is a way to express a player's performance over several seasons in a form that is immediately understandable: In essence, it shows what the player does every 162 games.

The wise Rotisserian knows not to take this at face value—seasonal notation does not account for platoon differentials, physical problems, or other reasons why a player does not generally play full time. The wise Rotisserian also knows that there's bound to be two or three schmucks in his league who won't realize this, and really believe that Lloyd McClendon would hit 30 home runs if only he played full time. Do not disabuse them.

Unless Cy Young or Iron Joe McGinnity comes out of retirement, no big league pitcher these days is a threat to log 162 games, so the formula applied to derive seasonal notation for position players is not applicable. For the pitchers rated below, seasonal notation is simply an annual average of numbers posted in the applicable years.

ON THE MOUND

Strange doings indeed. The National League gets Hurst, Langston, and Viola and the American League gets Hawkins, LaPoint, and Moyer. Such inter-league buffoonery keeps playing havoc with the prudent Rotisserian's strategic planning process. As it is, it's tough enough to figure out pitchers in the first place. A staff of Doc Gooden and Danny Jackson sure looked like the nucleus of a pennant winner last spring. On the other hand, teams stuck with Rick Sutcliffe and Scott Garrelts seemed doomed to the nether regions.

But the meaning of your team's pitching goes far beyond its mere place in the standings. It's a test of character. When you have good pitching, you feel pristine and pure—above the tawdry troubles of your peers laboring to keep their ERAs below 3.75. Teams with the best pitching numbers seem to possess the secrets of the universe, their owners capable of developing cold fusion, even. To heck with offense, they say, that's the work of the surly and ignorant, like drag racing and mud wrestling.

So, let us now praise fine young arms. And a few older ones, as well.

On the other hand, a pitching staff that blows up in your face, like the cigar from the joke shop, makes you feel like a gullible fool. "You really believe Tim Leary's for real? Here, let me give you a light, buddy." Bad pitching is unseemly; it's simply not for the genteel Rotisserian.

But how do you know it's Garrelts's season of rebirth and Leary's season of regression? How do you know its Bielecki's time to flourish and Robinson's (Jeff or Don) time to flounder? How do you know that Jack Morris is no longer money in the bank but Bert Blyleven is again? Where is it written? Right here, of course. By the way, we have a fresh cigar for you.

NATIONAL LEAGUE

TIM BELCHER   Age 30/R $13

By early September, he had six shutouts and only a dozen wins. Of course, in 1952, Virgil Trucks had two no-hitters and only *five* wins. We say buy Belcher, who throws hard and has only recently learned how to pitch, and stay away from Trucks, who turns 71 this season.

Year	Team	Lg.	G	IP	H	BB	SO	W	L	ERA	SV	Ratio
1987	Los Angeles	NL	6	34.0	30	7	23	4	2	2.38	0	1.088
1988	Los Angeles	NL	36	179.2	143	51	152	12	6	2.91	4	1.080
1989	Los Angeles	NL	39	230.0	182	80	200	15	12	2.82	1	1.139
Seasonal Notation				147.0	118	46	125	10	7	2.82	2	1.111

ANDY BENES   Age 22/R $8

The real thing, but still a couple of years away from maturity. If you're playing for this year, spend **$6**; if your eyes are on the future, go up to **$10**.

Year	Team	Lg.	G	IP	H	BB	SO	W	L	ERA	SV	Ratio
1989	San Diego	NL	10	66.2	51	31	66	6	3	3.51	0	1.230
Seasonal Notation				66.0	51	31	66	6	3	3.51	0	1.230

MIKE BIELECKI   Age 30/R $7

What's the difference between Bob Milacki and Mike Bielecki? Used to be about a dollar. But four good months in 1989 will wash away four years of contrary evidence. Worth maybe **$5**, but will go higher.

Year	Team	Lg.	G	IP	H	BB	SO	W	L	ERA	SV	Ratio
1986	Pittsburgh	NL	31	148.2	149	83	83	6	11	4.66	0	1.561
1987	Pittsburgh	NL	8	45.2	43	12	25	2	3	4.73	0	1.205
1988	Chicago	NL	19	48.1	55	16	33	2	2	3.35	0	1.469
1989	Chicago	NL	33	212.1	187	81	147	18	7	3.14	0	1.262
Seasonal Notation				113.0	109	48	72	7	6	3.82	0	1.376

TOM BROWNING   Age 29/L $15

There are only two kinds of pitching lines for the Browning Automatic: 9-3-1-0-2-5 or 3-8-6-6-3-1. Happily for the Browning children, the former outnumber the latter.

Year	Team	Lg.	G	IP	H	BB	SO	W	L	ERA	SV	Ratio
1986	Cincinnati	NL	39	243.1	225	70	147	14	13	3.81	0	1.212
1987	Cincinnati	NL	32	183.0	201	61	117	10	13	5.02	0	1.432
1988	Cincinnati	NL	36	250.2	205	64	124	18	5	3.41	0	1.073
1989	Cincinnati	NL	37	249.2	241	64	118	15	12	3.39	0	1.222
Seasonal Notation				231.0	218	65	127	14	11	3.83	0	1.221

JOHN CANDELARIA   Age 36/L $1

The Candy Man finished 1989 as a seldom-used middle reliever for the Expos. Where he goes from there is worth about $1 to find out.

Year	Team	Lg.	G	IP	H	BB	SO	W	L	ERA	SV	Ratio
1986	California	AL	16	91.2	68	26	81	10	2	2.55	0	1.026
1987	California	AL	20	116.2	127	20	74	8	6	4.71	0	1.260
1987	New York	NL	3	12.1	17	3	10	2	0	5.84	0	1.622
1988	New York	AL	25	157.0	150	23	121	13	7	3.38	1	1.102
1989	New York	AL	10	49.0	49	12	37	3	3	5.14	0	1.245
1989	Montreal	NL	12	16.1	17	4	14	0	2	3.31	0	1.286
Seasonal Notation				110.0	107	22	84	9	5	3.82	0	1.165

JIM CLANCY   Age 34/R $1

The Astros thought that Ryan was too old and Clancy was just right.

Year	Team	Lg.	G	IP	H	BB	SO	W	L	ERA	SV	Ratio
1986	Toronto	AL	34	219.1	202	63	126	14	14	3.94	0	1.208
1987	Toronto	AL	37	241.1	234	80	180	15	11	3.54	0	1.301
1988	Toronto	AL	36	196.1	207	47	118	11	13	4.49	1	1.294
1989	Houston	NL	33	147.0	155	66	91	7	14	5.08	0	1.503
Seasonal Notation				200.0	200	64	129	12	13	4.16	0	1.311

MARTY CLARY   Age 29/R $4

He's been bopping around the minors for so long that the Braves didn't even have him on their 40-man roster. But Clary was all but untouchable in AAA early last season, and pretty solid in the bigs later in the year. Think "Tim Leary."

Year	Team	Lg.	G	IP	H	BB	SO	W	L	ERA	SV	Ratio
1987	Atlanta	NL	7	14.2	20	4	7	0	1	6.14	0	1.637
1989	Atlanta	NL	18	108.2	103	31	30	4	3	3.15	0	1.233
Seasonal Notation				61.0	62	18	19	2	2	3.50	0	1.281

DAVID CONE   Age 27/R $13

After his immense 1988 season, this man bragged to reporters that
he had been a great Rotisserie bargain. For his fairly pallid performance in 1989, we put him at $8; for his public recognition of The
Greatest Game for Baseball Fans Since Baseball, we add another
five boccabellas.

Year	Team	Lg.	G	IP	H	BB	SO	W	L	ERA	SV	Ratio
1986	Kansas City	AL	11	22.2	29	13	21	0	0	5.56	0	1.853
1987	New York	NL	21	99.1	87	44	68	5	6	3.71	1	1.319
1988	New York	NL	35	231.1	178	80	213	20	3	2.22	0	1.115
1989	New York	NL	34	219.2	183	74	190	14	8	3.52	0	1.170
Seasonal Notation				143.0	119	53	123	10	4	3.11	0	1.201

DENNIS COOK   Age 27/L $2

After only half a season, the living embodiment of the phrase
"Phillies pitcher."

Year	Team	Lg.	G	IP	H	BB	SO	W	L	ERA	SV	Ratio
1988	San Francisco	NL	4	22.0	9	11	13	2	1	2.86	0	0.909
1989	San Francisco	NL	2	15.0	13	5	9	1	0	1.80	0	1.200
1989	Philadelphia	NL	21	106.0	97	33	58	6	8	3.99	0	1.226
Seasonal Notation				71.0	60	25	40	5	5	3.59	0	1.175

DANNY COX   Age 30/R $5

Whitey pieced together a staff last year without Danny and without Greg Mathews. Now he has to choose between the guys who
used to do it for him and those who are doing it now. We say
Whitey keeps the best major league player born in Northampton,
England, if only to avoid becoming known as a Cox-sacker.

Year	Team	Lg.	G	IP	H	BB	SO	W	L	ERA	SV	Ratio
1986	St. Louis	NL	32	220.0	189	60	108	12	13	2.90	0	1.132
1987	St. Louis	NL	31	199.1	224	71	101	11	9	3.88	0	1.480
1988	St. Louis	NL	13	86.0	89	25	47	3	8	3.98	0	1.326
Seasonal Notation				168.0	167	52	85	9	10	3.47	0	1.302

RON DARLING   Age 29/R $6

Just when he got over his tendency to issue walks, he developed a
tendency to issue hits. Ronnie is on the decline, one of several
candidates to be dropped from the Mets rotation.

Year	Team	Lg.	G	IP	H	BB	SO	W	L	ERA	SV	Ratio
1986	New York	NL	34	237.0	203	81	184	15	6	2.81	0	1.198
1987	New York	NL	32	207.2	183	96	167	12	8	4.29	0	1.344
1988	New York	NL	34	240.2	218	60	161	17	9	3.25	0	1.155
1989	New York	NL	33	217.1	214	70	153	14	14	3.52	0	1.307
Seasonal Notation				225.0	205	77	166	15	9	3.44	0	1.246

JOSE DELEON   Age 29/R $17

Suddenly, a ratio from heaven, a manager who knows how to win games, and still only 29 years old. Whitey's next great pitching star.

Year	Team	Lg.	G	IP	H	BB	SO	W	L	ERA	SV	Ratio
1986	Pittsburgh	NL	9	16.1	17	17	11	1	3	8.27	1	2.082
1986	Chicago	AL	13	79.0	49	42	68	4	5	2.96	0	1.152
1987	Chicago	AL	33	206.0	177	97	153	11	12	4.02	0	1.330
1988	St. Louis	NL	34	225.1	198	86	208	13	10	3.67	0	1.260
1989	St. Louis	NL	36	244.2	173	80	201	16	12	3.05	0	1.034
Seasonal Notation				192.0	154	81	160	11	11	3.59	0	1.214

JIM DESHAIES   Age 29/L $7

Pretty good pitcher.

Year	Team	Lg.	G	IP	H	BB	SO	W	L	ERA	SV	Ratio
1986	Houston	NL	26	144.0	124	59	128	12	5	3.25	0	1.271
1987	Houston	NL	26	152.0	149	57	104	11	6	4.62	0	1.355
1988	Houston	NL	31	207.0	164	72	127	11	14	3.00	0	1.140
1989	Houston	NL	34	225.2	180	79	153	15	10	2.91	0	1.148
Seasonal Notation				182.0	154	67	128	12	9	3.36	0	1.213

KELLY DOWNS   Age 29/R $2

The injury he suffered at the end of the 1988 season appears to be permanently debilitating. A good risk for an Ultra rotation roster, but not worth more than a couple of bucks on your big team.

Year	Team	Lg.	G	IP	H	BB	SO	W	L	ERA	SV	Ratio
1986	San Francisco	NL	14	88.1	78	30	64	4	4	2.75	0	1.223
1987	San Francisco	NL	41	186.0	185	67	137	12	9	3.63	1	1.355
1988	San Francisco	NL	27	168.0	140	47	118	13	9	3.32	0	1.113
1989	San Francisco	NL	18	82.2	82	26	49	4	8	4.79	0	1.307
Seasonal Notation				131.0	121	43	92	8	8	3.57	0	1.248

DOUG DRABEK   Age 27/R $16

Two straight excellent seasons, which is a rare accomplishment in Pittsburgh.

Year	Team	Lg.	G	IP	H	BB	SO	W	L	ERA	SV	Ratio
1986	New York	AL	27	131.2	126	50	76	7	8	4.10	0	1.337
1987	Pittsburgh	NL	29	176.1	165	46	120	11	12	3.88	0	1.197
1988	Pittsburgh	NL	33	219.1	194	50	127	15	7	3.08	0	1.112
1989	Pittsburgh	NL	35	244.1	215	69	123	14	12	2.80	0	1.162
Seasonal Notation				192.0	175	54	112	12	10	3.35	0	1.186

DAVE DRAVECKY   Age 34/L $4

It was enthralling and heart-breaking to watch his 1989 comeback. Keep an eye on spring training. It seems clear that if he's capable of pitching, he'll be good.

Year	Team	Lg.	G	IP	H	BB	SO	W	L	ERA	SV	Ratio
1986	San Diego	NL	26	161.1	149	54	87	9	11	3.07	0	1.258
1987	San Diego	NL	30	79.0	71	31	60	3	7	3.76	0	1.291
1987	San Francisco	NL	18	112.1	115	33	78	7	5	3.20	0	1.318
1988	San Francisco	NL	7	37.0	33	8	19	2	2	3.16	0	1.108
1989	San Francisco	NL	2	13.0	8	4	5	2	0	3.46	0	0.923
Seasonal Notation				100.0	94	33	62	6	6	3.26	0	1.257

SID FERNANDEZ   Age 27/L $16

His Corpulence continues to be a great numbers guy, even without as many victories as he ought to have. One of these years, he'll win 23 games—but not, of course, the year the Cary Nations own him.

Year	Team	Lg.	G	IP	H	BB	SO	W	L	ERA	SV	Ratio
1986	New York	NL	32	204.1	161	91	200	16	6	3.52	1	1.233
1987	New York	NL	28	156.0	130	67	134	12	8	3.81	0	1.263
1988	New York	NL	31	187.0	127	70	189	12	10	3.03	0	1.053
1989	New York	NL	35	219.1	157	75	198	14	5	2.83	0	1.058
Seasonal Notation				191.0	144	76	180	14	7	3.26	0	1.145

SCOTT GARRELTS   Age 28/R $15

If Roger Craig is so smart, why did he keep this born starter in the bullpen for so long? Maybe Rog was remembering Paul Richards' last tenure with the White Sox, when he tried to make Rich Gossage a starter and Pete Vuckovich a reliever.

Year	Team	Lg.	G	IP	H	BB	SO	W	L	ERA	SV	Ratio
1986	San Francisco	NL	53	173.2	144	74	125	13	9	3.11	10	1.255
1987	San Francisco	NL	64	106.1	70	55	127	11	7	3.22	12	1.176
1988	San Francisco	NL	65	98.0	80	46	86	5	9	3.58	13	1.286
1989	San Francisco	NL	30	193.1	149	46	119	14	5	2.28	0	1.009
Seasonal Notation				142.0	111	55	114	11	8	2.93	9	1.162

TOM GLAVINE   Age 24/L $3

That's his Atlanta price. Elsewhere, $8.

Year	Team	Lg.	G	IP	H	BB	SO	W	L	ERA	SV	Ratio
1987	Atlanta	NL	9	50.1	55	33	20	2	4	5.54	0	1.748
1988	Atlanta	NL	34	195.1	201	63	84	7	17	4.56	0	1.352
1989	Atlanta	NL	29	186.0	172	40	90	14	8	3.68	0	1.140
Seasonal Notation				143.0	143	45	65	8	10	4.30	0	1.307

DWIGHT GOODEN — Age 25/R — $25

The tyrannical team of Waggoner-Sklar, not to mention the football fans who run Bantam Books, are compelling these words to be written before the Doctor's mid-September comeback. However, in early September he really *sounded* good.

Year	Team	Lg.	G	IP	H	BB	SO	W	L	ERA	SV	Ratio
1986	New York	NL	33	250.0	197	80	200	17	6	2.84	0	1.108
1987	New York	NL	25	179.2	162	53	148	15	7	3.21	0	1.197
1988	New York	NL	34	248.1	242	57	175	18	9	3.19	0	1.204
1989	New York	NL	19	118.1	93	47	101	9	4	2.89	1	1.183
Seasonal Notation				199.0	174	59	156	15	7	3.04	0	1.169

KEVIN GROSS — Age 28/R — $3

Still writing his novel (even though there's no evidence he's ever read one).

Year	Team	Lg.	G	IP	H	BB	SO	W	L	ERA	SV	Ratio
1986	Philadelphia	NL	37	241.2	240	94	154	12	12	4.02	0	1.382
1987	Philadelphia	NL	34	200.2	205	87	110	9	16	4.35	0	1.455
1988	Philadelphia	NL	33	231.2	209	89	162	12	14	3.69	0	1.286
1989	Montreal	NL	31	201.1	188	88	158	11	12	4.38	0	1.371
Seasonal Notation				218.0	211	90	146	11	14	4.09	0	1.371

OREL HERSHISER — Age 31/R — $27

Forget about his incredible 1988. In his "mediocre" 1989, he was among the NL's ERA leaders and had a superb ratio. The best pitcher in the league should always be paid $30. But you'll get him for less because of the team behind him.

Year	Team	Lg.	G	IP	H	BB	SO	W	L	ERA	SV	Ratio
1986	Los Angeles	NL	35	231.1	213	86	153	14	14	3.85	0	1.293
1987	Los Angeles	NL	37	264.2	247	74	190	16	16	3.06	1	1.213
1988	Los Angeles	NL	35	267.0	208	73	178	23	8	2.26	1	1.052
1989	Los Angeles	NL	35	256.2	226	77	178	15	15	2.31	0	1.181
Seasonal Notation				254.0	224	78	175	17	13	2.84	1	1.181

KEN HOWELL — Age 29/R — $5

Extremely hard to hit, very easy to get walks off of. The Raven will either become Sid Fernandez or Charles Hudson.

Year	Team	Lg.	G	IP	H	BB	SO	W	L	ERA	SV	Ratio
1986	Los Angeles	NL	62	97.2	86	63	104	6	12	3.87	12	1.526
1987	Los Angeles	NL	40	55.0	54	29	60	3	4	4.91	1	1.509
1988	Los Angeles	NL	4	12.2	16	4	12	0	1	6.40	0	1.580
1989	Philadelphia	NL	33	204.0	155	86	164	12	12	3.44	0	1.181
Seasonal Notation				92.0	78	46	85	5	7	3.87	3	1.335

BRUCE HURST   Age 32/L $18

His career figures are deceptive—ERA and ratio plummeted the moment he left Fenway. Last year's numbers represent the real Hurst.

Year	Team	Lg.	G	IP	H	BB	SO	W	L	ERA	SV	Ratio
1986	Boston	AL	25	174.1	169	50	167	13	8	2.99	0	1.256
1987	Boston	AL	33	238.2	239	76	190	15	13	4.41	0	1.320
1988	Boston	AL	33	216.2	222	65	166	18	6	3.66	0	1.325
1989	San Diego	NL	33	244.2	214	66	179	15	11	2.69	0	1.144
Seasonal Notation				218.0	211	64	176	15	10	3.46	0	1.259

DANNY JACKSON   Age 28/L $15

Who knows? Either $3 or $25, or maybe $14.73. We think he'll come back, at least most of the way.

Year	Team	Lg.	G	IP	H	BB	SO	W	L	ERA	SV	Ratio
1986	Kansas City	AL	32	185.2	177	79	115	11	12	3.20	1	1.379
1987	Kansas City	AL	36	224.0	219	109	152	9	18	4.02	0	1.464
1988	Cincinnati	NL	35	260.2	206	71	161	23	8	2.73	0	1.063
1989	Cincinnati	NL	20	115.2	122	57	70	6	11	5.60	0	1.548
Seasonal Notation				196.0	181	79	125	12	12	3.63	0	1.323

PAUL KILGUS   Age 28/L $1

They wouldn't let him pitch the Cubs out of a division title. He went from the rotation to the minors in half a season, and his future—if he has one—is in mop-up work.

Year	Team	Lg.	G	IP	H	BB	SO	W	L	ERA	SV	Ratio
1987	Texas	AL	25	89.1	95	31	42	2	7	4.13	0	1.411
1988	Texas	AL	32	203.1	190	71	88	12	15	4.16	0	1.284
1989	Chicago	NL	35	145.2	164	49	61	6	10	4.39	2	1.462
Seasonal Notation				146.0	150	50	64	7	11	4.23	1	1.369

MIKE KRUKOW   Age 38/R $1

How many comeback pitchers of the year can the Giants have? Krukow will be a candidate if he returns from his rotator cuff injury.

Year	Team	Lg.	G	IP	H	BB	SO	W	L	ERA	SV	Ratio
1986	San Francisco	NL	34	245.0	204	55	178	20	9	3.05	0	1.057
1987	San Francisco	NL	30	163.0	182	46	104	5	6	4.80	0	1.399
1988	San Francisco	NL	20	124.2	111	31	75	7	4	3.54	0	1.139
1989	San Francisco	NL	8	43.0	37	18	18	4	3	3.98	0	1.279
Seasonal Notation				143.0	134	38	94	9	6	3.72	0	1.188

MARK LANGSTON   Age 29/L $26

A monster—one of those rare league-jumpers who turns out to be every bit as valuable as he was touted to be. However, Mr. Langston does like to walk people, and where will he be in 1990? The only French he learned was, "Adieu, Montreal."

Year	Team	Lg.	G	IP	H	BB	SO	W	L	ERA	SV	Ratio
1986	Seattle	AL	37	239.1	234	123	245	12	14	4.85	0	1.492
1987	Seattle	AL	35	272.0	242	114	262	19	13	3.84	0	1.309
1988	Seattle	AL	35	261.1	222	110	235	15	11	3.34	0	1.270
1989	Seattle	AL	10	73.1	60	19	60	4	5	3.56	0	1.077
1989	Montreal	NL	24	176.2	138	93	175	12	9	2.39	0	1.308
Seasonal Notation				255.0	224	115	244	16	13	3.68	0	1.325

TIM LEARY   Age 31/R $4

Never has there been better evidence of the effect that Dodger Stadium has on a pitcher's numbers. Away from Chavez, a classic fourth or fifth starter. Think "Marty Clary."

Year	Team	Lg.	G	IP	H	BB	SO	W	L	ERA	SV	Ratio
1986	Milwaukee	AL	33	188.1	216	53	110	12	12	4.21	0	1.428
1987	Los Angeles	NL	39	107.2	121	36	61	3	11	4.77	1	1.458
1988	Los Angeles	NL	35	228.2	201	56	180	17	11	2.91	0	1.124
1989	Los Angeles	NL	19	117.1	107	37	59	6	7	3.38	0	1.227
1989	Cincinnati	NL	14	89.2	98	31	64	2	7	3.71	0	1.439
Seasonal Notation				182.0	186	53	119	10	12	3.69	0	1.307

DEREK LILLIQUIST   Age 24/L $3

In any other organization, he'd be in the minors. Hardly walks anybody, largely because he gives up so many hits. Then why $3, when he appears to be worth $1? Because his last name is so pretty.

Year	Team	Lg.	G	IP	H	BB	SO	W	L	ERA	SV	Ratio
1989	Atlanta	NL	32	165.2	202	34	79	8	10	3.97	0	1.425
Seasonal Notation				165.0	202	34	79	8	10	3.97	0	1.425

GREG MADDUX   Age 23/R $8

Uh-oh. Zim's attempt last September to imitate the Gene Mauch of 1964 showed he'd learned very little from Maddux's awful second half in 1988. Greg's a tough customer, but crafty young-sters without fastballs often turn into Lary Sorensen. It probably won't happen for another year, though, so buy him for under $10—and when August comes, look for someone, *anyone* to pick up on waivers.

Year	Team	Lg.	G	IP	H	BB	SO	W	L	ERA	SV	Ratio
1986	Chicago	NL	6	31.0	44	11	20	2	4	5.52	0	1.774
1987	Chicago	NL	30	155.2	181	74	101	6	14	5.61	0	1.638
1988	Chicago	NL	34	249.0	230	81	140	18	8	3.18	0	1.249
1989	Chicago	NL	35	238.1	222	82	135	19	12	2.95	0	1.276
Seasonal Notation				168.0	169	62	99	11	10	3.77	0	1.372

JOE MAGRANE   Age 25/L $21

Take his numbers from 1988 and his victories from 1989, hope that
he puts them together in 1990—and open your wallet.

Year	Team	Lg.	G	IP	H	BB	SO	W	L	ERA	SV	Ratio
1987	St. Louis	NL	27	170.1	157	60	101	9	7	3.54	0	1.274
1988	St. Louis	NL	24	165.1	133	51	100	5	9	2.18	0	1.113
1989	St. Louis	NL	34	234.2	219	72	127	18	9	2.91	0	1.240
Seasonal Notation				190.0	170	61	109	11	8	2.89	0	1.213

RICK MAHLER   Age 36/R $1

On Draft Day, 1989, Michael Pollet (who sometimes isn't certain
what city the Padres come from) put in a bid for Rick Mahler, and
then justified it by quoting his excellent lifetime ERA in Riverfront.
None of us knew what had happened: whether Mahler had been
eating differently whenever he reached Cincinnati, or whether
Pollet's body had been possessed by an incubus. If the former,
Rick's connection skipped town last year.

Year	Team	Lg.	G	IP	H	BB	SO	W	L	ERA	SV	Ratio
1986	Atlanta	NL	39	237.2	283	95	137	14	18	4.89	0	1.591
1987	Atlanta	NL	39	197.0	212	85	95	8	13	4.98	0	1.508
1988	Atlanta	NL	39	249.0	279	42	131	9	16	3.69	0	1.289
1989	Cincinnati	NL	40	220.2	242	51	102	9	13	3.83	0	1.328
Seasonal Notation				226.0	254	68	116	10	15	4.32	0	1.425

DENNIS MARTINEZ   Age 34/R $13

Dennis turns 35 this year. This means he is likely to be over-
priced, and eligible to run for President—of Nicaragua.

Year	Team	Lg.	G	IP	H	BB	SO	W	L	ERA	SV	Ratio
1986	Baltimore	AL	4	6.2	11	2	2	0	0	6.76	0	1.952
1986	Montreal	NL	19	98.0	103	28	63	3	6	4.59	0	1.337
1987	Montreal	NL	22	144.2	133	40	84	11	4	3.30	0	1.196
1988	Montreal	NL	34	235.1	215	55	120	15	13	2.72	0	1.147
1989	Montreal	NL	34	232.0	227	49	142	16	7	3.18	0	1.190
Seasonal Notation				179.0	172	44	103	11	8	3.28	0	1.204

RAMON MARTINEZ   Age 22/R $7

At 6'4", 172 pounds, Ramon weights 2.25 pounds per inch. In other words, his specific gravity is 28% less than Rick Reuschel's.

Year	Team	Lg.	G	IP	H	BB	SO	W	L	ERA	SV	Ratio
1988	Los Angeles	NL	9	35.2	27	22	23	1	3	3.79	0	1.374
1989	Los Angeles	NL	15	98.2	79	41	89	6	4	3.19	0	1.216
Seasonal Notation				67.0	53	32	56	4	4	3.35	0	1.258

GREG MATHEWS   Age 26/L $2

Fundamentally, who really cares?

Year	Team	Lg.	G	IP	H	BB	SO	W	L	ERA	SV	Ratio
1986	St. Louis	NL	23	145.1	139	44	67	11	8	3.65	0	1.259
1987	St. Louis	NL	32	197.2	184	71	108	11	11	3.73	0	1.290
1988	St. Louis	NL	13	68.0	61	33	31	4	6	4.24	0	1.382
Seasonal Notation				136.0	128	49	69	9	8	3.79	0	1.294

MIKE MORGAN   Age 30/R $5

Do not be fooled by the numbers Morgan put up on the way to his sub-.500 1989 season. The man's been a professional pitcher for 12 years and still hasn't won 50 major league games. And he hasn't even won 40 in the minors. File under "generic Dodger pitcher," and get him to improve your ERA.

Year	Team	Lg.	G	IP	H	BB	SO	W	L	ERA	SV	Ratio
1986	Seattle	AL	37	216.1	243	86	116	11	17	4.53	1	1.521
1987	Seattle	AL	34	207.0	245	53	85	12	17	4.65	0	1.440
1988	Baltimore	AL	22	71.1	70	23	29	1	6	5.43	1	1.304
1989	Los Angeles	NL	40	152.2	130	33	72	8	11	2.54	0	1.068
Seasonal Notation				161.0	172	49	76	8	13	4.20	1	1.364

TERRY MULHOLLAND   Age 27/L $2

The move to Philadelphia will only help Terry compile a larger number of mediocre outings.

Year	Team	Lg.	G	IP	H	BB	SO	W	L	ERA	SV	Ratio
1986	San Francisco	NL	15	54.2	51	35	27	1	7	4.94	0	1.573
1988	San Francisco	NL	9	46.0	50	7	18	2	1	3.72	0	1.239
1989	San Francisco	NL	5	11.0	15	4	6	0	0	4.09	0	1.727
1989	Philadelphia	NL	20	104.1	122	32	60	4	7	5.00	0	1.476
Seasonal Notation				71.0	79	26	37	2	5	4.67	0	1.463

BOBBY OJEDA   Age 32/L $12

A year ago, we questioned his fingers. Now, we question his status. Something has to give on the Mets staff, and of all their starters Ojeda would suffer most in another ballpark. $12 at Shea, $10 at Busch, $5 at Wrigley.

Year	Team	Lg.	G	IP	H	BB	SO	W	L	ERA	SV	Ratio
1986	New York	NL	32	217.1	185	52	148	18	5	2.57	0	1.091
1987	New York	NL	10	46.1	45	10	21	3	5	3.89	0	1.187
1988	New York	NL	29	190.1	158	33	133	10	13	2.88	0	1.004
1989	New York	NL	31	192.0	179	78	95	13	11	3.47	0	1.339
Seasonal Notation				161.0	142	43	99	11	9	3.02	0	1.146

PASCUAL PEREZ   Age 32/R $14

Did you know his middle name is *Gross*? Specific gravity only barely higher than Ramon Martinez's. This year—his performance level is usually dependent on planetary movements—looks like a good one if Pluto barks.

Year	Team	Lg.	G	IP	H	BB	SO	W	L	ERA	SV	Ratio
1987	Montreal	NL	10	70.1	52	16	58	7	0	2.30	0	0.967
1988	Montreal	NL	27	188.0	133	44	131	12	8	2.44	0	0.941
1989	Montreal	NL	33	198.1	178	45	152	9	13	3.31	0	1.124
Seasonal Notation				152.0	121	35	114	9	7	2.80	0	1.025

MARK PORTUGAL   Age 27/R $3

Portugal, a democratic republic on the western edge of the Iberian peninsula, is known for its flowers, its dessert wines, and its sunny beaches. You can travel there for $3, but beware of devaluation.

Year	Team	Lg.	G	IP	H	BB	SO	W	L	ERA	SV	Ratio
1986	Minnesota	AL	27	112.2	112	50	67	6	10	4.31	1	1.438
1987	Minnesota	AL	13	44.0	58	24	28	1	3	7.77	0	1.864
1988	Minnesota	AL	26	57.2	60	17	31	3	3	4.53	3	1.335
1989	Houston	NL	20	108.0	91	37	86	7	1	2.75	0	1.185
Seasonal Notation				80.0	80	32	53	4	4	4.30	1	1.393

DENNIS RASMUSSEN   Age 30/L $5

Every even-numbered year, Rasmussen has a three-month stretch in which he's unhittable. Unfortunately, the baseball season has six months.

Year	Team	Lg.	G	IP	H	BB	SO	W	L	ERA	SV	Ratio
1986	New York	AL	31	202.0	160	74	131	18	6	3.88	0	1.158
1987	New York	AL	26	146.0	145	55	89	9	7	4.75	0	1.370
1987	Cincinnati	NL	7	45.1	39	12	39	4	1	3.97	0	1.125
1988	Cincinnati	NL	11	56.1	68	22	27	2	6	5.75	0	1.598
1988	San Diego	NL	20	148.1	131	36	85	14	4	2.55	0	1.126
1989	San Diego	NL	33	183.2	190	72	87	10	10	4.26	0	1.427
Seasonal Notation				195.0	183	68	115	14	9	4.02	0	1.284

RICK REUSCHEL   Age 40/R $17

A bloody wonder. As physical condition appears to have nothing to
do with Reuschel's performance, there's no reason why he shouldn't
be able to win 14-18 games, with good numbers—even if he does
turn 40 this year. Expect fewer innings from him, virtually no
complete games, a heavy reliance on Craig Lefferts to finish his
work—and expect, also, to pay dearly to watch it all happen.

Year	Team	Lg.	G	IP	H	BB	SO	W	L	ERA	SV	Ratio
1986	Pittsburgh	NL	35	215.2	232	57	125	9	16	3.96	0	1.340
1987	Pittsburgh	NL	25	177.0	163	35	80	8	6	2.75	0	1.119
1987	San Francisco	NL	9	50.0	44	7	27	5	3	4.32	0	1.020
1988	San Francisco	NL	36	245.0	242	42	92	19	11	3.12	0	1.159
1989	San Francisco	NL	32	208.1	195	54	111	17	8	2.94	0	1.195
Seasonal Notation				223.0	219	49	109	15	11	3.27	0	1.195

RICK RHODEN   Age 36/R $2

The other old Rick among National League starters. Hopeless.
Half his salary is for the park he pitches in.

Year	Team	Lg.	G	IP	H	BB	SO	W	L	ERA	SV	Ratio
1986	Pittsburgh	NL	34	253.2	211	76	159	15	12	2.84	0	1.131
1987	New York	AL	30	181.2	184	61	107	16	10	3.86	0	1.349
1988	New York	AL	30	197.0	206	56	94	12	12	4.29	0	1.330
1989	Houston	NL	20	96.2	108	41	41	2	6	4.28	0	1.541
Seasonal Notation				182.0	177	59	100	11	10	3.68	0	1.294

JOSÉ RIJO   Age 24/R $14

May turn out to be the saddest story ever told—or at least since
Ford Madox Ford wrote *The Good Soldier*. If José is pitching well
in spring training, take a chance, because should he come back as
the same pitcher he was before the injury, he'll be great.

Year	Team	Lg.	G	IP	H	BB	SO	W	L	ERA	SV	Ratio
1986	Oakland	AL	39	193.2	172	108	176	9	11	4.65	1	1.446
1987	Oakland	AL	21	82.1	106	41	67	2	7	5.90	0	1.785
1988	Cincinnati	NL	49	162.0	120	63	160	13	8	2.39	0	1.130
1989	Cincinnati	NL	19	111.0	101	48	86	7	6	2.84	0	1.342
Seasonal Notation				137.0	125	65	122	8	8	3.80	0	1.383

BASEBALL ANAGRAM #1

Wade Boggs = We Bag Dogs.

DON ROBINSON Age 32/R $8

Sometime starter, sometime reliever, Robinson is pretty reliable.

Year	Team	Lg.	G	IP	H	BB	SO	W	L	ERA	SV	Ratio
1986	Pittsburgh	NL	50	69.1	61	27	53	3	4	3.38	14	1.269
1987	Pittsburgh	NL	42	65.1	66	22	53	6	6	3.86	12	1.347
1987	San Francisco	NL	25	42.2	39	18	26	5	1	2.74	7	1.336
1988	San Francisco	NL	51	176.2	152	49	122	10	5	2.45	6	1.138
1989	San Francisco	NL	34	197.0	184	37	96	12	11	3.43	0	1.122
Seasonal Notation				137.0	126	38	88	9	7	3.10	10	1.189

RON ROBINSON Age 28/R $4

Sometime starter, sometime reliever, Robinson is pretty reliable.

Year	Team	Lg.	G	IP	H	BB	SO	W	L	ERA	SV	Ratio
1986	Cincinnati	NL	70	116.2	110	43	117	10	3	3.24	14	1.312
1987	Cincinnati	NL	48	154.0	148	43	99	7	5	3.68	4	1.240
1988	Cincinnati	NL	17	78.2	88	26	38	3	7	4.12	0	1.449
1989	Cincinnati	NL	15	83.1	80	28	36	5	3	3.35	0	1.296
Seasonal Notation				108.0	107	35	73	6	5	3.58	5	1.308

MIKE SCOTT Age 34/R $28

In 1989, he won more games than he ever has before. His ratio was great. A couple of rocky spells hurt his ERA, but even so it was markedly better than the league average. Count on three things in baseball: Steinbrenner's offensiveness, Zimmer's steel plate, and Scott's skill.

Year	Team	Lg.	G	IP	H	BB	SO	W	L	ERA	SV	Ratio
1986	Houston	NL	37	275.1	182	72	306	18	10	2.22	0	0.923
1987	Houston	NL	36	247.2	199	79	233	16	13	3.23	0	1.123
1988	Houston	NL	32	218.2	162	53	190	14	8	2.92	0	0.983
1989	Houston	NL	33	229.0	180	62	172	20	10	3.10	0	1.057
Seasonal Notation				242.0	181	67	225	17	10	2.85	0	1.019

SCOTT SCUDDER Age 22/R $5

He turns 22 during spring training. Will be great; see Andy Benes, but discount for Reds' inevitable mishandling.

Year	Team	Lg.	G	IP	H	BB	SO	W	L	ERA	SV	Ratio
1989	Cincinnati	NL	23	100.1	91	61	66	4	9	4.49	0	1.515
Seasonal Notation				100.0	91	61	66	4	9	4.49	0	1.515

ERIC SHOW Age 33/R $6

The only other time Show has been on the disabled list, he came back to have an uncharacteristically poor year. Without making too big a thing of it, you might think that Eric the Arrogant just doesn't take too well to the advice of physicians, trainers, and others he deems to be his intellectual inferiors. But he does know how to pitch, he does have a good arm, and he does think that Joe Pass is a much better guitarist than Eric Clapton.

Year	Team	Lg.	G	IP	H	BB	SO	W	L	ERA	SV	Ratio
1986	San Diego	NL	24	136.1	109	69	94	9	5	2.97	0	1.306
1987	San Diego	NL	34	206.1	188	85	117	8	16	3.84	0	1.323
1988	San Diego	NL	32	234.2	201	53	144	16	11	3.26	0	1.082
1989	San Diego	NL	16	106.1	113	39	66	8	6	4.23	0	1.430
Seasonal Notation				170.0	153	62	105	10	10	3.53	0	1.254

JOHN SMILEY   Age 25/L $16

He's getting better and better—probably the NL's next great ace.

Year	Team	Lg.	G	IP	H	BB	SO	W	L	ERA	SV	Ratio
1986	Pittsburgh	NL	12	11.2	4	4	9	1	0	3.86	0	0.686
1987	Pittsburgh	NL	63	75.0	69	50	58	5	5	5.76	4	1.587
1988	Pittsburgh	NL	34	205.0	185	46	129	13	11	3.25	0	1.127
1989	Pittsburgh	NL	28	205.1	174	49	123	12	8	2.81	0	1.086
Seasonal Notation				124.0	108	37	80	8	6	3.46	1	1.169

BRYN SMITH   Age 34/R $11

His wife actually told *Sports Illustrated* that Montreal's a nice place, but to purchase staples—Cheetos, Hamburger Helper, other culinary necessities—she drives more than an hour each way to Plattsburgh, New York. $8 for Bryn, 15 cents for Mrs. Bryn.

Year	Team	Lg.	G	IP	H	BB	SO	W	L	ERA	SV	Ratio
1986	Montreal	NL	30	187.1	182	63	105	10	8	3.94	0	1.308
1987	Montreal	NL	26	150.1	164	31	94	10	9	4.37	0	1.297
1988	Montreal	NL	32	198.0	179	32	122	12	10	3.00	0	1.066
1989	Montreal	NL	33	215.2	177	54	129	10	11	2.84	0	1.071
Seasonal Notation				187.0	176	45	113	11	10	3.46	0	1.174

PETE SMITH   Age 24/R $0

Do not mention his name in the presence of BFFCL Daniel Okrent. Smith's great second half in 1988 cost the Fenokees big money in 1989. No price; trading stopped by order of the SEC.

Year	Team	Lg.	G	IP	H	BB	SO	W	L	ERA	SV	Ratio
1987	Atlanta	NL	6	31.2	39	14	11	1	2	4.83	0	1.674
1988	Atlanta	NL	32	195.1	183	88	124	7	15	3.69	0	1.387
1989	Atlanta	NL	28	142.0	144	57	115	5	14	4.75	0	1.415
Seasonal Notation				122.0	122	53	83	4	10	4.20	0	1.423

JOHN SMOLTZ   Age 22/R $6

If you're named after a variety of herring, why don't you play for
the Fish? The National League's hardest thrower looks good in
seasonal notation, but just get a load of his second half stats for
1989: this herring got creamed. Still, a great arm, which may
interest those of you who trade in body parts.

Year	Team	Lg.	G	IP	H	BB	SO	W	L	ERA	SV	Ratio
1988	Atlanta	NL	12	64.0	74	33	37	2	7	5.48	0	1.672
1989	Atlanta	NL	29	208.0	160	72	168	12	11	2.94	0	1.115
Seasonal Notation				136.0	117	53	103	7	9	3.54	0	1.246

RICK SUTCLIFFE   Age 33/R $10

Some of you may remember that last year's book said Rick would
be out of the rotation by August 1. For twelve months we've had
to hold our tongues, but now the truth can be told: a rumor had
spread around baseball that Don Zimmer was making all of his
moves based on what the Rotisserie League Baseball book predicted each year. Approached by the Commissioner's Office, we
were asked to make a prediction so outlandish, so foolish, so
transparently silly that even Zimbo wouldn't follow it. You *may*
have noticed that Don Zimmer was *not* suspended from baseball
last summer. Draw your own conclusions.

Year	Team	Lg.	G	IP	H	BB	SO	W	L	ERA	SV	Ratio
1986	Chicago	NL	28	176.2	166	96	122	5	14	4.64	0	1.483
1987	Chicago	NL	34	237.1	223	106	174	18	10	3.68	0	1.386
1988	Chicago	NL	32	226.0	232	70	144	13	14	3.86	0	1.336
1989	Chicago	NL	35	229.0	202	69	153	16	11	3.66	0	1.183
Seasonal Notation				217.0	206	85	148	13	12	3.91	0	1.339

SCOTT TERRY   Age 30/R $4

Hit 12 home runs for Cedar Rapids of the Midwest League in
1982. As a pitcher, he's a pretty good outfielder. Worth having if
only for his ballpark and his manager.

Year	Team	Lg.	G	IP	H	BB	SO	W	L	ERA	SV	Ratio
1986	Cincinnati	NL	28	55.2	66	32	32	1	2	6.14	0	1.761
1987	St. Louis	NL	11	13.1	13	8	9	0	0	3.38	0	1.575
1988	St. Louis	NL	51	129.1	119	34	65	9	6	2.92	3	1.183
1989	St. Louis	NL	31	148.2	142	43	69	8	10	3.57	2	1.244
Seasonal Notation				86.0	85	29	44	5	5	3.74	1	1.317

FERNANDO VALENZUELA   Age 29/L $5

The miracle of 'Nando's second half is less impressive than it might
at first appear: While starting to win, and simultaneously bringing
down his ERA, he nonetheless failed to bring his ratio into polite
company. He's smart enough to be a good pitcher, but his arm is
too far gone for him ever to be great again.

Year	Team	Lg.	G	IP	H	BB	SO	W	L	ERA	SV	Ratio
1986	Los Angeles	NL	34	269.1	226	85	242	21	11	3.14	0	1.155
1987	Los Angeles	NL	34	251.0	254	124	190	14	14	3.98	0	1.506
1988	Los Angeles	NL	23	142.1	142	76	64	5	8	4.24	1	1.532
1989	Los Angeles	NL	31	196.2	185	98	116	10	13	3.43	0	1.439
Seasonal Notation				214.0	202	96	153	13	12	3.63	0	1.385

FRANK VIOLA   Age 29/L $27

"Sweet Music" indeed. As Gooden was in 1985, as Ojeda was in
1986, as Cone was in 1988, so will 1990 be Viola's year at Shea.

Year	Team	Lg.	G	IP	H	BB	SO	W	L	ERA	SV	Ratio
1986	Minnesota	AL	37	245.2	257	83	191	16	13	4.51	0	1.384
1987	Minnesota	AL	36	251.2	230	66	197	17	10	2.90	0	1.176
1988	Minnesota	AL	35	255.1	236	54	193	24	7	2.64	0	1.136
1989	Minnesota	AL	24	175.2	171	47	138	8	12	3.79	0	1.241
1989	New York	NL	12	85.1	75	27	73	5	5	3.38	0	1.195
Seasonal Notation				253.0	242	69	198	18	12	3.42	0	1.229

BOB WALK   Age 33/R $1

Should be named Bob Hit. His 1988 performance will keep him in
the majors for another four years, for which Mrs. Walk and all the
little Walks should be grateful.

Year	Team	Lg.	G	IP	H	BB	SO	W	L	ERA	SV	Ratio
1986	Pittsburgh	NL	44	141.2	129	64	78	7	8	3.75	2	1.362
1987	Pittsburgh	NL	39	117.0	107	51	78	8	2	3.31	0	1.350
1988	Pittsburgh	NL	32	212.2	183	65	81	12	10	2.71	0	1.166
1989	Pittsburgh	NL	33	196.0	208	65	83	13	10	4.41	0	1.393
Seasonal Notation				166.0	157	61	80	10	8	3.53	1	1.307

JOHN WETTELAND   Age 23/R $3

Plays the saxophone, pitches in Dodger Stadium. Shaky control
his only debit. Touted as the next Hershiser. But when?

Year	Team	Lg.	G	IP	H	BB	SO	W	L	ERA	SV	Ratio
1989	Los Angeles	NL	31	102.2	81	34	96	5	8	3.77	1	1.120
Seasonal Notation				102.0	81	34	96	5	8	3.77	1	1.120

ED WHITSON   Age 34/R $9

Pitched so well in 1989, Steinbrenner should sign him.

Year	Team	Lg.	G	IP	H	BB	SO	W	L	ERA	SV	Ratio
1986	New York	AL	14	37.0	54	23	27	5	2	7.54	0	2.081
1986	San Diego	NL	17	75.2	85	37	46	1	7	5.59	0	1.612
1987	San Diego	NL	36	205.2	197	64	135	10	13	4.73	0	1.269
1988	San Diego	NL	34	205.1	202	45	118	13	11	3.77	0	1.203
1989	San Diego	NL	33	227.0	198	48	117	16	11	2.66	0	1.084
Seasonal Notation				187.0	184	54	111	11	11	4.06	0	1.270

AMERICAN LEAGUE

Some pretty good northpaws and portsiders toed the turtleback during the last campaign: Bret Saberhagen, Dave Stewart, Jeff Ballard, Bert Blyleven, Mike Moore, Chuck Finley, Tom Gordon, Kirk McCaskill, Nolan Ryan, Dave Stieb, Chris Bosio. And a lot of aces had off-years: Roger Clemens, Mark Gubicza, Mike Witt, Jack Morris, Greg Swindell, Jeff Robinson, Jimmy Key, Teddy Higuera. So you have a lot to choose from and no excuses if you end up with Dave Schmidt.

JIM ABBOTT   Age 22/L $7

For the same reason people are curious about him, Rotisserie people will be reluctant to pay big bucks for him. That's right. Nobody's ever seen a good lefthander come out of Michigan.

Year	Team	Lg.	G	IP	H	BB	SO	W	L	ERA	SV	Ratio
1989	California	AL	29	181.1	190	74	115	12	12	3.92	0	1.456
Seasonal Notation				181.0	190	74	115	12	12	3.92	0	1.456

RICK AGUILERA   Age 28/R $8

The Twins have always liked ex-Met pitchers, most notably Jerry Koosman and Jeff Reardon. Aguilera's the best of the three hurlers acquired for Frank Viola. Twelve wins easy.

Year	Team	Lg.	G	IP	H	BB	SO	W	L	ERA	SV	Ratio
1986	New York	NL	28	141.2	145	36	104	10	7	3.88	0	1.278
1987	New York	NL	18	115.0	124	33	77	11	3	3.60	0	1.365
1988	New York	NL	11	24.2	29	10	16	0	4	6.93	0	1.582
1989	New York	NL	36	69.1	59	21	80	6	6	2.34	7	1.154
1989	Minnesota	AL	11	75.2	71	17	57	3	5	3.21	0	1.163
Seasonal Notation				106.0	107	29	84	8	6	3.61	2	1.278

DOYLE ALEXANDER   Age 39/R $2

One of the worst ratios in the league, with very little to show in the way of wins. Alexander the Mediocre should be pitching for the St. Lucie entry in the over-35 league. To give you some idea of how long Doyle has been around, here is an all-star team of players with and for whom he has been traded:

1b-Royle Stillman	of-Ted Wilborn
2b-Larvell Blanks	of-Frank Robinson
ss-Pepe Frias	of-Craig Landis
3b-Rick Dempsey (played it once)	sp-Ken Holtzman
c-Elrod Hendricks	rp-Pete Richert

Year	Team	Lg.	G	IP	H	BB	SO	W	L	ERA	SV	Ratio
1986	Toronto	AL	17	111.0	120	20	65	5	4	4.46	0	1.261
1986	Atlanta	NL	17	117.1	135	17	74	6	6	3.84	0	1.295
1987	Atlanta	NL	16	117.2	115	27	64	5	10	4.13	0	1.207
1987	Detroit	AL	11	88.1	63	26	44	9	0	1.53	0	1.008
1988	Detroit	AL	34	229.0	260	46	126	14	11	4.32	0	1.336
1989	Detroit	AL	33	223.0	245	76	95	6	18	4.44	0	1.439
Seasonal Notation				221.0	235	53	117	11	12	4.00	0	1.297

ALLAN ANDERSON   Age 26/L $15

An effective pitcher but a sloppy ratio. If he ever pitches to Andy Allanson, what you would have is a Double A battery.

Year	Team	Lg.	G	IP	H	BB	SO	W	L	ERA	SV	Ratio
1986	Minnesota	AL	21	84.1	106	30	51	3	6	5.55	0	1.613
1987	Minnesota	AL	4	12.1	20	10	3	1	0	10.95	0	2.433
1988	Minnesota	AL	30	202.1	199	37	83	16	9	2.45	0	1.166
1989	Minnesota	AL	33	196.2	214	53	69	17	10	3.80	0	1.358
Seasonal Notation				123.0	135	33	52	9	6	3.72	0	1.350

DON AUGUST   Age 26/R $3

The poor man's Doyle Alexander.

Year	Team	Lg.	G	IP	H	BB	SO	W	L	ERA	SV	Ratio
1988	Milwaukee	AL	24	148.1	137	48	66	13	7	3.09	0	1.247
1989	Milwaukee	AL	31	142.1	175	58	51	12	12	5.31	0	1.637
Seasonal Notation				145.0	156	53	59	13	10	4.18	0	1.438

JEFF BALLARD   Age 26/L $13

His season can best be summed up by this extraordinary pitching line last September: 9-7-0-0-0-0. Nothing fancy or overpowering, just smart pitching. Hearty congratulations to those of you who picked him up in last year's draft because nothing in his past indicated he would become an ace.

Year	Team	Lg.	G	IP	H	BB	SO	W	L	ERA	SV	Ratio
1987	Baltimore	AL	14	69.2	100	35	27	2	8	6.59	0	1.938
1988	Baltimore	AL	25	153.1	167	42	41	8	12	4.40	0	1.363
1989	Baltimore	AL	35	215.1	240	57	62	18	8	3.43	0	1.379
Seasonal Notation				146.0	169	45	43	9	9	4.27	0	1.462

SCOTT BANKHEAD   Age 26/R $8

The Danny Tartabull trade doesn't look so bad anymore. Just think what Bankhead could do if he was still with the Royals.

Year	Team	Lg.	G	IP	H	BB	SO	W	L	ERA	SV	Ratio
1986	Kansas City	AL	24	121.0	121	37	94	8	9	4.61	0	1.306
1987	Seattle	AL	27	149.1	168	37	95	9	8	5.42	0	1.373
1988	Seattle	AL	21	135.0	115	38	102	7	9	3.07	0	1.133
1989	Seattle	AL	33	210.1	187	63	140	14	6	3.34	0	1.189
Seasonal Notation				153.0	148	44	108	10	8	4.03	0	1.244

FLOYD BANNISTER   Age 34/L $3

Stop living in the past. If you're intent on picking up a heart-breaking lefthander, there are plenty of younger ones around.

Year	Team	Lg.	G	IP	H	BB	SO	W	L	ERA	SV	Ratio
1986	Chicago	AL	28	165.1	162	48	92	10	14	3.54	0	1.270
1987	Chicago	AL	34	228.2	216	49	124	16	11	3.58	0	1.159
1988	Kansas City	AL	31	189.1	182	68	113	12	13	4.33	0	1.320
1989	Kansas City	AL	14	75.1	87	18	35	4	1	4.66	0	1.394
Seasonal Notation				164.0	162	46	91	11	10	3.91	0	1.260

BUD BLACK   Age 32/L $5

As in "paints the . . ." A return to form for an old favorite.

Year	Team	Lg.	G	IP	H	BB	SO	W	L	ERA	SV	Ratio
1986	Kansas City	AL	56	121.0	100	43	68	5	10	3.20	9	1.182
1987	Kansas City	AL	29	122.1	126	35	61	8	6	3.61	1	1.316
1988	Kansas City	AL	17	22.0	23	11	19	2	1	4.91	0	1.545
1988	Cleveland	AL	16	59.0	59	23	44	2	3	5.03	1	1.390
1989	Cleveland	AL	33	222.1	213	52	88	12	11	3.36	0	1.192
Seasonal Notation				136.0	130	41	70	7	8	3.62	3	1.253

BERT BLYLEVEN   Age 38/R $10

It's going to kill a lot of writers, but he's headed for 300 wins and the Hall of Fame. He won't be as good as he was in 1989, but he won't be as bad as he was in 1988.

Year	Team	Lg.	G	IP	H	BB	SO	W	L	ERA	SV	Ratio
1986	Minnesota	AL	36	271.2	262	58	215	17	14	4.01	0	1.178
1987	Minnesota	AL	37	267.0	249	101	196	15	12	4.01	0	1.311
1988	Minnesota	AL	33	207.1	240	51	145	10	17	5.43	0	1.404
1989	California	AL	33	241.0	225	44	131	17	5	2.73	0	1.116
Seasonal Notation				246.0	244	64	172	15	12	3.99	0	1.246

MIKE BODDICKER   Age 32/R $6

The rich man's Don August.

Year	Team	Lg.	G	IP	H	BB	SO	W	L	ERA	SV	Ratio
1986	Baltimore	AL	33	218.1	214	74	175	14	12	4.70	0	1.319
1987	Baltimore	AL	33	226.0	212	78	152	10	12	4.18	0	1.283
1988	Baltimore	AL	21	147.0	149	51	100	6	12	3.86	0	1.361
1988	Boston	AL	15	89.0	85	26	56	7	3	2.63	0	1.247
1989	Boston	AL	34	211.2	217	71	145	15	11	4.00	0	1.361
Seasonal Notation				222.0	219	75	157	13	13	4.06	0	1.320

CHRIS BOSIO   Age 27/R $12

The stuff of a 20-game winner, but we worry because he pitched 50 more innings than he ever had before in a season.

Year	Team	Lg.	G	IP	H	BB	SO	W	L	ERA	SV	Ratio
1986	Milwaukee	AL	10	34.2	41	13	29	0	4	7.01	0	1.558
1987	Milwaukee	AL	46	170.0	187	50	150	11	8	5.24	2	1.394
1988	Milwaukee	AL	38	182.0	190	38	84	7	15	3.36	6	1.253
1989	Milwaukee	AL	33	234.2	225	48	173	15	10	2.95	0	1.163
Seasonal Notation				155.0	161	37	109	8	9	3.93	2	1.275

OIL CAN BOYD   Age 30/R $2

Oil Can't is more like it.

Year	Team	Lg.	G	IP	H	BB	SO	W	L	ERA	SV	Ratio
1986	Boston	AL	30	214.1	222	45	129	16	10	3.78	0	1.246
1987	Boston	AL	7	36.2	47	9	12	1	3	5.89	0	1.528
1988	Boston	AL	23	129.2	147	41	71	9	7	5.34	0	1.450
1989	Boston	AL	10	59.0	57	19	26	3	2	4.42	0	1.288
Seasonal Notation				109.0	118	29	60	7	6	4.50	0	1.335

KEVIN BROWN   Age 25/R $10

Not to be confused with Kevin Brown or Kevin Brown. The Milwaukee Brewers were: In their 1989 press guide they accidentally combined all the statistics of the three Kevin Browns in organized ball and *voila,* they had a pitcher who started 58 games for four different teams, with 431 innings pitched and a won-loss record of 19-27. This particular Kevin Brown's real name is James Brown, which causes a whole different confusion. But he made a name for himself with some very fine pitching in his rookie year. He'll get even better.

Year	Team	Lg.	G	IP	H	BB	SO	W	L	ERA	SV	Ratio
1986	Texas	AL	1	5.0	6	0	4	1	0	3.60	0	1.200
1988	Texas	AL	4	23.1	33	8	12	1	1	4.24	0	1.757
1989	Texas	AL	28	191.0	167	70	104	12	9	3.35	0	1.241
Seasonal Notation				73.0	69	26	40	5	3	3.45	0	1.295

TOM CANDIOTTI   Age 32/R $8

As with the knuckleball he throws, unpredictable.

Year	Team	Lg.	G	IP	H	BB	SO	W	L	ERA	SV	Ratio
1986	Cleveland	AL	36	252.1	234	106	167	16	12	3.57	0	1.347
1987	Cleveland	AL	32	201.2	193	93	111	7	18	4.78	0	1.418
1988	Cleveland	AL	31	216.2	225	53	137	14	8	3.28	0	1.283
1989	Cleveland	AL	31	206.0	188	55	124	13	10	3.10	0	1.180
Seasonal Notation				219.0	210	77	135	13	12	3.67	0	1.308

JOHN CERUTTI   Age 29/L $8

He deserved to win many more. He can not only paint the black, but according to the Blue Jays media guide, he can do landscapes, as well. Sure beats the traditional pursuits of major leaguers: hunting, fishing and room service.

Year	Team	Lg.	G	IP	H	BB	SO	W	L	ERA	SV	Ratio
1986	Toronto	AL	34	145.1	150	47	89	9	4	4.15	1	1.356
1987	Toronto	AL	44	151.1	144	59	92	11	4	4.40	0	1.341
1988	Toronto	AL	46	123.2	120	42	65	6	7	3.13	1	1.310
1989	Toronto	AL	33	205.1	214	53	69	11	11	3.07	0	1.300
Seasonal Notation				156.0	157	50	79	9	7	3.65	1	1.325

ROGER CLEMENS   Age 27/R $27

He's worth that much even in an off-year. The best starting pitcher available, bar none.

Year	Team	Lg.	G	IP	H	BB	SO	W	L	ERA	SV	Ratio
1986	Boston	AL	33	254.0	179	67	238	24	4	2.48	0	0.969
1987	Boston	AL	36	281.2	248	83	256	20	9	2.97	0	1.175
1988	Boston	AL	35	264.0	217	62	291	18	12	2.93	0	1.057
1989	Boston	AL	35	253.1	215	93	230	17	11	3.13	0	1.216
Seasonal Notation				263.0	215	76	254	20	9	2.88	0	1.105

STORM DAVIS   Age 28/R $8

He got some consideration for the Cy Young Award, but he was much more deserving of the Jim Merritt Award, given to that pitcher whose win total far exceeds his actual performance.

Year	Team	Lg.	G	IP	H	BB	SO	W	L	ERA	SV	Ratio
1986	Baltimore	AL	25	154.0	166	49	96	9	12	3.62	0	1.396
1987	San Diego	NL	21	62.2	70	36	37	2	7	6.18	0	1.692
1987	Oakland	AL	5	30.1	28	11	28	1	1	3.26	0	1.286
1988	Oakland	AL	33	201.2	211	91	127	16	7	3.70	0	1.498
1989	Oakland	AL	31	169.1	187	68	91	19	7	4.36	0	1.506
Seasonal Notation				154.0	166	64	95	12	9	4.09	0	1.484

JOHN DOPSON   Age 26/R $4
Sort of a cross between Pat Dobson and Rich Dotson.

Year	Team	Lg.	G	IP	H	BB	SO	W	L	ERA	SV	Ratio
1988	Montreal	NL	26	168.2	150	58	101	3	11	3.04	0	1.233
1989	Boston	AL	29	169.1	166	69	95	12	8	3.99	0	1.388
Seasonal Notation				168.0	158	64	98	8	10	3.51	0	1.311

RICH DOTSON   Age 31/R $1
Speak of the devil.

Year	Team	Lg.	G	IP	H	BB	SO	W	L	ERA	SV	Ratio
1986	Chicago	AL	34	197.0	226	69	110	10	17	5.48	0	1.497
1987	Chicago	AL	31	211.1	201	86	114	11	12	4.17	0	1.358
1988	New York	AL	32	171.0	178	72	77	12	9	5.00	0	1.462
1989	New York	AL	11	51.2	69	17	14	2	5	5.57	0	1.665
1989	Chicago	AL	17	99.2	112	41	55	3	7	3.88	0	1.535
Seasonal Notation				182.0	197	71	93	10	13	4.78	0	1.466

JOHN FARRELL   Age 27/R $5
The poor man's Mike Boddicker.

Year	Team	Lg.	G	IP	H	BB	SO	W	L	ERA	SV	Ratio
1987	Cleveland	AL	10	69.0	68	22	28	5	1	3.39	0	1.304
1988	Cleveland	AL	31	210.1	216	67	92	14	10	4.24	0	1.346
1989	Cleveland	AL	31	208.0	196	71	132	9	14	3.63	0	1.284
Seasonal Notation				162.0	160	53	84	9	8	3.86	0	1.313

CHUCK FINLEY   Age 27/L $11
Like Ballard, a lefthander who suddenly blossomed. Marcel
Lachemann, the Angels pitching coach, must be a genius, what
with the turnarounds of Blyleven, Kirk McCaskill, and Finley and
the emergence of Abbott.

Year	Team	Lg.	G	IP	H	BB	SO	W	L	ERA	SV	Ratio
1986	California	AL	25	46.1	40	23	37	3	1	3.30	0	1.360
1987	California	AL	35	90.2	102	43	63	2	7	4.67	0	1.599
1988	California	AL	31	194.1	191	82	111	9	15	4.17	0	1.405
1989	California	AL	29	199.2	171	82	156	16	9	2.57	0	1.267
Seasonal Notation				132.0	126	58	92	8	8	3.58	0	1.382

MIKE FLANAGAN   Age 38/L $4
He is now 10 years removed from his last good season, the one in
which he won the Cy Young. Cy Onara.

Year	Team	Lg.	G	IP	H	BB	SO	W	L	ERA	SV	Ratio
1986	Baltimore	AL	29	172.0	179	66	96	7	11	4.24	0	1.424
1987	Baltimore	AL	16	94.2	102	36	50	3	6	4.94	0	1.458
1987	Toronto	AL	7	49.1	46	15	43	3	2	2.37	0	1.237
1988	Toronto	AL	34	211.0	220	80	99	13	13	4.18	0	1.422
1989	Toronto	AL	30	171.2	186	47	47	8	10	3.93	0	1.357
Seasonal Notation				174.0	183	61	84	9	11	4.11	0	1.398

WES GARDNER   Age 28/R $1

When told that Gardner had been charged with beating his wife in
a Baltimore hotel last year, a Red Sox writer said, "Well, at least
he can beat someone."

Year	Team	Lg.	G	IP	H	BB	SO	W	L	ERA	SV	Ratio
1986	Boston	AL	1	1.0	1	0	1	0	0	9.00	0	1.000
1987	Boston	AL	49	89.2	98	42	70	3	6	5.42	10	1.561
1988	Boston	AL	36	149.0	119	64	106	8	6	3.50	2	1.228
1989	Boston	AL	22	86.0	97	47	81	3	7	5.97	0	1.674
Seasonal Notation				81.0	79	38	65	4	5	4.70	3	1.437

TOM GORDON   Age 22/R $12

The little guy with the big curve ran into a rough stretch at the
end. We hope it's not because he threw one too many breaking
balls, because for most of the summer, he was a joy to behold.

Year	Team	Lg.	G	IP	H	BB	SO	W	L	ERA	SV	Ratio
1988	Kansas City	AL	5	15.2	16	7	18	0	2	5.17	0	1.469
1989	Kansas City	AL	49	163.0	122	86	153	17	9	3.64	1	1.276
Seasonal Notation				89.0	69	47	86	9	6	3.78	1	1.293

MARK GUBICZA   Age 27/R $18

Gubicza and Saberhagen are like the Trammell and Whitaker of
pitchers. Both hurlers broke in with the Royals in 1984, and since
then, they have nearly identical records and ERAs. Gubicza is the
safer bet of the two, but Saberhagen offers brilliance.

Year	Team	Lg.	G	IP	H	BB	SO	W	L	ERA	SV	Ratio
1986	Kansas City	AL	35	180.2	155	84	118	12	6	3.64	0	1.323
1987	Kansas City	AL	35	241.2	231	120	166	13	18	3.98	0	1.452
1988	Kansas City	AL	35	269.2	237	83	183	20	8	2.70	0	1.187
1989	Kansas City	AL	36	255.0	252	63	173	15	11	3.04	0	1.235
Seasonal Notation				236.0	219	88	160	15	11	3.30	0	1.294

ERIK HANSON   Age 24/R $8

Downstairs, he has all the equipment. Upstairs, though, there are
cobwebs.

Year	Team	Lg.	G	IP	H	BB	SO	W	L	ERA	SV	Ratio
1988	Seattle	AL	6	41.2	35	12	36	2	3	3.24	0	1.128
1989	Seattle	AL	17	113.1	103	32	75	9	5	3.18	0	1.191
Seasonal Notation				77.0	69	22	56	6	4	3.19	0	1.174

PETE HARNISCH   Age 23/R $6

If he could harnisch hish talent, he'd be a shertainty to win the
Shy Young Award. (Spoken as either Foster Brooks or Yosemite Sam.)

Year	Team	Lg.	G	IP	H	BB	SO	W	L	ERA	SV	Ratio
1988	Baltimore	AL	2	13.0	13	9	10	0	2	5.54	0	1.692
1989	Baltimore	AL	18	103.1	97	64	70	5	9	4.62	0	1.558
Seasonal Notation				58.0	55	37	40	3	6	4.72	0	1.573

ANDY HAWKINS   Age 30/R $8

The rich man's John Farrell.

Year	Team	Lg.	G	IP	H	BB	SO	W	L	ERA	SV	Ratio
1986	San Diego	NL	37	209.1	218	75	117	10	8	4.30	0	1.400
1987	San Diego	NL	24	117.2	131	49	51	3	10	5.05	0	1.530
1988	San Diego	NL	33	217.2	196	76	91	14	11	3.35	0	1.250
1989	New York	AL	34	208.1	238	76	98	15	15	4.80	0	1.507
Seasonal Notation				188.0	196	69	89	11	11	4.28	0	1.406

GREG HIBBARD   Age 25/L $2

Someone to take in the last throes of the draft. He came to the
White Sox from the Royals along with Melido Perez for Floyd
Bannister. It's a trade that will haunt KC the way Tartabull for
Bankhead haunts Seattle.

Year	Team	Lg.	G	IP	H	BB	SO	W	L	ERA	SV	Ratio
1989	Chicago	AL	23	137.1	142	41	55	6	7	3.21	0	1.333
Seasonal Notation				137.0	142	41	55	6	7	3.21	0	1.333

TED HIGUERA   Age 31/L $20

If his back is fine, take advantage of his smaller price. He pitched
fine last year. He just didn't pitch enough.

Year	Team	Lg.	G	IP	H	BB	SO	W	L	ERA	SV	Ratio
1986	Milwaukee	AL	34	248.1	226	74	207	20	11	2.79	0	1.208
1987	Milwaukee	AL	35	261.2	236	87	240	18	10	3.85	0	1.234
1988	Milwaukee	AL	31	227.1	168	59	192	16	9	2.45	0	0.999
1989	Milwaukee	AL	22	135.1	125	48	91	9	6	3.46	0	1.278
Seasonal Notation				218.0	189	67	183	16	9	3.12	0	1.172

BRIAN HOLMAN   Age 25/R $3

The best of the pitchers Seattle got for Mark Langston.

Year	Team	Lg.	G	IP	H	BB	SO	W	L	ERA	SV	Ratio
1988	Montreal	NL	18	100.1	101	34	58	4	8	3.23	0	1.346
1989	Montreal	NL	10	31.2	34	15	23	1	2	4.83	0	1.548
1989	Seattle	AL	23	159.2	160	62	82	8	10	3.44	0	1.390
Seasonal Notation				145.0	148	56	82	7	10	3.52	0	1.392

CHARLIE HOUGH   Age 42/R $3

If you're intent on getting a knuckleballer, try Candiotti. Hough's wins are no longer worth his ERA or his ratio.

Year	Team	Lg.	G	IP	H	BB	SO	W	L	ERA	SV	Ratio
1986	Texas	AL	33	230.1	188	89	146	17	10	3.79	0	1.203
1987	Texas	AL	40	285.1	238	124	223	18	13	3.79	0	1.269
1988	Texas	AL	34	252.0	202	126	174	15	16	3.32	0	1.302
1989	Texas	AL	30	182.0	168	95	94	10	13	4.35	0	1.445
Seasonal Notation				237.0	199	109	159	15	13	3.77	0	1.295

DAVE JOHNSON   Age 30/R $2

The poor man's Andy Hawkins.

Year	Team	Lg.	G	IP	H	BB	SO	W	L	ERA	SV	Ratio
1987	Pittsburgh	NL	5	6.1	13	2	4	0	0	9.95	0	2.370
1989	Baltimore	AL	14	89.1	90	28	26	4	7	4.23	0	1.321
Seasonal Notation				47.0	52	15	15	2	4	4.61	0	1.390

RANDY JOHNSON   Age 26/L $2

The 6'10" Johnson resembles a brontosaurus in both size and brain volume.

Year	Team	Lg.	G	IP	H	BB	SO	W	L	ERA	SV	Ratio
1988	Montreal	NL	4	26.0	23	7	25	3	0	2.42	0	1.154
1989	Montreal	NL	7	29.2	29	26	26	0	4	6.68	0	1.854
1989	Seattle	AL	22	131.0	118	70	104	7	9	4.40	0	1.435
Seasonal Notation				93.0	85	52	78	5	7	4.48	0	1.463

JIMMY KEY   Age 28/L $15

His arm was just tired. When he came back after missing a month, he was his old self. The best control in baseball.

Year	Team	Lg.	G	IP	H	BB	SO	W	L	ERA	SV	Ratio
1986	Toronto	AL	36	232.0	222	74	141	14	11	3.57	0	1.276
1987	Toronto	AL	36	261.0	210	66	161	17	8	2.76	0	1.057
1988	Toronto	AL	21	131.1	127	30	65	12	5	3.29	0	1.195
1989	Toronto	AL	33	216.0	226	27	118	13	14	3.88	0	1.171
Seasonal Notation				210.0	196	49	121	14	10	3.35	0	1.169

ERIC KING

Age 25/R $3

White Sox GM Larry Himes takes a lot of heat, but he does a good job of acquiring pitchers. King is a bit of a head case, but the Tigers wish they had him back instead of Kenny Williams.

Year	Team	Lg.	G	IP	H	BB	SO	W	L	ERA	SV	Ratio
1986	Detroit	AL	33	138.1	108	63	79	11	4	3.51	3	1.236
1987	Detroit	AL	55	116.0	111	60	89	6	9	4.89	9	1.474
1988	Detroit	AL	23	68.2	60	34	45	4	1	3.41	3	1.369
1989	Chicago	AL	25	159.1	144	64	72	9	10	3.39	0	1.305
Seasonal Notation				120.0	106	55	71	8	6	3.79	4	1.335

DAVE LAPOINT

Age 30/L $2

A man dear to the heart of the Original Rotisserie League. That doesn't mean we want him on our team, however. To give Dave the benefit of the doubt, he has appeared washed up several times before.

Year	Team	Lg.	G	IP	H	BB	SO	W	L	ERA	SV	Ratio
1986	Detroit	AL	16	67.2	85	32	36	3	6	5.72	0	1.729
1986	San Diego	NL	24	61.1	67	24	41	1	4	4.26	0	1.484
1987	St. Louis	NL	6	16.0	26	5	8	1	1	6.75	0	1.938
1987	Chicago	AL	14	82.2	69	31	43	6	3	2.94	0	1.210
1988	Chicago	AL	25	161.1	151	47	79	10	11	3.40	0	1.227
1988	Pittsburgh	NL	8	52.0	54	10	19	4	2	2.77	0	1.231
1989	New York	AL	20	113.2	146	45	51	6	9	5.62	0	1.680
Seasonal Notation				138.0	150	49	69	8	9	4.20	0	1.428

CHARLIE LEIBRANDT

Age 33/L $1

Lost it all of a sudden. A big gamble, but one that might be worth taking.

Year	Team	Lg.	G	IP	H	BB	SO	W	L	ERA	SV	Ratio
1986	Kansas City	AL	35	231.1	238	63	108	14	11	4.09	0	1.301
1987	Kansas City	AL	35	240.1	235	74	151	16	11	3.41	0	1.286
1988	Kansas City	AL	35	243.0	244	62	125	13	12	3.19	0	1.259
1989	Kansas City	AL	33	161.0	196	54	73	5	11	5.14	0	1.553
Seasonal Notation				218.0	228	63	114	12	11	3.84	0	1.332

KIRK MCCASKILL

Age 28/R $13

It took him two years to recover from the strain of 1986. In fact, a Rotisserian we know noticed that he was bouncing his curve in warmups before Game 7 of the 1986 ALCS and resolved to trade him while his value was high. Sure enough, McCaskill got shelled in that game and shelved in 1987, and our friend swung a very sweet deal involving him. Which just goes to prove that you can actually learn things from going to real live games. So don't just sit at home poring over boxscores.

Year	Team	Lg.	G	IP	H	BB	SO	W	L	ERA	SV	Ratio
1986	California	AL	34	246.1	207	92	202	17	10	3.36	0	1.214
1987	California	AL	14	74.2	84	34	56	4	6	5.67	0	1.580
1988	California	AL	23	146.1	155	61	98	8	6	4.31	0	1.476
1989	California	AL	32	212.0	202	59	107	15	10	2.93	0	1.231
Seasonal Notation				169.0	162	62	116	11	8	3.68	0	1.316

BOB MILACKI   Age 25/R $7

His stuff isn't as good as Harnisch's, but he has a better idea of what he is doing out there.

Year	Team	Lg.	G	IP	H	BB	SO	W	L	ERA	SV	Ratio
1988	Baltimore	AL	3	25.0	9	9	18	2	0	0.72	0	0.720
1989	Baltimore	AL	37	243.0	233	88	113	14	12	3.74	0	1.321
Seasonal Notation				134.0	121	49	66	8	6	3.46	0	1.265

MIKE MOORE   Age 30/R $23

The best pitcher on the best staff in baseball, and the real MVP of the Athletics. We often wondered what he could do once he got to a good team, and now we know. May the same fate befall Scott Bankhead.

Year	Team	Lg.	G	IP	H	BB	SO	W	L	ERA	SV	Ratio
1986	Seattle	AL	38	266.0	279	94	146	11	13	4.30	1	1.402
1987	Seattle	AL	33	231.0	268	84	115	9	19	4.71	0	1.524
1988	Seattle	AL	37	228.2	196	63	182	9	15	3.78	1	1.133
1989	Oakland	AL	35	241.2	193	83	172	19	11	2.61	0	1.142
Seasonal Notation				241.0	234	81	154	12	15	3.85	1	1.303

JACK MORRIS   Age 34/R $12

He should benefit from being idle for half a season. From 1979 to 1988 he had averaged 247.2 innings a year, and he still has a few years left.

Year	Team	Lg.	G	IP	H	BB	SO	W	L	ERA	SV	Ratio
1986	Detroit	AL	35	267.0	229	82	223	21	8	3.27	0	1.165
1987	Detroit	AL	34	266.0	227	93	208	18	11	3.38	0	1.203
1988	Detroit	AL	34	235.0	225	83	168	15	13	3.94	0	1.311
1989	Detroit	AL	24	170.1	189	59	115	6	14	4.86	0	1.456
Seasonal Notation				234.0	218	79	179	15	12	3.76	0	1.265

JAIME NAVARRO   Age 23/R $3

A son of a gun. Namely, Julio Navarro.

Year	Team	Lg.	G	IP	H	BB	SO	W	L	ERA	SV	Ratio
1989	Milwaukee	AL	19	109.2	119	32	56	7	8	3.12	0	1.377
Seasonal Notation				109.0	119	32	56	7	8	3.12	0	1.377

CLAY PARKER   Age 32/R $1

The poor man's Dave Johnson.

Year	Team	Lg.	G	IP	H	BB	SO	W	L	ERA	SV	Ratio
1987	Seattle	AL	3	7.2	15	4	8	0	0	10.57	0	2.480
1989	New York	AL	22	120.0	123	31	53	4	5	3.67	0	1.283
Seasonal Notation				63.0	69	18	31	2	3	4.09	0	1.355

MELIDO PEREZ   Age 24/R $4

He had a pretty good second half after driving thousands of his Rotisserie owners to distraction the first half. But then what do you expect from Pascual's younger brother?

Year	Team	Lg.	G	IP	H	BB	SO	W	L	ERA	SV	Ratio
1987	Kansas City	AL	3	10.1	18	5	5	1	1	7.84	0	2.227
1988	Chicago	AL	32	197.0	186	72	138	12	10	3.79	0	1.310
1989	Chicago	AL	31	183.1	187	90	141	11	14	5.01	0	1.511
Seasonal Notation				130.0	130	56	95	8	8	4.47	0	1.428

SHANE RAWLEY   Age 34/L $1

He once wrote a script for *Miami Vice*. So we suggest he enroll in the Screen Writers Guild and withdraw his membership in the Players Association.

Year	Team	Lg.	G	IP	H	BB	SO	W	L	ERA	SV	Ratio
1986	Philadelphia	NL	23	157.2	166	50	73	11	7	3.54	0	1.370
1987	Philadelphia	NL	36	229.2	250	86	123	17	11	4.39	0	1.463
1988	Philadelphia	NL	32	198.0	220	78	87	8	16	4.18	0	1.505
1989	Minnesota	AL	27	145.0	167	60	68	5	12	5.21	0	1.566
Seasonal Notation				182.0	201	69	88	10	12	4.31	0	1.475

JERRY REUSS   Age 40/L $1

You don't want him, but since he's about to pitch in his fourth decade, we thought we'd leave you with this Jerry Reuss anecdote. Back when he was with the Dodgers, Reuss, a practical joker, wrote on one of the game balls, "Dear Frank, God bless you. Tommy." He showed the ball to manager Tommy Lasorda, then put it in the ball bag meant for home plate umpire Frank Pulli. During the course of the game, nobody seemed to notice the ball. But afterwards, reliever Tom Niedenfuer asked Lasorda if he had written on a ball. Lasorda explained that it was a prank played by Reuss and asked Niedenfuer what happened to the ball. "I threw it and the batter fouled it back," said Niedenfuer.

The story doesn't end there. When Lasorda got home that night, his wife Jo, who had been at the game, said, "Tommy, I almost caught a foul ball tonight." Tommy said, "That's nice, dear." She then said, "But Tommy. The man behind me caught it, and it had some writing on it: Dear Frank, God bless you. Tommy." As if that wasn't coincidence enough, Jo revealed the kicker. "Tommy," she said, "the man who caught the ball was named Frank."

Year	Team	Lg.	G	IP	H	BB	SO	W	L	ERA	SV	Ratio
1986	Los Angeles	NL	19	74.0	96	17	29	2	6	5.84	1	1.527
1987	Los Angeles	NL	1	2.0	2	0	2	0	0	4.50	0	1.000
1987	Cincinnati	NL	7	34.2	52	12	10	0	5	7.79	0	1.847
1987	California	AL	17	82.1	112	17	37	4	5	5.25	0	1.567
1988	Chicago	AL	32	183.0	183	43	73	13	9	3.44	0	1.235
1989	Chicago	AL	23	106.2	135	21	27	8	5	5.06	0	1.463
1989	Milwaukee	AL	7	33.2	36	13	13	1	4	5.35	0	1.456
Seasonal Notation				129.0	154	31	48	7	9	4.83	0	1.431

JEFF ROBINSON   Age 28/R $5

Sorry we don't have any Jeff Robinson anecdotes. But you might want to take a chance on this guy. For a few months in 1988, he was the most overpowering pitcher in the league.

Year	Team	Lg.	G	IP	H	BB	SO	W	L	ERA	SV	Ratio
1987	Detroit	AL	29	127.1	132	54	98	9	6	5.37	0	1.461
1988	Detroit	AL	24	172.0	121	72	114	13	6	2.98	0	1.122
1989	Detroit	AL	16	78.0	76	46	40	4	5	4.73	0	1.564
Seasonal Notation				125.0	110	57	84	9	6	4.15	0	1.328

STEVE ROSENBERG   Age 25/L $1

A Jewish pitcher like Sandy Koufax, Ken Holtzman, Steve Stone and Larry Sherry. Actually, he's more like Jewish pitchers Barry Latman, Marv Rotblatt and Ross Baumgarten. That brings to mind this story from *Jeopardy*. On one show, one of the categories was "Jews In Sports." The answer was "This pitcher was the youngest man ever inducted into the Hall of Fame." The contestant rang his buzzer and said, "Who is Hank Aaron?" Host Alex Trebek coolly said, "No, I'm sorry. Hank Aaron was not a pitcher."

Year	Team	Lg.	G	IP	H	BB	SO	W	L	ERA	SV	Ratio
1988	Chicago	AL	33	46.0	53	19	28	0	1	4.30	1	1.565
1989	Chicago	AL	38	142.0	148	58	77	4	13	4.94	0	1.451
Seasonal Notation				94.0	101	39	53	2	7	4.79	1	1.479

NOLAN RYAN   Age 43/R $12

Ordinarily, we would never tell you to spend this much on a 43-year-old pitcher. But there is nothing ordinary about this guy. His first strikeout back in 1966 was Pat Jarvis. His last strikeout will probably be Jarvis's grandson.

Year	Team	Lg.	G	IP	H	BB	SO	W	L	ERA	SV	Ratio
1986	Houston	NL	30	178.0	119	82	194	12	8	3.34	0	1.129
1987	Houston	NL	34	211.2	154	87	270	8	16	2.76	0	1.139
1988	Houston	NL	33	220.0	186	87	228	12	11	3.52	0	1.241
1989	Texas	AL	32	239.1	162	98	301	16	10	3.20	0	1.086
Seasonal Notation				212.0	155	89	248	12	11	3.20	0	1.148

BRET SABERHAGEN   Age 25/R $24

The wins were nice, and the ERA was sensational. But the most staggering thing about his season is that after 262⅓ innings, his ratio was still below one runner per inning. Bret does have a tendency to let down.

Year	Team	Lg.	G	IP	H	BB	SO	W	L	ERA	SV	Ratio
1986	Kansas City	AL	30	156.0	165	29	112	7	12	4.15	0	1.244
1987	Kansas City	AL	33	257.0	246	53	163	18	10	3.36	0	1.163
1988	Kansas City	AL	35	260.2	271	59	171	14	16	3.80	0	1.266
1989	Kansas City	AL	36	262.1	209	43	193	23	6	2.16	0	0.961
Seasonal Notation				233.0	223	46	160	16	11	3.28	0	1.149

ROY SMITH   Age 28/R $4

A very funny guy—his imitations of contemporary sportscasters are excellent. He's also one of the fastest workers in the game. Nobody's ever done this kind of study, but we would be willing to bet that faster workers get better support, offensive and defensive, than slower workers. That said, we should point out that Roy is not a great pitcher.

Year	Team	Lg.	G	IP	H	BB	SO	W	L	ERA	SV	Ratio
1986	Minnesota	AL	5	10.1	13	5	8	0	2	6.97	0	1.742
1987	Minnesota	AL	7	16.1	20	6	8	1	0	4.96	0	1.592
1988	Minnesota	AL	9	37.0	29	12	17	3	0	2.68	0	1.108
1989	Minnesota	AL	32	172.1	180	51	92	10	6	3.92	1	1.340
Seasonal Notation				58.0	61	19	31	4	2	3.93	0	1.339

DAVE STEWART   Age 33/R $25

Three straight 20-win seasons. The last pitcher to do that was Jim Palmer. If you think Smoke can make it four in a row, be our guest. To look at his ERA, you wonder how he managed to get even one.

Year	Team	Lg.	G	IP	H	BB	SO	W	L	ERA	SV	Ratio
1986	Oakland	AL	29	149.1	137	65	102	9	5	3.74	0	1.353
1986	Philadelphia	NL	8	12.1	15	4	9	0	0	6.57	0	1.541
1987	Oakland	AL	37	261.1	224	105	205	20	13	3.68	0	1.259
1988	Oakland	AL	37	275.2	240	110	192	21	12	3.23	0	1.270
1989	Oakland	AL	36	257.2	260	69	155	21	9	3.32	0	1.277
Seasonal Notation				239.0	219	88	166	18	10	3.50	0	1.285

DAVE STIEB   Age 32/R $12

All of his near no-hitters lead us to this suggestion: Why not have a no-hit bonus in your Rotisserie League? The award could either be monetary or statistical. For instance, a no-hitter could be counted twice; or better yet, a no-hitter would allow you to throw out your pitcher's worst outing.

Year	Team	Lg.	G	IP	H	BB	SO	W	L	ERA	SV	Ratio
1986	Toronto	AL	37	205.0	239	87	127	7	12	4.74	1	1.590
1987	Toronto	AL	33	185.0	164	87	115	13	9	4.09	0	1.357
1988	Toronto	AL	32	207.1	157	79	147	16	8	3.04	0	1.138
1989	Toronto	AL	33	206.2	164	76	101	17	8	3.35	0	1.161
Seasonal Notation				200.0	181	82	123	13	9	3.79	0	1.310

TODD STOTTLEMYRE   Age 24/R $3

It looks like Mel's boy may finally be coming around.

Year	Team	Lg.	G	IP	H	BB	SO	W	L	ERA	SV	Ratio
1988	Toronto	AL	28	98.0	109	46	67	4	8	5.69	0	1.582
1989	Toronto	AL	27	127.2	137	44	63	7	7	3.88	0	1.418
Seasonal Notation				112.0	123	45	65	6	8	4.67	0	1.489

BILLY SWIFT   Age 28/R $1

The poor man's Dave Schmidt.

Year	Team	Lg.	G	IP	H	BB	SO	W	L	ERA	SV	Ratio
1986	Seattle	AL	29	115.1	148	55	55	2	9	5.46	0	1.760
1988	Seattle	AL	38	174.2	199	65	47	8	12	4.59	0	1.512
1989	Seattle	AL	37	130.0	140	38	45	7	3	4.43	1	1.369
Seasonal Notation				139.0	162	53	49	6	8	4.78	0	1.536

GREG SWINDELL   Age 25/L $15

If his arm is sound, he's a $20 pitcher at least. But that's a big if.

Year	Team	Lg.	G	IP	H	BB	SO	W	L	ERA	SV	Ratio
1986	Cleveland	AL	9	61.2	57	15	46	5	2	4.23	0	1.168
1987	Cleveland	AL	16	102.1	112	37	97	3	8	5.10	0	1.456
1988	Cleveland	AL	33	242.0	234	45	180	18	14	3.20	0	1.153
1989	Cleveland	AL	28	184.1	170	51	129	13	6	3.37	0	1.199
Seasonal Notation				147.0	143	37	113	10	8	3.69	0	1.221

FRANK TANANA   Age 36/L $4

If he had been pitching for a better team last year, he might have had 15 wins. You can probably get him cheap, and he won't hurt you.

Year	Team	Lg.	G	IP	H	BB	SO	W	L	ERA	SV	Ratio
1986	Detroit	AL	32	188.1	196	65	119	12	9	4.16	0	1.386
1987	Detroit	AL	34	218.2	216	56	146	15	10	3.91	0	1.244
1988	Detroit	AL	32	203.0	213	64	127	14	11	4.21	0	1.365
1989	Detroit	AL	33	223.2	227	74	147	10	14	3.58	0	1.346
Seasonal Notation				208.0	213	65	135	13	11	3.95	0	1.333

BOB WELCH   Age 33/R $16

A pitcher this good has to win 20 games some time.

Year	Team	Lg.	G	IP	H	BB	SO	W	L	ERA	SV	Ratio
1986	Los Angeles	NL	33	235.2	227	55	183	7	13	3.28	0	1.197
1987	Los Angeles	NL	35	251.2	204	86	196	15	9	3.22	0	1.152
1988	Oakland	AL	36	244.2	237	81	158	17	9	3.64	0	1.300
1989	Oakland	AL	33	209.2	191	78	137	17	8	3.00	0	1.283
Seasonal Notation				235.0	215	75	169	14	10	3.30	0	1.231

DAVID WEST   Age 25/L $2

The Twins were appalled by his lack of mechanics after acquiring him from the Mets. But he does have a first class arm, and with the proper coaching, he might be a gem.

Year	Team	Lg.	G	IP	H	BB	SO	W	L	ERA	SV	Ratio
1988	New York	NL	2	6.0	6	3	3	1	0	3.00	0	1.500
1989	New York	NL	11	24.1	25	14	19	0	2	7.40	0	1.603
1989	Minnesota	AL	10	39.1	48	19	31	3	2	6.41	0	1.704
Seasonal Notation				34.0	40	18	27	2	2	6.46	0	1.651

BOBBY WITT   Age 25/R $2

Since brevity is the soul of wit: Pass.

Year	Team	Lg.	G	IP	H	BB	SO	W	L	ERA	SV	Ratio
1986	Texas	AL	31	157.2	130	143	174	11	9	5.48	0	1.732
1987	Texas	AL	26	143.0	114	140	160	8	10	4.91	0	1.776
1988	Texas	AL	22	174.1	134	101	148	8	10	3.92	0	1.348
1989	Texas	AL	31	194.1	182	114	166	12	13	5.14	0	1.523
Seasonal Notation				167.0	140	125	162	10	11	4.85	0	1.581

MIKE WITT   Age 29/R $7

Take a chance.

Year	Team	Lg.	G	IP	H	BB	SO	W	L	ERA	SV	Ratio
1986	California	AL	34	269.0	218	73	208	18	10	2.84	0	1.082
1987	California	AL	36	247.0	252	84	192	16	14	4.01	0	1.360
1988	California	AL	34	249.2	263	87	133	13	16	4.15	0	1.402
1989	California	AL	33	220.0	252	48	123	9	15	4.54	0	1.364
Seasonal Notation				246.0	246	73	164	14	14	3.84	0	1.296

CURT YOUNG   Age 29/L $2

We've always liked him for no apparent reason. Perhaps it's the idea of the headline: C. Young Wins C. Young.

Year	Team	Lg.	G	IP	H	BB	SO	W	L	ERA	SV	Ratio
1986	Oakland	AL	29	198.0	176	57	116	13	9	3.45	0	1.177
1987	Oakland	AL	31	203.0	194	44	124	13	7	4.08	0	1.172
1988	Oakland	AL	26	156.1	162	50	69	11	8	4.15	0	1.356
1989	Oakland	AL	25	111.0	117	47	55	5	9	3.73	0	1.477
Seasonal Notation				167.0	162	50	91	11	8	3.85	0	1.267

OUT OF THE BULLPEN

With the arrival of Mitch Williams in Chicago, the emergence of Joe Boever in Atlanta and Bill Landrum in Pittsburgh, and the trades of Steve Bedrosian to the Giants and Roger McDowell to the Phillies, something very peculiar happened. By our count, at least, every National League team possesses a legitimate stopper—a guy capable of 25 saves or more. The American League may not be as blessed, but it's close.

This fact brings us to our basic point. The relative plenitude of stoppers means you are expected to have at least one on your staff. A couple of teams will have lucked into two of these guys. Therefore, more than ever before, the key to the category lies not in the stoppers, but in the quality of the set-up men you can acquire. Look, anyone can pay $40 for Bedrosian or Eckersley. But you need a couple of Craig Leffertses and Rick Honeycutts to separate you from the pack.

The problem is, you can just as easily end up with Dale Mohorcics or Andy McGaffigans—guys with few saves and terrible numbers. Your best bet here is to watch those ratios over the last few years and hope the ones you pick, through trade or injury, become the top dogs before the season ends. Just ask Roger McDowell or Jeff Montgomery.

Does R. J. Reynolds smoke?

NATIONAL LEAGUE

DON AASE   Age 35/R $2

The first pitcher listed in *The Baseball Encyclopedia* is Don Aase.
The first non-pitcher is Henry Aaron. Spooky, or what?

Year	Team	Lg.	G	IP	H	BB	SO	W	L	ERA	SV	Ratio
1986	Baltimore	AL	66	81.2	71	28	67	6	7	2.98	34	1.212
1987	Baltimore	AL	7	8.0	8	4	3	1	0	2.25	2	1.500
1988	Baltimore	AL	35	46.2	40	37	28	0	0	4.05	0	1.650
1989	New York	NL	49	59.1	56	26	34	1	5	3.94	2	1.382
Seasonal Notation				48.0	44	24	33	2	3	3.50	10	1.380

JUAN AGOSTO   Age 32/L $2

While none of us was watching, this winter Juan Agosto prepared
for his sixteenth season in professional baseball. The long and
winding road has taken him from the cane fields of his native
Puerto Rico to the orange groves of Winter Haven; from the
factories of Elmira to the tobacco barns of Winston-Salem; from
the eastern remoteness of Glens Falls to the midwestern sweetness
of Appleton; from gutsy, brawling Edmonton to gutsy, brawling
Chicago; from the oxygen-thin heights of Denver to the gritty
depths of Buffalo; from Minneapolis by the Mississippi to Toledo by
the Maumee; from the the saguaro-covered mountains of Tucson to
the petroleum byproduct-covered infields of Houston. Juan, we
salute you: the Ryder Rent-a-Truck player of the decade.

Year	Team	Lg.	G	IP	H	BB	SO	W	L	ERA	SV	Ratio
1986	Chicago	AL	9	4.2	6	4	3	0	2	7.73	0	2.146
1986	Minnesota	AL	17	20.1	43	14	9	1	2	8.85	1	2.804
1987	Houston	NL	27	27.1	26	10	6	1	1	2.63	2	1.317
1988	Houston	NL	75	91.2	74	30	33	10	2	2.26	4	1.135
1989	Houston	NL	71	83.0	81	32	46	4	5	2.93	1	1.361
Seasonal Notation				56.0	58	23	24	4	3	3.25	2	1.410

PAUL ASSENMACHER   Age 29/L $3

Peculiarly, middle relievers get more valuable when they move to
Wrigley. They're the guys on the mound when the Cubbies are
trailing 7-2 and stage one of their late-inning ambushes, and they're
also the guys managers look to when the bullpen ace has blown his
third save in a row.

Year	Team	Lg.	G	IP	H	BB	SO	W	L	ERA	SV	Ratio
1986	Atlanta	NL	61	68.1	61	26	56	7	3	2.50	7	1.273
1987	Atlanta	NL	52	54.2	58	24	39	1	1	5.10	2	1.500
1988	Atlanta	NL	64	79.1	72	32	71	8	7	3.06	5	1.311
1989	Atlanta	NL	49	57.2	55	16	64	1	3	3.59	0	1.231
1989	Chicago	NL	14	19.0	19	12	15	2	1	5.21	0	1.632
Seasonal Notation				69.0	66	28	61	5	4	3.58	4	1.344

STEVE BEDROSIAN   Age 32/R $28

Sharing the burden with Craig Lefferts will reduce Bedrock's save situations, but enhance his effectiveness. Good career move, tolerable Rotisserie move.

Year	Team	Lg.	G	IP	H	BB	SO	W	L	ERA	SV	Ratio
1986	Philadelphia	NL	68	90.1	79	34	82	8	6	3.39	29	1.251
1987	Philadelphia	NL	65	89.0	79	28	74	5	3	2.83	40	1.202
1988	Philadelphia	NL	57	74.1	75	27	61	6	6	3.75	28	1.372
1989	Philadelphia	NL	28	33.2	21	17	24	2	3	3.21	6	1.129
1989	San Francisco	NL	40	51.0	35	22	34	1	4	2.65	17	1.118
Seasonal Notation				84.0	72	32	69	6	6	3.19	30	1.233

JOE BOEVER   Age 29/R $20

Started 1989 as if his name was Sutter. Ended 1989 unsure whether his name should be Ethyl or Premium. He's the sort of player Ultra was invented for: buy him for **$20**, and if he continues his late-season pyromania, bring up Dwayne Henry in his place.

Year	Team	Lg.	G	IP	H	BB	SO	W	L	ERA	SV	Ratio
1986	St. Louis	NL	11	21.2	19	11	8	0	1	1.66	0	1.385
1987	Atlanta	NL	14	18.1	29	12	18	1	0	7.36	0	2.237
1988	Atlanta	NL	16	20.1	12	1	7	0	2	1.77	1	0.639
1989	Atlanta	NL	66	82.1	78	34	68	4	11	3.94	21	1.360
Seasonal Notation				35.0	35	15	25	1	4	3.72	6	1.374

JEFF BRANTLEY   Age 26/R $1

Unowned and untouchable for most of last season; after the Gazers picked him up in mid-year, all that distinguished him was his ordinariness.

Year	Team	Lg.	G	IP	H	BB	SO	W	L	ERA	SV	Ratio
1988	San Francisco	NL	9	20.2	22	6	11	0	1	5.66	1	1.355
1989	San Francisco	NL	59	97.1	101	37	69	7	1	4.07	0	1.418
Seasonal Notation				58.0	62	22	40	4	1	4.35	1	1.407

TIM BURKE   Age 31/R $35

Has finally lived up to the role he inherited when Jeff Reardon went westward. Good thing, too, as the 'Spos have no one else to turn to.

Year	Team	Lg.	G	IP	H	BB	SO	W	L	ERA	SV	Ratio
1986	Montreal	NL	68	101.1	103	46	82	9	7	2.93	4	1.470
1987	Montreal	NL	55	91.0	64	17	58	7	0	1.19	18	0.890
1988	Montreal	NL	61	82.0	84	25	42	3	5	3.40	18	1.329
1989	Montreal	NL	68	84.2	68	22	54	9	3	2.55	28	1.063
Seasonal Notation				89.0	80	28	59	7	4	2.51	17	1.195

DON CARMAN   Age 30/L $0

If he's in the Phillies rotation, the Phillies are in deep trouble. The
Phillies are in deep trouble anyway, but that's another story.

Year	Team	Lg.	G	IP	H	BB	SO	W	L	ERA	SV	Ratio
1986	Philadelphia	NL	50	134.1	113	52	98	10	5	3.22	1	1.228
1987	Philadelphia	NL	35	211.0	194	69	125	13	11	4.22	0	1.246
1988	Philadelphia	NL	36	201.1	211	70	116	10	14	4.29	0	1.396
1989	Philadelphia	NL	49	149.1	152	86	81	5	15	5.24	0	1.594
Seasonal Notation				173.0	168	69	105	10	11	4.27	0	1.361

NORM CHARLTON   Age 33/L $3

Actually graduated from Rice University with a triple major in
political science, religion, and physical education. We wonder
about two things: when will the Reds put him in the rotation and
leave him there; and what foreign language did he study?

Year	Team	Lg.	G	IP	H	BB	SO	W	L	ERA	SV	Ratio
1988	Cincinnati	NL	10	61.1	60	20	39	4	5	3.96	0	1.304
1989	Cincinnati	NL	69	95.1	67	40	98	8	3	2.93	0	1.122
Seasonal Notation				78.0	64	30	69	6	4	3.33	0	1.194

DANNY DARWIN   Age 34/R $11

Great, great season—so great that to take him out of his swingman
role would seem crazy. The Darwin of 1989 was the closest thing that
Rotisserie Baseball has ever had to a "four-category" pitcher. Price
that low only because of the sheer unlikeliness of his accomplishment.

Year	Team	Lg.	G	IP	H	BB	SO	W	L	ERA	SV	Ratio
1986	Milwaukee	AL	27	130.1	120	35	80	6	8	3.52	0	1.189
1986	Houston	NL	12	54.1	50	9	40	5	2	2.32	0	1.086
1987	Houston	NL	33	195.2	184	69	134	9	10	3.59	0	1.293
1988	Houston	NL	44	192.0	189	48	129	8	13	3.84	3	1.234
1989	Houston	NL	68	122.0	92	33	104	11	4	2.36	7	1.025
Seasonal Notation				173.0	159	49	122	10	9	3.33	3	1.194

MARK DAVIS   Age 29/L $43

He seemed to have 20 saves by the end of April, and then he
quieted down. We should all encounter such quietness: When the
Padres came back in August, so did Davis. He's the new Worrell.

Year	Team	Lg.	G	IP	H	BB	SO	W	L	ERA	SV	Ratio
1986	San Francisco	NL	67	84.1	63	34	90	5	7	2.99	4	1.150
1987	San Francisco	NL	20	70.2	72	28	51	4	5	4.71	0	1.415
1987	San Diego	NL	43	62.1	51	31	47	5	3	3.18	2	1.316
1988	San Diego	NL	62	98.1	70	42	102	5	10	2.01	28	1.139
1989	San Diego	NL	70	92.2	66	31	92	4	3	1.85	44	1.047
Seasonal Notation				102.0	81	42	96	6	7	2.82	20	1.195

KEN DAYLEY   Age 31/L $16

No reason to think Whitey won't use him at least as much as he did in 1989; if anything, given Worrell's recent fragility, Dayley's saves should increase.

Year	Team	Lg.	G	IP	H	BB	SO	W	L	ERA	SV	Ratio
1986	St. Louis	NL	31	38.2	42	11	33	0	3	3.26	5	1.371
1987	St. Louis	NL	53	61.0	52	33	63	9	5	2.66	4	1.393
1988	St. Louis	NL	54	55.1	48	19	38	2	7	2.77	5	1.211
1989	St. Louis	NL	71	75.1	63	30	40	4	3	2.87	12	1.235
Seasonal Notation				57.0	51	23	44	4	5	2.85	7	1.294

ROB DIBBLE   Age 26/R $15

Unbelievable. Watching him pitch is like watching the Chinese tanks roll into Tienanmen Square. Will *have* to become someone's stopper within another season or two. Buy him now, before he's unaffordable.

Year	Team	Lg.	G	IP	H	BB	SO	W	L	ERA	SV	Ratio
1988	Cincinnati	NL	37	59.1	43	21	59	1	1	1.82	0	1.079
1989	Cincinnati	NL	74	99.0	62	39	141	10	5	2.09	2	1.020
Seasonal Notation				79.0	53	30	100	6	3	1.99	1	1.042

FRANK DIPINO   Age 33/L $2

Reliable.

Year	Team	Lg.	G	IP	H	BB	SO	W	L	ERA	SV	Ratio
1986	Houston	NL	31	40.1	27	16	27	1	3	3.57	3	1.066
1986	Chicago	NL	30	40.0	47	14	43	2	4	5.18	0	1.525
1987	Chicago	NL	69	80.0	75	34	61	3	3	3.15	4	1.362
1988	Chicago	NL	63	90.1	102	32	69	2	3	4.98	6	1.483
1989	St. Louis	NL	67	88.1	73	20	44	9	0	2.45	0	1.053
Seasonal Notation				84.0	81	29	61	4	3	3.74	3	1.298

MARK EICHHORN   Age 29/R $1

Unreliable.

Year	Team	Lg.	G	IP	H	BB	SO	W	L	ERA	SV	Ratio
1986	Toronto	AL	69	157.0	105	45	166	14	6	1.72	10	0.955
1987	Toronto	AL	89	127.2	110	52	96	10	6	3.17	4	1.269
1988	Toronto	AL	37	66.2	79	27	28	0	3	4.19	1	1.590
1989	Atlanta	NL	45	68.1	70	19	49	5	5	4.35	0	1.303
Seasonal Notation				104.0	91	36	85	7	5	2.98	4	1.208

JOHN FRANCO   Age 29/L $40

For five straight seasons, until last year, his save total increased. His only new record best in 1989 was losses. Still, he's John Franco.

Year	Team	Lg.	G	IP	H	BB	SO	W	L	ERA	SV	Ratio
1986	Cincinnati	NL	74	101.0	90	44	84	6	6	2.94	29	1.327
1987	Cincinnati	NL	68	82.0	76	27	61	8	5	2.52	32	1.256
1988	Cincinnati	NL	70	86.0	60	27	46	6	6	1.57	39	1.012
1989	Cincinnati	NL	60	80.2	77	36	60	4	8	3.12	32	1.401
Seasonal Notation				87.0	76	34	63	6	6	2.55	33	1.250

TODD FROHWIRTH   Age 27/R $1

Inconsequential.

Year	Team	Lg.	G	IP	H	BB	SO	W	L	ERA	SV	Ratio
1987	Philadelphia	NL	10	11.0	12	2	9	1	0	0.00	0	1.273
1988	Philadelphia	NL	12	12.0	16	11	11	1	2	8.25	0	2.250
1989	Philadelphia	NL	45	62.2	56	18	39	1	0	3.59	0	1.181
Seasonal Notation				28.0	28	10	20	1	1	3.78	0	1.343

JIM GOTT   Age 30/R $?

Who knows? It was unlikely enough when he became a star stopper, and unlikelier still when Bill Landrum stepped into his shoes and did even better. Until we see what Gott, Leyland, and the Pirates do in spring training, this is a limb we will not walk out on.

Year	Team	Lg.	G	IP	H	BB	SO	W	L	ERA	SV	Ratio
1986	San Francisco	NL	9	13.0	16	13	9	0	0	7.62	1	2.231
1987	San Francisco	NL	30	56.0	53	32	63	1	0	4.50	0	1.518
1987	Pittsburgh	NL	25	31.0	28	8	27	0	2	1.45	13	1.161
1988	Pittsburgh	NL	67	77.1	68	22	76	6	6	3.49	34	1.164
1989	Pittsburgh	NL	1	0.2	1	1	1	0	0	0.00	0	3.030
Seasonal Notation				44.0	42	19	44	2	2	3.74	12	1.360

MARK GRANT   Age 26/R $3

In-and-out. Doomed to middle relief, but will do fairly well for you there.

Year	Team	Lg.	G	IP	H	BB	SO	W	L	ERA	SV	Ratio
1986	San Francisco	NL	4	10.0	6	5	5	0	1	3.60	0	1.100
1987	San Francisco	NL	16	61.0	66	21	32	1	2	3.54	1	1.426
1987	San Diego	NL	17	102.1	104	52	58	6	7	4.66	0	1.524
1988	San Diego	NL	33	97.2	97	36	61	2	8	3.69	0	1.362
1989	San Diego	NL	50	116.1	105	32	69	8	2	3.33	2	1.178
Seasonal Notation				96.0	95	37	56	4	5	3.81	1	1.353

ATLEE HAMMAKER   Age 32/L $2

His real first name is "Charlton." True fact. No relation to Heston.

Year	Team	Lg.	G	IP	H	BB	SO	W	L	ERA	SV	Ratio
1987	San Francisco	NL	31	168.1	159	57	107	10	10	3.58	0	1.283
1988	San Francisco	NL	43	144.2	136	41	65	9	9	3.73	5	1.224
1989	San Francisco	NL	28	76.2	78	23	30	6	6	3.76	0	1.318
Seasonal Notation				129.0	124	40	67	8	8	3.67	2	1.268

GREG W. HARRIS   Age 26/R $8

The only remaining Greg Harris in the National League may not
be ambidextrous like the AL version, but he's eight years younger
and a hell of a good pitcher. His day will come, and you could do
worse than invest now.

Year	Team	Lg.	G	IP	H	BB	SO	W	L	ERA	SV	Ratio
1988	San Diego	NL	3	18.0	13	3	15	2	0	1.50	0	0.889
1989	San Diego	NL	56	135.0	106	52	106	8	9	2.60	6	1.170
Seasonal Notation				76.0	60	28	61	5	5	2.47	3	1.137

JOE HESKETH   Age 31/L $1

Once upon a time, we thought he was gonna be a contenduh.

Year	Team	Lg.	G	IP	H	BB	SO	W	L	ERA	SV	Ratio
1986	Montreal	NL	15	82.2	92	31	67	6	5	5.01	0	1.488
1987	Montreal	NL	18	28.2	23	15	31	0	0	3.14	1	1.326
1988	Montreal	NL	60	72.2	63	35	64	4	3	2.85	9	1.349
1989	Montreal	NL	43	48.1	54	26	44	6	4	5.77	3	1.655
Seasonal Notation				58.0	58	27	52	4	3	4.26	3	1.459

JAY HOWELL   Age 34/R $35

If someone had asked you what pitcher would finally persuade
Tommy Lasorda to go with one big guy in the bullpen, would you
possibly have guessed Jay Howell? He set a new LA saves record
in early August, and that was in a season in which the Dodgers
were rarely winning. Phenomenal numbers, but he's had five
appearances on the DL since 1983, and he turns 35 this year.

Year	Team	Lg.	G	IP	H	BB	SO	W	L	ERA	SV	Ratio
1986	Oakland	AL	38	53.1	53	23	42	3	6	3.38	16	1.425
1987	Oakland	AL	36	44.1	48	21	35	3	4	5.89	16	1.557
1988	Los Angeles	NL	50	65.0	44	21	70	5	3	2.08	21	1.000
1989	Los Angeles	NL	56	79.2	60	22	55	5	3	1.58	28	1.029
Seasonal Notation				60.0	51	22	51	4	4	2.90	20	1.205

BOB KIPPER   Age 25/L $1
Looks better than he is.

Year	Team	Lg.	G	IP	H	BB	SO	W	L	ERA	SV	Ratio
1986	Pittsburgh	NL	20	114.0	123	34	81	6	8	4.03	0	1.377
1987	Pittsburgh	NL	24	110.2	117	52	83	5	9	5.94	0	1.527
1988	Pittsburgh	NL	50	65.0	54	26	39	2	6	3.74	0	1.231
1989	Pittsburgh	NL	52	83.0	55	33	58	3	4	2.93	4	1.060
Seasonal Notation				93.0	87	36	65	4	7	4.30	1	1.326

LES LANCASTER   Age 27/R $3
Utterly impossible to predict how Zimmer will use him. But be
assured: last year's ERA will never occur again.

Year	Team	Lg.	G	IP	H	BB	SO	W	L	ERA	SV	Ratio
1987	Chicago	NL	27	132.1	138	51	78	8	3	4.90	0	1.428
1988	Chicago	NL	44	85.2	89	34	36	4	6	3.78	5	1.436
1989	Chicago	NL	42	72.2	60	15	56	4	2	1.36	8	1.032
Seasonal Notation				96.0	96	33	57	5	4	3.68	4	1.331

BILL LANDRUM   Age 32/R $32
Is Jim Gott the new Wally Pipp? If you think "yes," pay the price.

Year	Team	Lg.	G	IP	H	BB	SO	W	L	ERA	SV	Ratio
1986	Cincinnati	NL	10	13.1	23	4	14	0	0	6.75	0	2.026
1987	Cincinnati	NL	44	65.0	68	34	42	3	2	4.71	2	1.569
1988	Chicago	NL	7	12.1	19	3	6	1	0	5.84	0	1.784
1989	Pittsburgh	NL	56	81.0	60	28	51	2	3	1.67	26	1.086
Seasonal Notation				42.0	43	17	28	2	1	3.51	7	1.392

CRAIG LEFFERTS   Age 32/L $12
Excellent, reliable, brave, trustworthy, reverent, true. He's only
had one bad year, and even that wasn't a calamity. A Lefferts in
the pen helps managers sleep, and Rotisserians win. Still, a full
season of Bedrosian will cut Craig's saves in half.

Year	Team	Lg.	G	IP	H	BB	SO	W	L	ERA	SV	Ratio
1986	San Diego	NL	83	107.2	98	44	72	9	8	3.09	4	1.319
1987	San Diego	NL	33	51.1	56	15	39	2	2	4.38	2	1.383
1987	San Francisco	NL	44	47.1	36	18	18	3	3	3.23	4	1.141
1988	San Francisco	NL	64	92.1	74	23	58	3	8	2.92	11	1.051
1989	San Francisco	NL	70	107.0	93	22	71	2	4	2.69	20	1.075
Seasonal Notation				101.0	89	31	65	5	6	3.13	10	1.181

ROGER MCDOWELL   Age 29/R $15

Reborn in Philadelphia. But how much longer will his sinker sink?
And how much longer will Parrett stay in middle relief?

Year	Team	Lg.	G	IP	H	BB	SO	W	L	ERA	SV	Ratio
1986	New York	NL	75	128.0	107	42	65	14	9	3.02	22	1.164
1987	New York	NL	56	88.2	95	28	32	7	5	4.16	25	1.387
1988	New York	NL	62	89.0	80	31	46	5	5	2.63	16	1.247
1989	New York	NL	25	35.1	34	16	15	1	5	3.31	4	1.415
1989	Philadelphia	NL	44	56.2	45	22	32	3	3	1.11	19	1.182
Seasonal Notation				99.0	90	35	48	8	7	2.94	22	1.257

JEFF MUSSELMAN   Age 26/L $1

So he got a degree from Harvard—big deal. George Bush got a
degree from Yale, and how smart is he?

Year	Team	Lg.	G	IP	H	BB	SO	W	L	ERA	SV	Ratio
1986	Toronto	AL	6	5.1	8	5	4	0	0	10.13	0	2.439
1987	Toronto	AL	68	89.0	75	54	54	12	5	4.15	3	1.449
1988	Toronto	AL	15	85.0	80	30	39	8	5	3.18	0	1.294
1989	Toronto	AL	5	11.0	19	9	3	0	1	10.64	0	2.545
1989	New York	NL	20	26.1	27	14	11	3	2	3.08	0	1.557
Seasonal Notation				54.0	52	28	28	6	3	4.11	1	1.482

RANDY MYERS   Age 27/L $42

Money in the bank, especially with McDowell gone.

Year	Team	Lg.	G	IP	H	BB	SO	W	L	ERA	SV	Ratio
1986	New York	NL	10	10.2	11	9	13	0	0	4.22	0	1.876
1987	New York	NL	54	75.0	61	30	92	3	6	3.96	6	1.213
1988	New York	NL	55	68.0	45	17	69	7	3	1.72	26	0.912
1989	New York	NL	65	84.1	62	40	88	7	4	2.35	24	1.210
Seasonal Notation				59.0	45	24	66	4	3	2.76	14	1.156

JEFF PARRETT   Age 28/R $15

Along with Dibble, the middle reliever most likely to become an
effective short man. A key man for a team looking beyond this
year.

Year	Team	Lg.	G	IP	H	BB	SO	W	L	ERA	SV	Ratio
1986	Montreal	NL	12	20.1	19	13	21	0	1	4.87	0	1.574
1987	Montreal	NL	45	62.0	53	30	56	7	6	4.21	6	1.339
1988	Montreal	NL	61	91.2	66	45	62	12	4	2.65	6	1.211
1989	Philadelphia	NL	72	105.2	90	44	98	12	6	2.98	6	1.268
Seasonal Notation				69.0	57	33	59	8	4	3.28	5	1.287

ALEJANDRO PENA   Age 30/R $7

Still an excellent numbers man. Will help in two categories, possibly three.

Year	Team	Lg.	G	IP	H	BB	SO	W	L	ERA	SV	Ratio
1986	Los Angeles	NL	24	70.0	74	30	46	1	2	4.89	1	1.486
1987	Los Angeles	NL	37	87.1	82	37	76	2	7	3.50	11	1.363
1988	Los Angeles	NL	60	94.1	75	27	83	6	7	1.91	12	1.081
1989	Los Angeles	NL	53	76.0	62	18	75	4	3	2.13	5	1.053
Seasonal Notation				81.0	73	28	70	3	5	3.02	7	1.236

JEFF PICO   Age 24/R $1

Yawn.

Year	Team	Lg.	G	IP	H	BB	SO	W	L	ERA	SV	Ratio
1988	Chicago	NL	29	112.2	108	37	57	6	7	4.15	1	1.287
1989	Chicago	NL	53	90.2	99	31	38	3	1	3.77	2	1.434
Seasonal Notation				101.0	104	34	48	5	4	3.98	2	1.353

DAN QUISENBERRY   Age 37/R $2

Watching Quiz contribute in St. Louis was the happiest story of the year. He will, however, turn 37 the week before the pitchers and catchers report.

Year	Team	Lg.	G	IP	H	BB	SO	W	L	ERA	SV	Ratio
1986	Kansas City	AL	62	81.1	92	24	36	3	7	2.77	12	1.426
1987	Kansas City	AL	47	49.0	58	10	17	4	1	2.76	8	1.388
1988	Kansas City	AL	20	25.1	32	5	9	0	1	3.55	1	1.461
1988	St. Louis	NL	33	38.0	54	6	19	2	0	6.16	0	1.579
1989	St. Louis	NL	63	78.1	78	14	37	3	1	2.64	6	1.175
Seasonal Notation				67.0	79	15	30	3	3	3.28	7	1.371

DAVE SMITH   Age 35/R $31

Has been between 24 and 33 saves for six straight years. Just don't let him do any heavy lifting in the off-season.

Year	Team	Lg.	G	IP	H	BB	SO	W	L	ERA	SV	Ratio
1986	Houston	NL	54	56.0	39	22	46	4	7	2.73	33	1.089
1987	Houston	NL	50	60.0	39	21	73	2	3	1.65	24	1.000
1988	Houston	NL	51	57.1	60	19	38	4	5	2.67	27	1.378
1989	Houston	NL	52	58.0	49	19	31	3	4	2.64	25	1.172
Seasonal Notation				57.0	47	20	47	3	5	2.41	27	1.159

ZANE SMITH   Age 29/L $2

After years of striving to be the ugliest starter in baseball, Zane finally realized that Rick Mahler just wouldn't relinquish the crown. Consequently, asked management to change his role when he got to Montreal, enabling him to win "ugliest middle reliever in base-ball." By acclamation.

Year	Team	Lg.	G	IP	H	BB	SO	W	L	ERA	SV	Ratio
1986	Atlanta	NL	38	204.2	209	105	139	8	16	4.05	1	1.534
1987	Atlanta	NL	36	242.0	245	91	130	15	10	4.09	0	1.388
1988	Atlanta	NL	23	140.1	159	44	59	5	10	4.30	0	1.447
1989	Atlanta	NL	17	99.0	102	33	58	1	12	4.45	0	1.364
1989	Montreal	NL	31	48.0	39	19	35	0	1	1.50	2	1.208
Seasonal Notation				183.0	189	73	105	7	12	4.00	1	1.425

MIKE STANTON   Age 22/L $9

Came out of nowhere late in the season, a pretty easy task when the shoes to be filled are Joe Boever's. Pay especially close attention this spring.

Year	Team	Lg.	G	IP	H	BB	SO	W	L	ERA	SV	Ratio
1989	Atlanta	NL	20	24.0	17	8	27	0	1	1.50	7	1.042
Seasonal Notation				24.0	17	8	27	0	1	1.50	7	1.042

MITCH WILLIAMS   Age 25/L $33

Yow! At his very best, the James Brown of relief pitching will hurt your ratio and disturb your sleep. For this you should pay so much? Yep.

Year	Team	Lg.	G	IP	H	BB	SO	W	L	ERA	SV	Ratio
1986	Texas	AL	80	98.0	69	79	90	8	6	3.58	8	1.510
1987	Texas	AL	85	108.2	63	94	129	8	6	3.23	6	1.445
1988	Texas	AL	67	68.0	48	47	61	2	7	4.63	18	1.397
1989	Chicago	NL	76	81.2	71	52	67	4	4	2.65	36	1.506
Seasonal Notation				89.0	63	68	87	6	6	3.46	17	1.468

STEVE WILSON   Age 25/L $3

Who?

Year	Team	Lg.	G	IP	H	BB	SO	W	L	ERA	SV	Ratio
1988	Texas	AL	3	7.2	7	4	1	0	0	5.87	0	1.436
1989	Chicago	NL	53	85.2	83	31	65	6	4	4.20	2	1.331
Seasonal Notation				46.0	45	18	33	3	2	4.34	1	1.339

BASEBALL ANAGRAM #2

George Steinbrenner = Bring ego. Sneer. Reset!

TODD WORRELL   Age 30/R $39

Medic! Medic! If healthy in Florida, ante up per usual. He's still Todd Worrell.

Year	Team	Lg.	G	IP	H	BB	SO	W	L	ERA	SV	Ratio
1986	St. Louis	NL	74	103.2	86	41	73	9	10	2.08	36	1.225
1987	St. Louis	NL	75	94.2	86	34	92	8	6	2.66	33	1.268
1988	St. Louis	NL	68	90.0	69	34	78	5	9	3.00	32	1.144
1989	St. Louis	NL	47	51.2	42	26	41	3	5	2.96	20	1.316
Seasonal Notation				84.0	71	34	71	6	8	2.62	30	1.229

AMERICAN LEAGUE

Finding relief used to be much more a crap shoot than it is now. For some reason, the top relievers—Dennis Eckersley, Doug Jones, Jeff Reardon, Dan Plesac—are more reliable than they once were. And occasionally, you unearth a Jeff Montgomery or a Lee Guetterman. Be prepared to spend some heavy bucks for the saviors.

SCOTT BAILES   Age 28/L $2

Rhymes with fails.

Year	Team	Lg.	G	IP	H	BB	SO	W	L	ERA	SV	Ratio
1986	Cleveland	AL	62	112.2	123	43	60	10	10	4.95	7	1.473
1987	Cleveland	AL	39	120.1	145	47	65	7	8	4.64	6	1.596
1988	Cleveland	AL	37	145.0	149	46	53	9	14	4.90	0	1.345
1989	Cleveland	AL	34	113.2	116	29	47	5	9	4.28	0	1.276
Seasonal Notation				122.0	133	41	56	8	10	4.70	3	1.420

JUAN BERENGUER   Age 35/R $5

There are several reasons to get the Panamanian strongman. He's been averaging eight wins a year for the Twins. If Reardon goes down, the stopper role will fall to him. And if you're producing a Latino version of *Damn Yankees*, he would make a wonderful Devil.

Year	Team	Lg.	G	IP	H	BB	SO	W	L	ERA	SV	Ratio
1986	San Francisco	NL	46	73.1	64	44	72	2	3	2.70	4	1.473
1987	Minnesota	AL	47	112.0	100	47	110	8	1	3.94	4	1.313
1988	Minnesota	AL	57	100.0	74	61	99	8	4	3.96	2	1.350
1989	Minnesota	AL	56	106.0	96	47	93	9	3	3.48	3	1.349
Seasonal Notation				97.0	84	50	94	7	3	3.59	3	1.362

TODD BURNS   Age 30/R $6

A man caught in the middle because he's a good spot starter and an excellent setup man. If the Athletics ever find a role for him, his value will increase.

Year	Team	Lg.	G	IP	H	BB	SO	W	L	ERA	SV	Ratio
1988	Oakland	AL	17	102.2	93	34	57	8	2	3.16	1	1.237
1989	Oakland	AL	50	96.1	66	28	49	6	5	2.24	8	0.976
Seasonal Notation				99.0	80	31	53	7	4	2.71	5	1.111

GREG CADARET   Age 28/L $3

You loved the musical, now buy the pitcher. Life is a cadaret, old chum.

Year	Team	Lg.	G	IP	H	BB	SO	W	L	ERA	SV	Ratio
1987	Oakland	AL	29	39.2	37	24	30	6	2	4.54	0	1.538
1988	Oakland	AL	58	71.2	60	36	64	5	2	2.89	3	1.340
1989	Oakland	AL	26	27.2	21	19	14	0	0	2.28	0	1.446
1989	New York	AL	20	92.1	109	38	66	5	5	4.58	0	1.592
Seasonal Notation				77.0	76	39	58	5	3	3.77	1	1.487

CHUCK CARY   Age 30/L $4

Called up because everybody in the Yankees' rotation sucked, this career minor leaguer pitched some brilliant games. He might just be one of those late-blooming lefthanders like Ballard.

Year	Team	Lg.	G	IP	H	BB	SO	W	L	ERA	SV	Ratio
1986	Detroit	AL	22	31.2	33	15	21	1	2	3.41	0	1.516
1987	Atlanta	NL	13	16.2	17	4	15	1	1	3.78	1	1.261
1988	Atlanta	NL	7	8.1	8	4	7	0	0	6.48	0	1.441
1989	New York	AL	22	99.1	78	29	79	4	4	3.26	0	1.077
Seasonal Notation				38.0	34	13	31	2	2	3.52	0	1.205

CHUCK CRIM   Age 31/R $7

Plesac's understudy, he had more wins than all but two Brewer pitchers. Put a Crim in your plans.

Year	Team	Lg.	G	IP	H	BB	SO	W	L	ERA	SV	Ratio
1987	Milwaukee	AL	53	130.0	133	39	56	6	8	3.67	12	1.323
1988	Milwaukee	AL	70	105.0	95	28	58	7	6	2.91	9	1.171
1989	Milwaukee	AL	76	117.2	114	36	59	9	7	2.83	7	1.275
Seasonal Notation				117.0	114	34	58	7	7	3.16	9	1.262

DENNIS ECKERSLEY   Age 35/R $40

A lesser man would have crumbled after giving up that homer to
Kirk Gibson. If he hadn't missed a month, he might have won the
Cy Young Award. Not only is he a great relief pitcher—three
walks!—but he is used carefully by Tony LaRussa.

Year	Team	Lg.	G	IP	H	BB	SO	W	L	ERA	SV	Ratio
1986	Chicago	NL	33	201.0	226	43	137	6	11	4.57	0	1.338
1987	Oakland	AL	54	115.2	99	17	113	6	8	3.03	16	1.003
1988	Oakland	AL	60	72.2	52	11	70	4	2	2.35	45	0.867
1989	Oakland	AL	51	57.2	32	3	55	4	0	1.56	33	0.607
Seasonal Notation				111.0	102	19	94	5	5	3.42	24	1.081

STEVE FARR   Age 33/R $3

He lost his stopper role to Montgomery, but he could always get it
back. (Of course, we said the same thing when Dan Quisenberry
lost his role to Farr.)

Year	Team	Lg.	G	IP	H	BB	SO	W	L	ERA	SV	Ratio
1986	Kansas City	AL	56	109.1	90	39	83	8	4	3.13	8	1.180
1987	Kansas City	AL	47	91.0	97	44	88	4	3	4.15	1	1.549
1988	Kansas City	AL	62	82.2	74	30	72	5	4	2.50	20	1.258
1989	Kansas City	AL	51	63.1	75	22	56	2	5	4.12	18	1.532
Seasonal Notation				86.0	84	34	75	5	4	3.43	12	1.360

WILLIE FRASER   Age 25/R $4

There aren't many of these guys: pitchers born in New York City.
Willie is no Whitey Ford, a previous city lad, but he did turn out
to be a decent relief pitcher after a disastrous two-year-long turn in
the rotation. The reason to keep an eye on him is that Bryan
Harvey does not inspire a great deal of confidence, and that Greg
Minton and Bob McClure are no spring chickens.

Year	Team	Lg.	G	IP	H	BB	SO	W	L	ERA	SV	Ratio
1986	California	AL	1	4.1	6	1	2	0	0	8.31	0	1.617
1987	California	AL	36	176.2	160	63	106	10	10	3.92	1	1.262
1988	California	AL	34	194.2	203	80	86	12	13	5.41	0	1.454
1989	California	AL	44	91.2	80	23	46	4	7	3.24	2	1.124
Seasonal Notation				116.0	112	42	60	7	8	4.45	1	1.318

PAUL GIBSON   Age 30/L $1

Strictly an ort. Look it up.

Year	Team	Lg.	G	IP	H	BB	SO	W	L	ERA	SV	Ratio
1988	Detroit	AL	40	92.0	83	34	50	4	2	2.93	0	1.272
1989	Detroit	AL	45	132.0	129	57	77	4	8	4.64	0	1.409
Seasonal Notation				112.0	106	46	64	4	5	3.94	0	1.353

CECILIO GUANTE   Age 30/R $2

Throws hard. (Ask Tony Fernandez.) But as long as Jeff Russell is effective, there's not much for Guante to do.

Year	Team	Lg.	G	IP	H	BB	SO	W	L	ERA	SV	Ratio
1986	Pittsburgh	NL	52	78.0	65	29	63	5	2	3.35	4	1.205
1987	New York	AL	23	44.0	42	20	46	3	2	5.73	1	1.409
1988	New York	AL	56	75.0	59	22	61	5	6	2.88	11	1.080
1988	Texas	AL	7	4.2	8	4	4	0	0	1.93	1	2.575
1989	Texas	AL	50	69.0	66	36	69	6	6	3.91	2	1.478
Seasonal Notation				67.0	60	28	61	5	4	3.72	5	1.297

LEE GUETTERMAN   Age 31/L $3

Nearly took the job away from Dave Righetti. But soft-throwing lefthanders are not your classic stoppers.

Year	Team	Lg.	G	IP	H	BB	SO	W	L	ERA	SV	Ratio
1986	Seattle	AL	41	76.0	108	30	38	0	4	7.34	0	1.816
1987	Seattle	AL	25	113.1	117	35	42	11	4	3.81	0	1.341
1988	New York	AL	20	40.2	49	14	15	1	2	4.65	0	1.549
1989	New York	AL	70	103.0	98	26	51	5	5	2.45	13	1.204
Seasonal Notation				83.0	93	26	37	4	4	4.30	3	1.432

BRYAN HARVEY   Age 26/R $25

Averages three strikeouts every two innings. Also averages two walks every three innings. He should have had many more saves.

Year	Team	Lg.	G	IP	H	BB	SO	W	L	ERA	SV	Ratio
1987	California	AL	3	5.0	6	2	3	0	0	0.00	0	1.600
1988	California	AL	50	76.0	59	20	67	7	5	2.13	17	1.039
1989	California	AL	51	55.0	36	41	78	3	3	3.44	25	1.400
Seasonal Notation				45.0	34	21	49	3	3	2.58	14	1.206

TOM HENKE   Age 32/R $20

Some very impressive numbers, but that's only the half of it. The other half is Duane Ward, and you're going to have to go after him, too. The two of them had 35 saves. The Blue Jays are very lucky to have the two of them. They can go with the hot hand. But you may not be able to afford that luxury.

Year	Team	Lg.	G	IP	H	BB	SO	W	L	ERA	SV	Ratio
1986	Toronto	AL	63	91.1	63	32	118	9	5	3.35	27	1.040
1987	Toronto	AL	72	94.0	62	25	128	0	6	2.49	34	0.926
1988	Toronto	AL	52	68.0	60	24	66	4	4	2.91	25	1.235
1989	Toronto	AL	64	89.0	66	25	116	8	3	1.92	20	1.022
Seasonal Notation				85.0	63	27	107	5	5	2.66	27	1.043

MIKE HENNEMAN   Age 28/R $10

The worst All-Star selection in history—he had two saves at the time. Of course, the Tigers didn't give him much to save. He is still preferable to the man below.

Year	Team	Lg.	G	IP	H	BB	SO	W	L	ERA	SV	Ratio
1987	Detroit	AL	55	96.2	86	30	75	11	3	2.98	7	1.200
1988	Detroit	AL	65	91.1	72	24	58	9	6	1.87	22	1.051
1989	Detroit	AL	60	90.0	84	51	69	11	4	3.70	8	1.500
Seasonal Notation				92.0	81	35	67	10	4	2.85	12	1.248

GUILLERMO HERNANDEZ   Age 34/L $5

If you got his 15 saves last year, shame on you.

Year	Team	Lg.	G	IP	H	BB	SO	W	L	ERA	SV	Ratio
1986	Detroit	AL	64	88.2	87	21	77	8	7	3.55	24	1.218
1987	Detroit	AL	45	49.0	53	20	30	3	4	3.67	8	1.490
1988	Detroit	AL	63	67.2	50	31	59	6	5	3.06	10	1.197
1989	Detroit	AL	32	31.1	36	16	30	2	2	5.75	15	1.660
Seasonal Notation				59.0	57	22	49	5	5	3.73	14	1.327

RICK HONEYCUTT   Age 35/L $5

Another reason the Athletics have the best bullpen in history.

Year	Team	Lg.	G	IP	H	BB	SO	W	L	ERA	SV	Ratio
1986	Los Angeles	NL	32	171.0	164	45	100	11	9	3.32	0	1.222
1987	Los Angeles	NL	27	115.2	133	45	92	2	12	4.59	0	1.539
1987	Oakland	AL	7	23.2	25	9	10	1	4	5.33	0	1.437
1988	Oakland	AL	55	79.2	74	25	47	3	2	3.50	7	1.243
1989	Oakland	AL	64	76.2	56	26	52	2	2	2.35	12	1.070
Seasonal Notation				116.0	113	38	75	5	7	3.61	5	1.290

MIKE JACKSON   Age 27/R $5

He walks too many batters, but he would step into the breach if Mike Schooler blew enough games.

Year	Team	Lg.	G	IP	H	BB	SO	W	L	ERA	SV	Ratio
1986	Philadelphia	NL	9	13.1	12	4	3	0	0	3.38	0	1.200
1987	Philadelphia	NL	55	109.1	88	56	93	3	10	4.20	1	1.317
1988	Seattle	AL	62	99.1	74	43	76	6	5	2.63	4	1.178
1989	Seattle	AL	65	99.1	81	54	94	4	6	3.17	7	1.359
Seasonal Notation				80.0	64	39	67	3	5	3.36	3	1.282

MIKE JEFFCOAT   Age 30/L $4

Yet another late-blooming lefty. On a staff with Nolan Ryan, Charlie Hough, Bobby Witt, and Kevin Brown, Jeffcoat led the Rangers in shutouts with two.

Year	Team	Lg.	G	IP	H	BB	SO	W	L	ERA	SV	Ratio
1987	Texas	AL	2	7.0	11	4	1	0	1	12.86	0	2.143
1988	Texas	AL	5	10.0	19	5	5	0	2	11.70	0	2.400
1989	Texas	AL	22	130.2	139	33	64	9	6	3.58	0	1.316
Seasonal Notation				49.0	56	14	23	3	3	4.57	0	1.429

BARRY JONES   Age 27/R $1

The one thing that can be said about Barry is that he has never been overworked: 193 innings in four seasons.

Year	Team	Lg.	G	IP	H	BB	SO	W	L	ERA	SV	Ratio
1986	Pittsburgh	NL	26	37.1	29	21	29	3	4	2.89	3	1.339
1987	Pittsburgh	NL	32	43.1	55	23	28	2	4	5.61	1	1.800
1988	Pittsburgh	NL	42	56.1	57	21	31	1	1	3.04	2	1.385
1988	Chicago	AL	17	26.0	15	17	17	2	2	2.42	1	1.231
1989	Chicago	AL	22	30.1	22	8	17	3	2	2.37	1	0.989
Seasonal Notation				48.0	45	23	31	3	3	3.40	2	1.386

DOUG JONES   Age 32/R $30

A few years ago, he was offered a job as a minor league pitching coach in the Cleveland organization. Now he's indispensable. He had a rough stretch in mid-season, but he's a solid pick.

Year	Team	Lg.	G	IP	H	BB	SO	W	L	ERA	SV	Ratio
1986	Cleveland	AL	11	18.0	18	6	12	1	0	2.50	1	1.333
1987	Cleveland	AL	49	91.1	101	24	87	6	5	3.15	8	1.369
1988	Cleveland	AL	51	83.1	69	16	72	3	4	2.27	37	1.020
1989	Cleveland	AL	59	80.2	76	13	65	7	10	2.34	32	1.103
Seasonal Notation				68.0	66	15	59	4	5	2.60	20	1.182

MARK KNUDSON   Age 29/R $2

You can probably eliminate this middle man.

Year	Team	Lg.	G	IP	H	BB	SO	W	L	ERA	SV	Ratio
1986	Milwaukee	AL	4	17.2	22	5	9	0	1	7.64	0	1.529
1986	Houston	NL	9	42.2	48	15	20	1	5	4.22	0	1.477
1987	Milwaukee	AL	15	62.0	88	14	26	4	4	5.37	0	1.645
1988	Milwaukee	AL	5	16.0	17	2	7	0	0	1.13	0	1.188
1989	Milwaukee	AL	40	123.2	110	29	47	8	5	3.35	0	1.124
Seasonal Notation				65.0	71	16	27	3	4	4.12	0	1.336

DENNIS LAMP   Age 37/R $1

Sure he had a fine year. And what did it get him? Four wins and two saves.

Year	Team	Lg.	G	IP	H	BB	SO	W	L	ERA	SV	Ratio
1986	Toronto	AL	40	73.0	93	23	30	2	6	5.05	2	1.589
1987	Oakland	AL	36	56.2	76	22	36	1	3	5.08	0	1.730
1988	Boston	AL	46	82.2	92	19	49	7	6	3.48	0	1.343
1989	Boston	AL	42	112.1	96	27	61	4	2	2.32	2	1.095
Seasonal Notation				81.0	89	23	44	4	4	3.71	1	1.380

BOB MCCLURE   Age 37/L $1

A lot of Rotisserians subscribe to the theory that if a team has just one lefty in the bullpen, you should get him. Well, here's the one in the Angels bullpen. He had a very good season. And all he has to show for it is three saves.

Year	Team	Lg.	G	IP	H	BB	SO	W	L	ERA	SV	Ratio
1986	Milwaukee	AL	13	16.1	18	10	11	2	1	3.86	0	1.715
1986	Montreal	NL	52	62.2	53	23	42	2	5	3.02	6	1.213
1987	Montreal	NL	52	52.1	47	20	33	6	1	3.44	5	1.280
1988	Montreal	NL	19	19.0	23	6	12	1	3	6.16	2	1.526
1988	New York	NL	14	11.0	12	2	7	1	0	4.09	1	1.273
1989	California	AL	48	52.1	39	15	36	6	1	1.55	3	1.032
Seasonal Notation				53.0	48	19	35	5	3	3.16	4	1.254

GREG MINTON   Age 38/R $5

A return to form for the Moon Man.

Year	Team	Lg.	G	IP	H	BB	SO	W	L	ERA	SV	Ratio
1986	San Francisco	NL	48	68.2	63	34	34	4	4	3.93	5	1.413
1987	San Francisco	NL	15	23.1	30	10	9	1	0	3.47	1	1.715
1987	California	AL	41	76.0	71	29	35	5	4	3.08	10	1.316
1988	California	AL	44	79.0	67	34	46	4	5	2.85	7	1.278
1989	California	AL	62	90.0	76	37	42	4	3	2.20	8	1.256
Seasonal Notation				84.0	77	36	42	5	4	2.99	8	1.338

JEFF MONTGOMERY   Age 28/R $30

The Royals make the best and worst trades. David Cone for Ed Hearn is an example of the latter. Van Snider to Cincinnati for Jeff Montgomery is an example of the former. You could hardly blame Farr for losing his job to this guy. His numbers were sensational.

Year	Team	Lg.	G	IP	H	BB	SO	W	L	ERA	SV	Ratio
1987	Cincinnati	NL	14	19.1	25	9	13	2	2	6.52	0	1.759
1988	Kansas City	AL	45	62.2	54	30	47	7	2	3.45	1	1.341
1989	Kansas City	AL	63	92.0	66	25	94	7	3	1.37	18	0.989
Seasonal Notation				57.0	48	21	51	5	2	2.69	6	1.201

ROB MURPHY   Age 29/L $10

Pete Rose overused him, and Murphy may never recover his
fastball. But he's still a formidable reliever, and Lee Smith had
better watch his step.

Year	Team	Lg.	G	IP	H	BB	SO	W	L	ERA	SV	Ratio
1986	Cincinnati	NL	34	50.1	26	21	36	6	0	0.72	1	0.934
1987	Cincinnati	NL	87	100.2	91	32	99	8	5	3.04	3	1.222
1988	Cincinnati	NL	76	84.2	69	38	74	0	6	3.08	3	1.264
1989	Boston	AL	74	105.0	97	41	107	5	7	2.74	9	1.314
Seasonal Notation				85.0	71	33	79	5	5	2.62	4	1.218

GENE NELSON   Age 29/R $3

Part of the left (Burns), right (Nelson), left (Honeycutt), right
(Eckersley) combination with which the A's knock out opponents.

Year	Team	Lg.	G	IP	H	BB	SO	W	L	ERA	SV	Ratio
1986	Chicago	AL	54	114.2	118	41	70	6	6	3.85	6	1.387
1987	Oakland	AL	54	123.2	120	35	94	6	5	3.93	3	1.253
1988	Oakland	AL	54	111.2	93	38	67	9	6	3.06	3	1.173
1989	Oakland	AL	50	80.0	60	30	70	3	5	3.26	3	1.125
Seasonal Notation				107.0	98	36	75	6	6	3.56	4	1.244

GREGG OLSON   Age 23/R $25

Frank Robinson brought him along beautifully. He eased him into
the stopper role so as not to risk his confidence, and then, when
Olson began to lose effectiveness after the All-Star break, Robinson stayed with Gregg and demonstrated his confidence in him.
The real question facing Olson is: How can someone so baby-faced
have a receding hairline?

Year	Team	Lg.	G	IP	H	BB	SO	W	L	ERA	SV	Ratio
1988	Baltimore	AL	10	11.0	10	10	9	1	1	3.27	0	1.818
1989	Baltimore	AL	64	85.0	57	46	90	5	2	1.69	27	1.212
Seasonal Notation				48.0	34	28	50	3	2	1.88	14	1.281

JESSE OROSCO   Age 32/L $3

He has become strictly a specialist against lefthanders.

Year	Team	Lg.	G	IP	H	BB	SO	W	L	ERA	SV	Ratio
1986	New York	NL	58	81.0	64	35	62	8	6	2.33	21	1.222
1987	New York	NL	58	77.0	78	31	78	3	9	4.44	16	1.416
1988	Los Angeles	NL	55	53.0	41	30	43	3	2	2.72	9	1.340
1989	Cleveland	AL	69	78.0	54	26	79	3	4	2.08	3	1.026
Seasonal Notation				72.0	59	31	66	4	5	2.90	12	1.242

DONN PALL   Age 28/R $3

He supposedly throws 150 miles an hour. But Bobby Thigpen's not moving.

Year	Team	Lg.	G	IP	H	BB	SO	W	L	ERA	SV	Ratio
1988	Chicago	AL	17	28.2	39	8	16	0	2	3.45	0	1.640
1989	Chicago	AL	53	87.0	90	19	58	4	5	3.31	6	1.253
Seasonal Notation				57.0	65	14	37	2	4	3.35	3	1.349

DAN PLESAC   Age 28/L $35

What we have here is a great reliever who seems to get better every year. It's only a matter of time before he breaks into the 40-save club.

Year	Team	Lg.	G	IP	H	BB	SO	W	L	ERA	SV	Ratio
1986	Milwaukee	AL	51	91.0	81	29	75	10	7	2.97	14	1.209
1987	Milwaukee	AL	57	79.1	63	23	89	5	6	2.61	23	1.084
1988	Milwaukee	AL	50	52.1	46	12	52	1	2	2.41	30	1.108
1989	Milwaukee	AL	52	61.1	47	17	52	3	4	2.35	33	1.044
Seasonal Notation				70.0	59	20	67	5	5	2.63	25	1.120

ERIC PLUNK   Age 26/R $5

Another pretender to Righetti's throne.

Year	Team	Lg.	G	IP	H	BB	SO	W	L	ERA	SV	Ratio
1986	Oakland	AL	26	120.1	91	102	98	4	7	5.31	0	1.604
1987	Oakland	AL	32	95.0	91	62	90	4	6	4.74	2	1.611
1988	Oakland	AL	49	78.0	62	39	79	7	2	3.00	5	1.295
1989	Oakland	AL	23	28.2	17	12	24	1	1	2.20	1	1.012
1989	New York	AL	27	75.2	65	52	61	7	5	3.69	0	1.546
Seasonal Notation				99.0	82	67	88	6	5	4.19	2	1.491

JEFF REARDON   Age 34/R $33

Not as overpowering as he once was, but still the top dog on the Twins.

Year	Team	Lg.	G	IP	H	BB	SO	W	L	ERA	SV	Ratio
1986	Montreal	NL	62	89.0	83	26	67	7	9	3.94	35	1.225
1987	Minnesota	AL	63	80.1	70	28	83	8	8	4.48	31	1.220
1988	Minnesota	AL	63	73.0	68	15	56	2	4	2.47	42	1.137
1989	Minnesota	AL	65	73.0	68	12	46	5	4	4.07	31	1.096
Seasonal Notation				78.0	72	20	63	6	6	3.77	35	1.173

JERRY REED   Age 34/R $1

Here's a unique novelty: a relief pitcher without a save. But he
does pitch okay; he picks up wins and he gives you innings.

Year	Team	Lg.	G	IP	H	BB	SO	W	L	ERA	SV	Ratio
1986	Seattle	AL	11	34.2	38	13	16	4	0	3.12	0	1.471
1987	Seattle	AL	39	81.2	79	24	51	1	2	3.42	7	1.261
1988	Seattle	AL	46	86.1	82	33	48	1	1	3.96	1	1.332
1989	Seattle	AL	52	101.2	89	43	50	7	7	3.19	0	1.298
Seasonal Notation				76.0	72	28	41	3	3	3.46	2	1.318

DAVE RIGHETTI   Age 31/L $25

Not a great season, but considering the way he was throwing at the
start, a season of retribution. $12 if he's in the rotation.

Year	Team	Lg.	G	IP	H	BB	SO	W	L	ERA	SV	Ratio
1986	New York	AL	74	106.2	88	35	83	8	8	2.45	46	1.153
1987	New York	AL	60	95.0	95	44	77	8	6	3.51	31	1.463
1988	New York	AL	60	87.0	86	37	70	5	4	3.52	25	1.414
1989	New York	AL	55	69.0	73	26	51	2	6	3.00	25	1.435
Seasonal Notation				89.0	86	36	70	6	6	3.10	32	1.353

KENNY ROGERS   Age 25/L $2

Hasn't done anything good since he left the First Edition (I Just
Dropped In To See What Condition My Condition Was In). Seriously, folks, the sole lefthander in the Texas bullpen.

Year	Team	Lg.	G	IP	H	BB	SO	W	L	ERA	SV	Ratio
1989	Texas	AL	73	73.2	60	42	63	3	4	2.93	2	1.385
Seasonal Notation				73.0	60	42	63	3	4	2.93	2	1.385

JEFF RUSSELL   Age 28/R $35

The Rangers made a great move. Like the Athletics with Eckersley,
they took a decent starter without much staying power and turned
him into a reliever. In this case, the best reliever in the league.

Year	Team	Lg.	G	IP	H	BB	SO	W	L	ERA	SV	Ratio
1986	Texas	AL	37	82.0	74	31	54	5	2	3.40	2	1.280
1987	Texas	AL	52	97.1	109	52	56	5	4	4.44	3	1.654
1988	Texas	AL	34	188.2	183	66	88	10	9	3.82	0	1.320
1989	Texas	AL	71	72.2	45	24	77	6	4	1.98	38	0.950
Seasonal Notation				110.0	103	43	69	7	5	3.57	11	1.325

MIKE SCHOOLER   Age 27/R $29

That many saves with a wretched club is a pretty good trick, but he should have had many more.

Year	Team	Lg.	G	IP	H	BB	SO	W	L	ERA	SV	Ratio
1988	Seattle	AL	40	48.1	45	24	54	5	8	3.54	15	1.428
1989	Seattle	AL	67	77.0	81	19	69	1	7	2.81	33	1.299
Seasonal Notation				62.0	63	22	62	3	8	3.09	24	1.348

LEE SMITH   Age 32/R $25

An amazing number of strikeouts for innings pitched, so he obviously has the old heater back. He just lacks a certain *je ne sais quoi*. Let's put it this way. He makes us Red Sox fans very nervous with the game on the line.

Year	Team	Lg.	G	IP	H	BB	SO	W	L	ERA	SV	Ratio
1986	Chicago	NL	66	90.1	69	42	93	9	9	3.09	31	1.229
1987	Chicago	NL	62	83.2	84	32	96	4	10	3.12	36	1.387
1988	Boston	AL	64	83.2	72	37	96	4	5	2.80	29	1.303
1989	Boston	AL	64	70.2	53	33	96	6	1	3.57	25	1.217
Seasonal Notation				82.0	70	36	95	6	6	3.13	30	1.285

BOBBY THIGPEN   Age 26/R $25

Not your classic stopper stats, but he gets the job done. He once wrote a poem to protest his salary negotiations, so in the same spirit:

Rose was a Red/Viola's in blue,
Thigpen's a cinch/To save 32.

Year	Team	Lg.	G	IP	H	BB	SO	W	L	ERA	SV	Ratio
1986	Chicago	AL	20	35.2	26	12	20	2	0	1.77	7	1.066
1987	Chicago	AL	51	89.0	86	24	52	7	5	2.73	16	1.236
1988	Chicago	AL	68	90.0	96	33	62	5	8	3.30	34	1.433
1989	Chicago	AL	61	79.0	62	40	47	2	6	3.76	34	1.291
Seasonal Notation				73.0	68	27	45	4	5	3.06	23	1.291

DUANE WARD   Age 25/R $18

Abbott and Costello. Ferrante and Teicher. Romulus and Remus. Henke and Ward.

Year	Team	Lg.	G	IP	H	BB	SO	W	L	ERA	SV	Ratio
1986	Atlanta	NL	10	16.0	22	8	8	0	1	7.31	0	1.875
1986	Toronto	AL	2	2.0	3	4	1	0	1	13.50	0	3.500
1987	Toronto	AL	12	11.2	14	12	10	1	0	6.95	0	2.230
1988	Toronto	AL	64	111.2	101	60	91	9	3	3.30	15	1.442
1989	Toronto	AL	66	114.2	94	58	122	4	10	3.77	15	1.326
Seasonal Notation				63.0	59	36	58	4	4	4.01	8	1.469

GARY WAYNE   Age 27/L $2

The Twins' lefty out of the pen, and a pretty impressive showing for a rookie.

Year	Team	Lg.	G	IP	H	BB	SO	W	L	ERA	SV	Ratio
1989	Minnesota	AL	60	71.0	55	36	41	3	4	3.30	1	1.282
Seasonal Notation				71.0	55	36	41	3	4	3.30	1	1.282

DAVID WELLS   Age 30/L $5

Not only did he show incredible ingenuity last year, but the guts of a cat burglar, as well. We're talking, of course, of his two alleged sleepwalking incidents, one of which resulted in a cut hand. If ever you told your teacher your cat ate your homework, this is the man for you.

Year	Team	Lg.	G	IP	H	BB	SO	W	L	ERA	SV	Ratio
1987	Toronto	AL	18	29.1	37	12	32	4	3	3.99	1	1.671
1988	Toronto	AL	41	64.1	65	31	56	3	5	4.62	4	1.492
1989	Toronto	AL	54	86.1	66	28	78	7	4	2.40	2	1.089
Seasonal Notation				59.0	56	24	55	5	4	3.45	2	1.328

FRANK WILLIAMS   Age 32/R $1

We had hopes he might become a stopper when he was over in the National League, but those hopes have all but faded.

Year	Team	Lg.	G	IP	H	BB	SO	W	L	ERA	SV	Ratio
1986	San Francisco	NL	36	52.1	35	21	33	3	1	1.20	1	1.070
1987	Cincinnati	NL	85	105.2	101	39	60	4	0	2.30	2	1.325
1988	Cincinnati	NL	60	62.2	59	35	43	3	2	2.59	1	1.500
1989	Detroit	AL	42	71.2	70	46	33	3	3	3.64	1	1.619
Seasonal Notation				73.0	66	35	42	3	2	2.49	1	1.389

MARK WILLIAMSON   Age 30/R $8

An extremely useful pitcher, the kind who gets to pitch the last three innings of games in which his team is losing or in which it has a big lead. Consequently, he nearly had double figures in both wins and saves.

Year	Team	Lg.	G	IP	H	BB	SO	W	L	ERA	SV	Ratio
1987	Baltimore	AL	61	125.0	122	41	73	8	9	4.03	3	1.304
1988	Baltimore	AL	37	117.2	125	40	69	5	8	4.90	2	1.402
1989	Baltimore	AL	65	107.1	105	30	55	10	5	2.93	9	1.258
Seasonal Notation				116.0	117	37	66	8	7	3.99	5	1.323

BEHIND THE PLATE

Watching a 25-year-old rerun of Home Run Derby brought it all home again. There was the Derby's six-time champ, Dick Stuart of the Bucs, defending his title against—no, not Aaron, Colavito, or even Johnny Callison—but Gus Triandos. Okay, so Dr. Strangeglove clobbered the Baltimore backstop. So what. The fact that Gus was even considered for the competition was a credit to his profession. Can you picture the show today? Glenn Wilson takes on Jeff Reed? No, neither can we.

Enough of this golden era stuff. In fact, we may be seeing a glimmer of hope for this much maligned position. Isn't Mickey Tettleton more than filling the shoes of Triandos and Hendricks? Carlton Fisk will probably be chewing and spitting and banging doubles off the wall until his age matches his uniform number. And look at the senior circuit. Craig Biggio can hit and steal bases. Damon Berryhill's ready to blossom. And Sandy Alomar, Jr. and Todd Zeile seem ready for the show.

Unfortunately, there are never enough of these guys to go around. That leaves you with some very tough calls come draft day. And that's why you throw your money away on other purported scouting reports like Gary Carter trying to cut down Vince Coleman. You want to separate the wheat from the chaff; the Pagnozzis from the Manwarings; the Lyonses from the Sassers. Read on, friends, and you will see how much we can help.

NATIONAL LEAGUE

SANDY ALOMAR   Age 23/R $9

Enough already. Let's see if he can play major league ball. We're always suspicious of Pacific Coast League numbers, especially Las Vegas.

Year	Team	Lg.	Pos.	G	AB	R	H	HR	RBI	SB	BA
1989	San Diego	NL	C	7	19	1	4	1	6	0	.211
Seasonal Notation					439	23	92	23	138	0	.211

BRUCE BENEDICT   Age 34/R $1

While most catchers with this Bruce's skills would be happy warming up relief pitchers, this guy is still a Braves starting catcher. But what would you expect from a team whose rebuilding program began by replacing the ebullient Chief Nok-A-Homa with the psychotic Homer the Brave?

Year	Team	Lg.	Pos.	G	AB	R	H	HR	RBI	SB	BA
1986	Atlanta	NL	C	64	160	11	36	0	13	1	.225
1987	Atlanta	NL	C	37	95	4	14	1	5	0	.147
1988	Atlanta	NL	C	90	236	11	57	0	19	0	.242
1989	Atlanta	NL	C	66	160	12	31	1	6	0	.194
Seasonal Notation					410	23	86	1	27	0	.212

DAMON BERRYHILL   Age 26/B $11

Short-circuited by a rotator problem last year, we still thought he'd
have banged a few more off the ivy in the Friendly Confines. Just
give him some more time.

Year	Team	Lg.	Pos.	G	AB	R	H	HR	RBI	SB	BA
1987	Chicago	NL	C	12	28	2	5	0	1	0	.179
1988	Chicago	NL	C	95	309	19	80	7	38	1	.259
1989	Chicago	NL	C	91	334	37	86	5	41	1	.257
Seasonal Notation					549	47	139	9	65	1	.255

CRAIG BIGGIO   Age 24/R $16

Most Rotisserians took it for granted that the Astros lead-off spot
belonged to Gerald Young, or maybe Billy Hatcher. Who could
figure that a catcher would snatch the job from the fleet-footed
outfielders? But, why not? Biggio runs just as well, plus he actually
gets on base. In fact his power numbers are pretty good, even for
the Dome. Right now, he's the best in the league and the first
backstop to lead off for the Astros since Ron Brand.

Year	Team	Lg.	Pos.	G	AB	R	H	HR	RBI	SB	BA
1988	Houston	NL	C	50	123	14	26	3	5	6	.211
1989	Houston	NL	C	134	443	64	114	13	60	21	.257
Seasonal Notation					498	68	123	14	57	23	.247

GARY CARTER   Age 35/R $1

You may be seeing Gary's grin behind a microphone instead of
taking curtain calls.

Year	Team	Lg.	Pos.	G	AB	R	H	HR	RBI	SB	BA
1986	New York	NL	C	132	490	81	125	24	105	1	.255
1987	New York	NL	C	139	523	55	123	20	83	0	.235
1988	New York	NL	C	130	455	39	110	11	46	0	.242
1989	New York	NL	C	50	153	14	28	2	15	0	.183
Seasonal Notation					582	67	138	20	89	0	.238

DARREN DAULTON   Age 28/L $2

Finally healthy after all these years, Dutch showed us what we already knew—he hits with power when he hits at all. Even platooned with Steve Lake, Daulton could barely crack the Mendoza Line. If you can package him with a backstop who hits for average, Daulton's taters might be worth a few bucks.

Year	Team	Lg.	Pos.	G	AB	R	H	HR	RBI	SB	BA
1986	Philadelphia	NL	C	49	138	18	31	8	21	2	.225
1987	Philadelphia	NL	C	53	129	10	25	3	13	0	.194
1988	Philadelphia	NL	C	58	144	13	30	1	12	2	.208
1989	Philadelphia	NL	C	131	368	29	74	8	44	2	.201
Seasonal Notation					433	38	89	11	50	3	.205

JODY DAVIS   Age 33/R $1

We thought Jody would take a liking to the Launching Pad. Wrong again. The ascendancy of Bruce Benedict tells you how far Jody has fallen from his salad days at Wrigley.

Year	Team	Lg.	Pos.	G	AB	R	H	HR	RBI	SB	BA
1986	Chicago	NL	C	148	528	61	132	21	74	0	.250
1987	Chicago	NL	C	125	428	57	106	19	51	1	.248
1988	Chicago	NL	C	88	249	19	57	6	33	0	.229
1988	Atlanta	NL	C	2	8	2	2	1	3	0	.250
1989	Atlanta	NL	C	78	231	12	39	4	19	0	.169
Seasonal Notation					530	55	123	18	66	0	.233

RICK DEMPSEY   Age 40/R $1

Great for your post-season play, but little else.

Year	Team	Lg.	Pos.	G	AB	R	H	HR	RBI	SB	BA
1986	Baltimore	AL	C	122	327	42	68	13	29	1	.208
1987	Cleveland	AL	C	60	141	16	25	1	9	0	.177
1988	Los Angeles	NL	C	77	167	25	42	7	30	1	.251
1989	Los Angeles	NL	C	79	151	16	27	4	16	1	.179
Seasonal Notation					376	47	77	11	40	1	.206

BO DIAZ   Age 37/R $1

We're surprised he's still around, too. Good chance he won't be come April.

Year	Team	Lg.	Pos.	G	AB	R	H	HR	RBI	SB	BA
1986	Cincinnati	NL	C	134	474	50	129	10	56	1	.272
1987	Cincinnati	NL	C	140	496	49	134	15	82	1	.270
1988	Cincinnati	NL	C	92	315	26	69	10	35	0	.219
1989	Cincinnati	NL	C	43	132	6	27	1	8	0	.205
Seasonal Notation					561	51	142	14	71	0	.253

TERRY KENNEDY　　　　　　Age 33/L　　　$3

Don't look for too much his second year in the cold.

Year	Team	Lg.	Pos.	G	AB	R	H	HR	RBI	SB	BA
1986	San Diego	NL	C	141	432	46	114	12	57	0	.264
1987	Baltimore	AL	C	143	512	51	128	18	62	1	.250
1988	Baltimore	AL	C	85	265	20	60	3	16	0	.226
1989	San Francisco	NL	C	125	355	19	85	5	34	1	.239
Seasonal Notation					512	44	126	12	55	0	.247

STEVE LAKE　　　　　　Age 33/R　　　$1

Great for your defense, but little else.

Year	Team	Lg.	Pos.	G	AB	R	H	HR	RBI	SB	BA
1986	Chicago	NL	C	10	19	4	8	0	4	0	.421
1986	St. Louis	NL	C	26	49	4	12	2	10	0	.245
1987	St. Louis	NL	C	74	179	19	45	2	19	0	.251
1988	St. Louis	NL	C	36	54	5	15	1	4	0	.278
1989	Philadelphia	NL	C	58	155	9	39	2	14	0	.252
Seasonal Notation					362	32	94	5	40	0	.261

MIKE LAVALLIERE　　　　Age 29/L　　　$2

When healthy, Spanky's a good average hitter at best. Seems like 1990 will be a make or break year.

Year	Team	Lg.	Pos.	G	AB	R	H	HR	RBI	SB	BA
1986	St. Louis	NL	C	110	303	18	71	3	30	0	.234
1987	Pittsburgh	NL	C	121	340	33	102	1	36	0	.300
1988	Pittsburgh	NL	C	120	352	24	92	2	47	3	.261
1989	Pittsburgh	NL	C	68	190	15	60	2	23	0	.316
Seasonal Notation					458	34	125	3	52	1	.274

BARRY LYONS　　　　　　Age 29/R　　　$1

See Steve Lake.

Year	Team	Lg.	Pos.	G	AB	R	H	HR	RBI	SB	BA
1986	New York	NL	C	6	9	1	0	0	2	0	.000
1987	New York	NL	C	53	130	15	33	4	24	0	.254
1988	New York	NL	C	50	91	5	21	0	11	0	.231
1989	New York	NL	C	79	235	15	58	3	27	0	.247
Seasonal Notation					400	31	96	6	55	0	.241

KIRT MANWARING　　　　Age 24/R　　　$1

See Barry Lyons.

Year	Team	Lg.	Pos.	G	AB	R	H	HR	RBI	SB	BA
1987	San Francisco	NL	C	6	7	0	1	0	0	0	.143
1988	San Francisco	NL	C	40	116	12	29	1	15	0	.250
1989	San Francisco	NL	C	85	200	14	42	0	18	2	.210
Seasonal Notation					399	32	89	1	40	2	.223

JUNIOR ORTIZ   Age 30/R $1
See Kirt Manwaring.

Year	Team	Lg.	Pos.	G	AB	R	H	HR	RBI	SB	BA
1986	Pittsburgh	NL	C	49	110	11	37	0	14	0	.336
1987	Pittsburgh	NL	C	75	192	16	52	1	22	0	.271
1988	Pittsburgh	NL	C	49	118	8	33	2	18	1	.280
1989	Pittsburgh	NL	C	91	230	16	50	1	22	2	.217
Seasonal Notation					398	31	105	2	46	1	.265

TOM PAGNOZZI   Age 27/R $1
See Junior Ortiz.

Year	Team	Lg.	Pos.	G	AB	R	H	HR	RBI	SB	BA
1987	St. Louis	NL	C	27	48	8	9	2	9	1	.188
1988	St. Louis	NL	1B	81	195	17	55	0	15	0	.282
1989	St. Louis	NL	C	52	80	3	12	0	3	0	.150
Seasonal Notation					327	28	76	2	27	1	.235

MARK PARENT   Age 28/R $1
See Tom Pag . . . Wait a minute! This guy's always good for 6-8
dingers, he doesn't play enough to hurt your BA, and you gotta have
a second catcher anyway. So be prepared to go all the way to **$2**.

Year	Team	Lg.	Pos.	G	AB	R	H	HR	RBI	SB	BA
1986	San Diego	NL	C	8	14	1	2	0	0	0	.143
1987	San Diego	NL	C	12	25	0	2	0	2	0	.080
1988	San Diego	NL	C	41	118	9	23	6	15	0	.195
1989	San Diego	NL	C	52	141	12	27	7	21	1	.191
Seasonal Notation					427	31	77	18	54	1	.181

TONY PENA   32/R $8
See ya later. A free-agent, Tony will likely move on to the Reds,
Red Sox, or Giants or any other team seeking another veteran
catcher whose offensive skills seem to decline every year.

Year	Team	Lg.	Pos.	G	AB	R	H	HR	RBI	SB	BA
1986	Pittsburgh	NL	C	144	510	56	147	10	52	9	.288
1987	St. Louis	NL	C	116	384	40	82	5	44	6	.214
1988	St. Louis	NL	C	149	505	55	133	10	51	6	.263
1989	St. Louis	NL	C	141	424	36	110	4	37	5	.259
Seasonal Notation					536	55	139	8	54	7	.259

JEFF REED   Age 27/L $1
Thought he'd at least hit for average. On second thought, see
Lake, Lyons, Manwaring and Co.

Year	Team	Lg.	Pos.	G	AB	R	H	HR	RBI	SB	BA
1986	Minnesota	AL	C	68	165	13	39	2	9	1	.236
1987	Montreal	NL	C	75	207	15	44	1	21	0	.213
1988	Montreal	NL	C	43	123	10	27	0	9	1	.220
1988	Cincinnati	NL	C	49	142	10	33	1	7	0	.232
1989	Cincinnati	NL	C	102	287	16	64	3	23	0	.223
Seasonal Notation					444	30	99	3	33	0	.224

BENITO SANTIAGO   Age 25/R $9

The Pods may have dangled Benito as trade bait for a bit long.
He's still better than most of this bunch, especially if he's hitting at
Fenway Park.

Year	Team	Lg.	Pos.	G	AB	R	H	HR	RBI	SB	BA
1986	San Diego	NL	C	17	62	10	18	3	6	0	.290
1987	San Diego	NL	C	146	546	64	164	18	79	21	.300
1988	San Diego	NL	C	139	492	49	122	10	46	15	.248
1989	San Diego	NL	C	129	462	50	109	16	62	11	.236
Seasonal Notation					587	65	155	17	72	17	.264

MACKEY SASSER   Age 27/L $1

See Steve Lake. Really.

Year	Team	Lg.	Pos.	G	AB	R	H	HR	RBI	SB	BA
1987	San Francisco	NL	C	2	4	0	0	0	0	0	.000
1987	Pittsburgh	NL	C	12	23	2	5	0	2	0	.217
1988	New York	NL	C	60	123	9	35	1	17	0	.285
1989	New York	NL	C	72	182	17	53	1	22	0	.291
Seasonal Notation					368	31	103	2	45	0	.280

MIKE SCIOSCIA   Age 31/L $4

In spite of his poor production—this guy used to hit for a decent
average, at least—the Dodgers signed him to a three-year contract
because he bleeds blue. Don't make the same mistake.

Year	Team	Lg.	Pos.	G	AB	R	H	HR	RBI	SB	BA
1986	Los Angeles	NL	C	122	374	36	94	5	26	3	.251
1987	Los Angeles	NL	C	142	461	44	122	6	38	7	.265
1988	Los Angeles	NL	C	130	408	29	105	3	35	0	.257
1989	Los Angeles	NL	C	133	408	40	102	10	44	0	.250
Seasonal Notation					507	45	130	7	43	3	.256

ALEX TREVINO   Age 32/R $1

This is another one the Mets let get away—and don't want back.
But someone had to fill Alan Ashby's shoes.

Year	Team	Lg.	Pos.	G	AB	R	H	HR	RBI	SB	BA
1986	Los Angeles	NL	C	89	202	31	53	4	26	0	.262
1987	Los Angeles	NL	C	72	144	16	32	3	16	1	.222
1988	Houston	NL	C	78	193	19	48	2	13	5	.249
1989	Houston	NL	C	59	131	15	38	2	16	0	.290
Seasonal Notation					364	44	92	5	38	3	.255

TODD ZEILE   Age 24/R $8

While the press, or at least the Padres, proclaimed Sandy, Jr. as
the catcher of the '90s, Zeile continued to flourish at Louisville. If
he can hit in St. Louis, he'll drive in a lot of runs. And he's hit
everywhere else. Don't expect a lot of homers, but do figure on
60+ ribbies.

Year	Team	Lg.	Pos.	G	AB	R	H	HR	RBI	SB	BA
1989	St. Louis	NL	C	28	82	7	21	1	8	0	.256
Seasonal Notation					474	40	121	5	46	0	.256

AMERICAN LEAGUE

Many people in and out of baseball attribute the out-of-nowhere
success of Baltimore catcher Mickey Tettleton to his well-publicized
penchant for Froot Loops, the cold cereal that turns your milk a
color not found in nature. We think his season had more to do with
the karma of him being a switch-hitter from Oklahoma named
Mickey. But just in case Froot Loops did the Trix, we are recom-
mending a brand of cereal for each of the AL catchers, most of
whom amount to plenty of Nut 'N Honey:

ANDY ALLANSON   Age 28/R $3

How can someone so big (6'5", 215) have so little power? He is
worth this much because 1) his backup is Joel Skinner, 2) like Jose
Canseco, Howard Johnson, and Bo Jackson, his home runs nearly
match his stolen bases, and 3) he has a certain trade value if you're
dealing with an airhead who thinks he's getting Allan Anderson.
Wheaties.

Year	Team	Lg.	Pos.	G	AB	R	H	HR	RBI	SB	BA
1986	Cleveland	AL	C	101	293	30	66	1	29	10	.225
1987	Cleveland	AL	C	50	154	17	41	3	16	1	.266
1988	Cleveland	AL	C	133	434	44	114	5	50	5	.263
1989	Cleveland	AL	C	111	323	30	75	3	17	4	.232
Seasonal Notation					493	49	121	4	45	8	.246

BOB BOONE   Age 42/R $3

We know, he's like fine wine. A future Hall of Famer. The best
receiver of his generation. All well and good, but the fact of the
matter is that he has never been much of a Rotisserie League
player, unless you like to go to bed at night thinking he's actually
handling your pitching staff. And HE WILL BE 42 YEARS OLD!
All-Bran.

Year	Team	Lg.	Pos.	G	AB	R	H	HR	RBI	SB	BA
1986	California	AL	C	144	442	48	98	7	49	1	.222
1987	California	AL	C	128	389	42	94	3	33	0	.242
1988	California	AL	C	122	352	38	104	5	39	2	.295
1989	Kansas City	AL	C	131	405	33	111	1	43	3	.274
Seasonal Notation					490	49	125	4	50	1	.256

PAT BORDERS   Age 26/R $3

Waiting in the wings for Whitt to wither. We think he'll be a
pretty good hitter, but there's no need to get into a bidding frenzy
over him. After all, it will only be a Borders war. Frosted
Mini-Wheats.

Year	Team	Lg.	Pos.	G	AB	R	H	HR	RBI	SB	BA
1988	Toronto	AL	C	56	154	15	42	5	21	0	.273
1989	Toronto	AL	C	94	241	22	62	3	29	2	.257
Seasonal Notation					426	39	112	8	54	2	.263

SCOTT BRADLEY   Age 30/L $3

A good hitter who doesn't play enough. If he gets traded to a team
that takes advantage of his versatility, he might be a real bargain.
This has nothing to do with Rotisserie baseball, but Peter Gam-
mons of *Sports Illustrated* thinks Bradley is intelligent and articu-
late enough to become the next Tim McCarver. Would that he
could play as well. Wheat Chex.

Year	Team	Lg.	Pos.	G	AB	R	H	HR	RBI	SB	BA
1986	Chicago	AL	C	9	21	3	6	0	0	0	.286
1986	Seattle	AL	C	68	199	17	60	5	28	1	.302
1987	Seattle	AL	C	102	342	34	95	5	43	0	.278
1988	Seattle	AL	C	103	335	45	86	4	33	1	.257
1989	Seattle	AL	C	103	270	21	74	3	37	1	.274
Seasonal Notation					491	50	135	7	59	1	.275

RICK CERONE   Age 35/R $3

That was quite a year he had in 1980. Last season was his best since then, but let's not forget one thing: He was third-string behind Ozzie Virgil and Bruce Benedict in Atlanta not too long ago. You might be interested to know that Rick is personally acquainted with the Chairman of the Board, and we don't mean Haywood Sullivan. Lucky Charms.

Year	Team	Lg.	Pos.	G	AB	R	H	HR	RBI	SB	BA
1986	Milwaukee	AL	C	68	216	22	56	4	18	1	.259
1987	New York	AL	C	113	284	28	69	4	23	0	.243
1988	Boston	AL	C	84	264	31	71	3	27	0	.269
1989	Boston	AL	C	102	296	28	72	4	48	0	.243
Seasonal Notation					467	48	118	6	51	0	.253

CARLTON FISK   Age 42/R $9

Healthy, he's $12 or more. Truly a physical marvel, Fisk is still one of the two or three best offensive catchers in the game. Equally offensive is his penchant for dragging games into their third hour, but that's neither here nor there. What is pertinent is that HE'S 41 YEARS OLD! Cracklin' Bran.

Year	Team	Lg.	Pos.	G	AB	R	H	HR	RBI	SB	BA
1986	Chicago	AL	C	125	457	42	101	14	63	2	.221
1987	Chicago	AL	C	135	454	68	116	23	71	1	.256
1988	Chicago	AL	C	76	253	37	70	19	50	0	.277
1989	Chicago	AL	C	103	375	47	110	13	68	1	.293
Seasonal Notation					567	71	146	25	92	1	.258

RICH GEDMAN   Age 30/L $2

Even sadder than Tinker to Evers to Chance are these words: Gedman comes to the plate. His plunge into ineptitude is as puzzling as it is poignant. Maybe if he found a new batting coach or a new therapist . . . He might benefit from a change of scene. Alpha-Bits.

Year	Team	Lg.	Pos.	G	AB	R	H	HR	RBI	SB	BA
1986	Boston	AL	C	135	462	49	119	16	65	1	.258
1987	Boston	AL	C	52	151	11	31	1	13	0	.205
1988	Boston	AL	C	95	299	33	69	9	39	0	.231
1989	Boston	AL	C	93	260	24	55	4	16	0	.212
Seasonal Notation					506	50	118	12	57	0	.234

BOB GEREN   Age 28/R $3

Encouraging but incomplete. He may indeed be the Yankees' best catcher since Rick Cerone. Then again, there may be a reason why he languished in the Yankees' farm system for so long. Those home runs are pretty tempting. Apple Jacks.

Year	Team	Lg.	Pos.	G	AB	R	H	HR	RBI	SB	BA
1988	New York	AL	C	10	10	0	1	0	0	0	.100
1989	New York	AL	C	65	205	26	59	9	27	0	.288
Seasonal Notation					464	56	129	19	58	0	.279

BRIAN HARPER   Age 30/R $5

He converted Gary Gaetti, then he converted us. Actually, he could always hit. He just found a team willing to put up with his defense behind the plate. He is thus the answer to the trivia question: Whatever happened to Tim Laudner? Honeycomb.

Year	Team	Lg.	Pos.	G	AB	R	H	HR	RBI	SB	BA
1986	Detroit	AL	OF	19	36	2	5	0	3	0	.139
1987	Oakland	AL	OF	11	17	1	4	0	3	0	.235
1988	Minnesota	AL	C	60	166	15	49	3	20	0	.295
1989	Minnesota	AL	C	126	385	43	125	8	57	2	.325
Seasonal Notation					453	45	137	8	62	1	.303

RON HASSEY   Age 37/L $2

We think he's through. But $2 says he isn't. Bran Chex.

Year	Team	Lg.	Pos.	G	AB	R	H	HR	RBI	SB	BA
1986	New York	AL	C	64	191	23	57	6	29	1	.298
1986	Chicago	AL	C	49	150	22	53	3	20	0	.353
1987	Chicago	AL	C	49	145	15	31	3	12	0	.214
1988	Oakland	AL	C	107	323	32	83	7	45	2	.257
1989	Oakland	AL	C	97	268	29	61	5	23	1	.228
Seasonal Notation					476	53	126	10	57	1	.265

MIKE HEATH   Age 35/R $3

One of the craziest competitors in the game, he experienced something of a rebirth last season. You might want to pair him with Matt Nokes to assure yourself of at least one everyday catcher with power. Corn Flakes.

Year	Team	Lg.	Pos.	G	AB	R	H	HR	RBI	SB	BA
1986	St. Louis	NL	C	65	190	19	39	4	25	2	.205
1986	Detroit	AL	C	30	98	11	26	4	11	4	.265
1987	Detroit	AL	C	93	270	34	76	8	33	1	.281
1988	Detroit	AL	C	86	219	24	54	5	18	1	.247
1989	Detroit	AL	C	122	396	38	104	10	43	7	.263
Seasonal Notation					479	51	122	12	53	6	.255

RON KARKOVICE · Age 26/R · $1

He hit beyond our wildest expectations last year, but that still isn't saying very much. According to the White Sox media guide, his nickname is "Karko," which goes to show you how clever baseball players can be. Special K.

Year	Team	Lg.	Pos.	G	AB	R	H	HR	RBI	SB	BA
1986	Chicago	AL	C	37	97	13	24	4	13	1	.247
1987	Chicago	AL	C	39	85	7	6	2	7	3	.071
1988	Chicago	AL	C	46	115	10	20	3	9	4	.174
1989	Chicago	AL	C	71	182	21	48	3	24	0	.264
Seasonal Notation					402	42	82	10	44	6	.205

CHAD KREUTER · Age 25/R · $.33

And not a penny more. A terrible hitter, but he is the only catcher in baseball named after a central north African republic. Belongs on a team with Chili Davis, Ricky Jordan, Mark Portugal, and Edwin Correa. Puffed Rice.

Year	Team	Lg.	Pos.	G	AB	R	H	HR	RBI	SB	BA
1988	Texas	AL	C	16	51	3	14	1	5	0	.275
1989	Texas	AL	C	87	158	16	24	5	9	0	.152
Seasonal Notation					328	29	59	9	22	0	.182

TIM LAUDNER · Age 31/R · $1

His occasional power is not worth carrying his batting average. Personally, we have a soft spot in our heart for this native Iowan, but we're still going to warn you off him. Corn Chex.

Year	Team	Lg.	Pos.	G	AB	R	H	HR	RBI	SB	BA
1986	Minnesota	AL	C	76	193	21	47	10	29	1	.244
1987	Minnesota	AL	C	113	288	30	55	16	43	1	.191
1988	Minnesota	AL	C	117	375	38	94	13	54	0	.251
1989	Minnesota	AL	C	100	239	24	53	6	27	1	.222
Seasonal Notation					436	45	99	17	61	1	.227

MIKE MACFARLANE · Age 25/R · $1

One of the reasons Bob Boone will be playing up until pension time. Basically, MacFarlane is just a body to fill up your catching slot—he won't hurt, he won't help. Puffed Wheat.

Year	Team	Lg.	Pos.	G	AB	R	H	HR	RBI	SB	BA
1987	Kansas City	AL	C	8	19	0	4	0	3	0	.211
1988	Kansas City	AL	C	70	211	25	56	4	26	0	.265
1989	Kansas City	AL	C	69	157	13	35	2	19	0	.223
Seasonal Notation					426	41	104	6	52	0	.245

BOB MELVIN   Age 28/R $1

Didn't you just love him when he was with the Blue Notes? Oh, that was Harold. This must be the one who once hit 11 dingers for the Giants. We wouldn't count on it happening again. Rice Krispies.

Year	Team	Lg.	Pos.	G	AB	R	H	HR	RBI	SB	BA
1986	San Francisco	NL	C	89	268	24	60	5	25	3	.224
1987	San Francisco	NL	C	84	246	31	49	11	31	0	.199
1988	San Francisco	NL	C	92	273	23	64	8	27	0	.234
1989	Baltimore	AL	C	85	278	22	67	1	32	1	.241
Seasonal Notation					492	46	111	11	53	1	.225

MATT NOKES   Age 26/L $5

Let's get serious here for a moment. He'll be undervalued due to an off-, oft-injured season, but he's a legitimate threat to hit 30 homers. He could be the bargain of the draft. Then again, we could be kidding. Sugar Smacks.

Year	Team	Lg.	Pos.	G	AB	R	H	HR	RBI	SB	BA
1986	Detroit	AL	C	7	24	2	8	1	2	0	.333
1987	Detroit	AL	C	135	461	69	133	32	87	2	.289
1988	Detroit	AL	C	122	382	53	96	16	53	0	.251
1989	Detroit	AL	C	87	268	15	67	9	39	1	.250
Seasonal Notation					523	64	140	26	83	1	.268

CHARLIE O'BRIEN   Age 29/R $1

His nose and foot speed are reminiscent of Ernie Lombardi, but the resemblance ends there. Lay off this latter-day Charlie O. Cheerios.

Year	Team	Lg.	Pos.	G	AB	R	H	HR	RBI	SB	BA
1987	Milwaukee	AL	C	10	35	2	7	0	0	0	.200
1988	Milwaukee	AL	C	40	118	12	26	2	9	0	.220
1989	Milwaukee	AL	C	62	188	22	44	6	35	0	.234
Seasonal Notation					493	52	111	11	63	0	.226

LANCE PARRISH   Age 33/R $13

His power figures are about half of what they once were, which still makes him a big dog among these mutts. We're softies for former bodyguards of Tina Turner. Count Chocula.

Year	Team	Lg.	Pos.	G	AB	R	H	HR	RBI	SB	BA
1986	Detroit	AL	C	91	327	53	84	22	62	0	.257
1987	Philadelphia	NL	C	130	466	42	114	17	67	0	.245
1988	Philadelphia	NL	C	123	424	44	91	15	60	0	.215
1989	California	AL	C	124	433	48	103	17	50	1	.238
Seasonal Notation					571	64	135	24	82	0	.238

GENO PETRALLI   Age 30/L $3

One of the bigger and nicer mysteries of baseball is how a guy who was loading soda crates a few summers ago could become a legitimate .300 hitter. Give him 500 at-bats and he might be exposed, but used on a limited basis, he's a boxscore surprise. No relation to Gino Marchetti, by the way. Rice Chex.

Year	Team	Lg.	Pos.	G	AB	R	H	HR	RBI	SB	BA
1986	Texas	AL	C	69	137	17	35	2	18	3	.255
1987	Texas	AL	C	101	202	28	61	7	31	0	.302
1988	Texas	AL	C	129	351	35	99	7	36	0	.282
1989	Texas	AL	C	70	184	18	56	4	23	0	.304
Seasonal Notation					383	43	110	8	47	1	.287

BILL SCHROEDER   Age 31/R $1

In 1987 he hit .332 with 14 homers and 42 RBIs for the Brewers, earning an entire chapter in the Time-Life volume on Unexplained Phenomena. If you're going to wait for the same thing to happen, bring plenty of canned goods. Shredded Wheat.

Year	Team	Lg.	Pos.	G	AB	R	H	HR	RBI	SB	BA
1986	Milwaukee	AL	C	64	217	32	46	7	19	1	.212
1987	Milwaukee	AL	C	75	250	35	83	14	42	5	.332
1988	Milwaukee	AL	C	41	122	9	19	5	10	0	.156
1989	California	AL	C	41	138	16	28	6	15	0	.203
Seasonal Notation					532	67	129	23	63	4	.242

JOEL SKINNER   Age 29/R $1

A model of consistency. He has proven he can't hit anywhere. Too bad Dad didn't pass along a batting gene or two. Sugar Pops.

Year	Team	Lg.	Pos.	G	AB	R	H	HR	RBI	SB	BA
1986	Chicago	AL	C	60	149	17	30	4	20	1	.201
1986	New York	AL	C	54	166	6	43	1	17	0	.259
1987	New York	AL	C	64	139	9	19	3	14	0	.137
1988	New York	AL	C	88	251	23	57	4	23	0	.227
1989	Cleveland	AL	C	79	178	10	41	1	13	1	.230
Seasonal Notation					414	30	89	6	40	0	.215

DON SLAUGHT   Age 31/R $3

He's always been a decent hitter, which means he must be an indecent catcher, since nobody seems willing to hand him the job on an everyday basis. Take away the D in his name—apparently he doesn't show any behind the plate—and you have On Slaught. Cocoa Krispies.

Year	Team	Lg.	Pos.	G	AB	R	H	HR	RBI	SB	BA
1986	Texas	AL	C	95	314	39	83	13	46	3	.264
1987	Texas	AL	C	95	237	25	53	8	16	0	.224
1988	New York	AL	C	97	322	33	91	9	43	1	.283
1989	New York	AL	C	117	350	34	88	5	38	1	.251
Seasonal Notation					490	52	126	14	57	2	.258

TERRY STEINBACH   Age 28/R $7

The surest thing among the catchers: .280, about 10 homers,
around 50 RBIs. He would've hit even better if Canseco had been
in the lineup all year and McGwire hadn't had a power outage. In
a bow to the Bay Area novelist of a similar name, feed Terry the
Grape-Nuts of Wrath.

Year	Team	Lg.	Pos.	G	AB	R	H	HR	RBI	SB	BA
1986	Oakland	AL	C	6	15	3	5	2	4	0	.333
1987	Oakland	AL	C	122	391	66	111	16	56	1	.284
1988	Oakland	AL	C	104	351	42	93	9	51	3	.265
1989	Oakland	AL	C	130	454	37	124	7	42	1	.273
Seasonal Notation					541	66	149	15	68	2	.275

B.J. SURHOFF   Age 25/L $7

A triple threat: He can drive in runs, steal bases, and converse on
the real estate prices in Rye, N.Y., the exclusive New York City
suburb whence he comes. Our only worry is that he should've
been a star by now. The potential is still there. S.W. Graham.

Year	Team	Lg.	Pos.	G	AB	R	H	HR	RBI	SB	BA
1987	Milwaukee	AL	C	115	395	50	118	7	68	11	.299
1988	Milwaukee	AL	C	139	493	47	121	5	38	21	.245
1989	Milwaukee	AL	C	126	436	42	108	5	55	14	.248
Seasonal Notation					564	59	147	7	68	19	.262

MICKEY TETTLETON   Age 29/B $14

You think we're going to tell you that his season was a fluke. You
think we're going to tell you to lay off the Mick. You think we're
going to tell you he'll be hitting homers for Rochester by June.
Well, you're wrong. He's very serious about his hitting, and he
looked pretty good the second time around the league. Froot Loops.

Year	Team	Lg.	Pos.	G	AB	R	H	HR	RBI	SB	BA
1986	Oakland	AL	C	90	211	26	43	10	35	7	.204
1987	Oakland	AL	C	82	211	19	41	8	26	1	.194
1988	Baltimore	AL	C	86	283	31	74	11	37	0	.261
1989	Baltimore	AL	C	117	411	72	106	26	65	3	.258
Seasonal Notation					482	63	114	23	70	4	.237

DAVE VALLE   Age 29/R $3

The Mariners are committed to Valle, for some reason, even
though he's nearly 30 ("How green is my Valle?" says GM Woody
Woodward) and can't hit the tough righthanders. He's all right if
all you want of your catcher is the occasional homer. Frosted
Flakes.

Year	Team	Lg.	Pos.	G	AB	R	H	HR	RBI	SB	BA
1986	Seattle	AL	C	22	53	10	18	5	15	0	.340
1987	Seattle	AL	C	95	324	40	83	12	53	2	.256
1988	Seattle	AL	C	92	290	29	67	10	50	0	.231
1989	Seattle	AL	C	94	316	32	75	7	34	0	.237
Seasonal Notation					525	59	129	18	81	1	.247

ERNIE WHITT   Age 37/L $5

The last of the original Jays, he was taken from the Red Sox in the
1976 expansion draft. (Say, Haywood, how about a platoon of Fisk
and Whitt for 13 years?) Ernie can still jack the ball out of the
park, even when it's a convertible. However, HE'LL BE 38 YEARS
OLD IN JUNE. Mueslix.

Year	Team	Lg.	Pos.	G	AB	R	H	HR	RBI	SB	BA
1986	Toronto	AL	C	131	395	48	106	16	56	0	.268
1987	Toronto	AL	C	135	446	57	120	19	75	0	.269
1988	Toronto	AL	C	127	398	63	100	16	70	4	.251
1989	Toronto	AL	C	129	385	42	101	11	53	5	.262
Seasonal Notation					504	65	132	19	78	2	.263

AT THE CORNERS

If you don't know by now, the gods who rule the fates of Rotisserians
are a fickle bunch. Remember how those with Chris Sabo and Ron
Gant on their rosters strutted around last spring knowing they had
the rights to the two best prospects in the league. And the teams
that counted on Vance Law producing great numbers at a bargain
basement salary. How can you protect yourself against such cruel
disappointments?

This is a particularly critical issue at the corner positions.
After all, at a time when outfields are populated by the kind of swift,
high average hitters who get excited about their on-base percent-
ages, you've got to get your boomers at first and third.

The simple truth is you must shell out for the blue-chip
boomers, and don't be shy about it. You've just got to pony up for
Will Clark, Glenn Davis, Mark McGwire, and, Great George Scott,

Nick Esasky. And of course, there's the remarkable Howard Johnson, who we all knew was on his way to Seattle and oblivion.

Most of us, however, will hedge our bets as usual. We'll hope that Galarraga, Murray, or Bonilla bounce back to full boomer status. Because if you don't pick up one of these guys, you'll be left praying that Pagliarulo takes a liking to San Diego, Sid Bream recovers from surgery, and Dale Berra has a kindly probation officer.

NATIONAL LEAGUE

TODD BENZINGER   Age 27/B $18

The Reds thought he'd drive in more runs than Nick Esasky, so they threw in Rob Murphy as a sweetener. DUH!

Year	Team	Lg.	Pos.	G	AB	R	H	HR	RBI	SB	BA
1987	Boston	AL	OF	73	223	36	62	8	43	5	.278
1988	Boston	AL	1B	120	405	47	103	13	70	2	.254
1989	Cincinnati	NL	1B	161	628	79	154	17	76	3	.245
Seasonal Notation					574	74	145	17	86	4	.254

JEFF BLAUSER   Age 24/R $6

Good little feller to have around at the right (low) price. He'll surprise with his pop, though it's not enough for a third sacker. Our hunch is that the Braves will deal the valuable but sleepwalking Andres Thomas and put Blauser at short.

Year	Team	Lg.	Pos.	G	AB	R	H	HR	RBI	SB	BA
1987	Atlanta	NL	SS	51	165	11	40	2	15	7	.242
1988	Atlanta	NL	2B	18	67	7	16	2	7	0	.239
1989	Atlanta	NL	3B	142	456	63	123	12	46	5	.270
Seasonal Notation					528	62	137	12	52	9	.260

BASEBALL ANAGRAM #3

Mookie Wilson = Look, women, is I!

BOBBY BONILLA   Age 27/B $30

He led the league in errors committed (not a Rotissecategory).
Still, he was the Pirates' all-everything offensively in 1989. They'll
move him off the hot corner, probably to first base, and he'll
respond like Pedro Guerrero. Look for even better numbers in
1990.

Year	Team	Lg.	Pos.	G	AB	R	H	HR	RBI	SB	BA
1986	Chicago	AL	OF	75	234	27	63	2	26	4	.269
1986	Pittsburgh	NL	3B	63	192	28	46	1	17	4	.240
1987	Pittsburgh	NL	3B	141	466	58	140	15	77	3	.300
1988	Pittsburgh	NL	3B	159	584	87	160	24	100	3	.274
1989	Pittsburgh	NL	3B	163	616	96	173	24	86	8	.281
Seasonal Notation					563	79	156	17	82	5	.278

SID BREAM   Age 29/L $12

1989 was a washout. Before that, he had consistently okay numbers: 10-17 homers, 65-77 ribbies a season. Ever since Pops hung
'em up, the Bucs have needed a little more pop at this position.
And so do you.

Year	Team	Lg.	Pos.	G	AB	R	H	HR	RBI	SB	BA
1986	Pittsburgh	NL	1B	154	522	73	140	16	77	13	.268
1987	Pittsburgh	NL	1B	149	516	64	142	13	65	9	.275
1988	Pittsburgh	NL	1B	148	462	50	122	10	65	9	.264
1989	Pittsburgh	NL	1B	19	36	3	8	0	4	0	.222
Seasonal Notation					529	65	142	13	72	10	.268

KEN CAMINITI   Age 26/B $13

Has won the job with solid but not arousing numbers. Will get
somewhat better. But don't take out a second mortgage just to get
him.

Year	Team	Lg.	Pos.	G	AB	R	H	HR	RBI	SB	BA
1987	Houston	NL	3B	63	203	10	50	3	23	0	.246
1988	Houston	NL	3B	30	83	5	15	1	7	0	.181
1989	Houston	NL	3B	161	585	71	149	10	72	4	.255
Seasonal Notation					555	54	136	8	65	2	.246

JACK CLARK   Age 34/R $31

This guy *never* hits in the spring, so let somebody else take the hit
on draft day, and you pick him up for a song about June 15.
Careful, though: Last season his "spring" lasted four months.

Year	Team	Lg.	Pos.	G	AB	R	H	HR	RBI	SB	BA
1986	St. Louis	NL	1B	65	232	34	55	9	23	1	.237
1987	St. Louis	NL	1B	131	419	93	120	35	106	1	.286
1988	New York	AL	OF	150	496	81	120	27	93	3	.242
1989	San Diego	NL	1B	142	455	76	110	26	94	6	.242
Seasonal Notation					531	94	134	32	104	3	.253

WILL CLARK   Age 26/L $44

Mr. Everything. Not too early to compare him to Williams and
Musial. So what if he's a little . . . ahh, confident. Wouldn't you
be, in his shoes?

Year	Team	Lg.	Pos.	G	AB	R	H	HR	RBI	SB	BA
1986	San Francisco	NL	1B	111	408	66	117	11	41	4	.287
1987	San Francisco	NL	1B	150	529	89	163	35	91	5	.308
1988	San Francisco	NL	1B	162	575	102	162	29	109	9	.282
1989	San Francisco	NL	1B	159	588	104	196	23	111	8	.333
Seasonal Notation					584	100	177	27	97	7	.304

GLENN DAVIS   Age 29/R $37

A super player, despite being sentenced to a vast, dead, ugly
ballpark and having nobody hitting after him. Glenn, this Bud's for
you!

Year	Team	Lg.	Pos.	G	AB	R	H	HR	RBI	SB	BA
1986	Houston	NL	1B	158	574	91	152	31	101	3	.265
1987	Houston	NL	1B	151	578	70	145	27	93	4	.251
1988	Houston	NL	1B	152	561	78	152	30	99	4	.271
1989	Houston	NL	1B	158	581	87	156	34	89	4	.269
Seasonal Notation					600	85	158	31	99	3	.264

ANDRES GALARRAGA   Age 28/R $35

His batting average was a pussy but the Cat will be back.

Year	Team	Lg.	Pos.	G	AB	R	H	HR	RBI	SB	BA
1986	Montreal	NL	1B	105	321	39	87	10	42	6	.271
1987	Montreal	NL	1B	147	551	72	168	13	90	7	.305
1988	Montreal	NL	1B	157	609	99	184	29	92	13	.302
1989	Montreal	NL	1B	152	572	76	147	23	85	12	.257
Seasonal Notation					592	82	169	21	89	10	.285

MARK GRACE   Age 25/L $29

The natural successor to Keith Hernandez, whose early numbers
he's a cinch to match or surpass. This guy comes guaranteed.

Year	Team	Lg.	Pos.	G	AB	R	H	HR	RBI	SB	BA
1988	Chicago	NL	1B	134	486	65	144	7	57	3	.296
1989	Chicago	NL	1B	142	510	74	160	13	79	14	.314
Seasonal Notation					584	81	178	11	79	9	.305

TY GRIFFIN   Age 23/B $12

Hotshot prospect who'll take over third or push Sandberg from second to third, which makes more sense. As can't-miss as they come. Particularly if you're rebuilding, he's a *must*.

[No major league experience prior to 1990.]

PEDRO GUERRERO   Age 33/R $32

His home runs were down, thanks to playing in Busch. But his ability to drive in runners from scoring position was the best in the league. Overall, a great year.

Year	Team	Lg.	Pos.	G	AB	R	H	HR	RBI	SB	BA
1986	Los Angeles	NL	OF	31	61	7	15	5	10	0	.246
1987	Los Angeles	NL	OF	152	545	89	184	27	89	9	.338
1988	Los Angeles	NL	3B	59	215	24	64	5	35	2	.298
1988	St. Louis	NL	1B	44	149	16	40	5	30	2	.268
1989	St. Louis	NL	1B	162	570	60	177	17	117	2	.311
Seasonal Notation					556	70	173	21	101	5	.312

JEFF HAMILTON   Age 26/R $11

Despite his decent HR total, his RBIs were paltry given his ABs. The Dodgers will improve on him if they can. Mr. Boggs?

Year	Team	Lg.	Pos.	G	AB	R	H	HR	RBI	SB	BA
1986	Los Angeles	NL	3B	71	147	22	33	5	19	0	.224
1987	Los Angeles	NL	3B	35	83	5	18	0	1	0	.217
1988	Los Angeles	NL	3B	111	309	34	73	6	33	0	.236
1989	Los Angeles	NL	3B	151	548	45	134	12	56	0	.245
Seasonal Notation					478	46	113	10	47	0	.237

CHARLIE HAYES   Age 24/R $11

Dunno. Has a pretty quick, slashing stroke, which should get better with time. Bad fielder. Held his own after getting the opportunity to play every day.

Year	Team	Lg.	Pos.	G	AB	R	H	HR	RBI	SB	BA
1988	San Francisco	NL	OF	7	11	0	1	0	0	0	.091
1989	San Francisco	NL	3B	3	5	0	1	0	0	0	.200
1989	Philadelphia	NL	3B	84	299	26	77	8	43	3	.258
Seasonal Notation					542	44	136	13	74	5	.251

KEITH HERNANDEZ   Age 36/L $12

Mex and the Apple: the end of a beautiful romance.

Year	Team	Lg.	Pos.	G	AB	R	H	HR	RBI	SB	BA
1986	New York	NL	1B	149	551	94	171	13	83	2	.310
1987	New York	NL	1B	154	587	87	170	18	89	0	.290
1988	New York	NL	1B	95	348	43	96	11	55	2	.276
1989	New York	NL	1B	75	215	18	50	4	19	0	.233
Seasonal Notation					582	82	166	15	84	1	.286

HOWARD JOHNSON   Age 29/B $38

Another great, great season. Outshone all the other New York
pretty boys and spoiled brats. Came within a whisker of 40-40.
He'll get close again.

Year	Team	Lg.	Pos.	G	AB	R	H	HR	RBI	SB	BA
1986	New York	NL	3B	88	220	30	54	10	39	8	.245
1987	New York	NL	3B	157	554	93	147	36	99	32	.265
1988	New York	NL	3B	148	495	85	114	24	68	23	.230
1989	New York	NL	3B	153	571	104	164	36	101	41	.287
Seasonal Notation					545	92	142	31	91	30	.260

RICKY JORDAN   Age 24/R $17

Settling in as a pretty solid run producer who should keep his
average close to .300. Recovered nicely last year from first-half
hand injuries.

Year	Team	Lg.	Pos.	G	AB	R	H	HR	RBI	SB	BA
1988	Philadelphia	NL	1B	69	273	41	84	11	43	1	.308
1989	Philadelphia	NL	1B	144	523	63	149	12	75	4	.285
Seasonal Notation					605	79	177	17	89	3	.293

JEFF KING   Age 25/R $5

It all depends on his winning a job. If Bonilla moves to the
outfield, then King takes over at third. If not, he'll platoon at first.
A disputable #-1 draft pick, he has shown flashes of power but not
much average. Will finally end up a utility-type player.

Year	Team	Lg.	Pos.	G	AB	R	H	HR	RBI	SB	BA
1989	Pittsburgh	NL	1B	75	215	31	42	5	19	4	.195
Seasonal Notation					464	66	90	10	41	8	.195

VANCE LAW   33/R $2

He'll put in one or two seasons as a Manny Trillo-type utility man.
Enough pop to be valuable.

Year	Team	Lg.	Pos.	G	AB	R	H	HR	RBI	SB	BA
1986	Montreal	NL	2B	112	360	37	81	5	44	3	.225
1987	Montreal	NL	2B	133	436	52	119	12	56	8	.273
1988	Chicago	NL	3B	151	556	73	163	11	78	1	.293
1989	Chicago	NL	3B	130	408	38	96	7	42	2	.235
Seasonal Notation					542	61	141	10	67	4	.261

DAVE MAGADAN   Age 27/L $10

Should be a regular something, we suppose, though his glove at third is execrable and not much better than that (though improving) at first. And who needs a singles hitter at either corner?

Year	Team	Lg.	Pos.	G	AB	R	H	HR	RBI	SB	BA
1986	New York	NL	1B	10	18	3	8	0	3	0	.444
1987	New York	NL	3B	85	192	21	61	3	24	0	.318
1988	New York	NL	1B	112	314	39	87	1	35	0	.277
1989	New York	NL	1B	127	374	47	107	4	41	1	.286
Seasonal Notation					435	53	127	3	49	0	.293

EDDIE MURRAY   Age 34/B $26

Last year we told you the move to L.A. would wake him up. Thirty-plus home runs, we told you. So sue us. And given who our lawyer is, sue us big.

Year	Team	Lg.	Pos.	G	AB	R	H	HR	RBI	SB	BA
1986	Baltimore	AL	1B	137	495	61	151	17	84	3	.305
1987	Baltimore	AL	1B	160	618	89	171	30	91	1	.277
1988	Baltimore	AL	1B	161	603	75	171	28	84	5	.284
1989	Los Angeles	NL	1B	160	594	66	147	20	88	7	.247
Seasonal Notation					605	76	167	24	90	4	.277

MIKE PAGLIARULO   Age 30/L $9

Don't expect his Yankee Stadium HR numbers to be approached in San Diego. Not even close. His BA has declined every year he's been in the majors, and it wasn't much to begin with. So what's keeping him in the starting lineup? His glove—for one more shot.

Year	Team	Lg.	Pos.	G	AB	R	H	HR	RBI	SB	BA
1986	New York	AL	3B	149	504	71	120	28	71	4	.238
1987	New York	AL	3B	150	522	76	122	32	87	1	.234
1988	New York	AL	3B	125	444	46	96	15	67	1	.216
1989	New York	AL	3B	74	223	19	44	4	16	1	.197
1989	San Diego	NL	3B	50	148	12	29	3	14	2	.196
Seasonal Notation					544	66	121	24	75	2	.223

TERRY PENDLETON   Age 29/B $15

Chronically bad wheels made him considerably less valuable than in the past, but he's still a solid RBI man.

Year	Team	Lg.	Pos.	G	AB	R	H	HR	RBI	SB	BA
1986	St. Louis	NL	3B	159	578	56	138	1	59	24	.239
1987	St. Louis	NL	3B	159	583	82	167	12	96	19	.286
1988	St. Louis	NL	3B	110	391	44	99	6	53	3	.253
1989	St. Louis	NL	3B	162	613	83	162	13	74	9	.264
Seasonal Notation					594	72	155	8	77	15	.261

GERALD PERRY   Age 29/L $15

Rumors abound. May well be ticketed to the American League, where his barely adequate defensive skills won't matter. Wherever he goes, he'll never be mistaken for Lou Gehrig. His replacement? Drew Denson, grab a glove!

Year	Team	Lg.	Pos.	G	AB	R	H	HR	RBI	SB	BA
1986	Atlanta	NL	OF	29	70	6	19	2	11	0	.271
1987	Atlanta	NL	1B	142	533	77	144	12	74	42	.270
1988	Atlanta	NL	1B	141	547	61	164	8	74	29	.300
1989	Atlanta	NL	1B	72	266	24	67	4	21	10	.252
Seasonal Notation					597	70	166	10	75	34	.278

RANDY READY   Age 30/R $2

Capable fill-in. The Vet will help his longball value.

Year	Team	Lg.	Pos.	G	AB	R	H	HR	RBI	SB	BA
1986	Milwaukee	AL	OF	23	79	8	15	1	4	2	.190
1986	San Diego	NL	3B	1	3	0	0	0	0	0	.000
1987	San Diego	NL	3B	124	350	69	108	12	54	7	.309
1988	San Diego	NL	3B	114	331	43	88	7	39	6	.266
1989	San Diego	NL	3B	28	67	4	17	0	5	0	.254
1989	Philadelphia	NL	OF	72	187	33	50	8	21	4	.267
Seasonal Notation					455	70	124	12	55	8	.273

ERNEST RILES   Age 29/L $2

A good twenty-third player.

Year	Team	Lg.	Pos.	G	AB	R	H	HR	RBI	SB	BA
1986	Milwaukee	AL	SS	145	524	69	132	9	47	7	.252
1987	Milwaukee	AL	3B	83	276	38	72	4	38	3	.261
1988	Milwaukee	AL	3B	41	127	7	32	1	9	2	.252
1988	San Francisco	NL	3B	79	187	26	55	3	28	1	.294
1989	San Francisco	NL	3B	122	302	43	84	7	40	0	.278
Seasonal Notation					488	63	129	8	55	4	.265

BIP ROBERTS   Age 26/B $11

Pesky, feisty, wherever they put him. He's found his role, which is role playing. Speed makes him worth the above ticket.

Year	Team	Lg.	Pos.	G	AB	R	H	HR	RBI	SB	BA
1986	San Diego	NL	2B	101	241	34	61	1	12	14	.253
1988	San Diego	NL	3B	5	9	1	3	0	0	0	.333
1989	San Diego	NL	OF	117	329	81	99	3	25	21	.301
Seasonal Notation					420	84	118	2	26	25	.282

CHRIS SABO
Age 28/R   **$19**

He's not as good as his rookie year and he's not as bad as last year, when injuries ruined everything.

Year	Team	Lg.	Pos.	G	AB	R	H	HR	RBI	SB	BA
1988	Cincinnati	NL	3B	137	538	74	146	11	44	46	.271
1989	Cincinnati	NL	3B	82	304	40	79	6	29	14	.260
Seasonal Notation					622	84	166	12	54	44	267

TIM WALLACH
Age 32/R   **$22**

Could be broomed as part of Expo housecleaning.

Year	Team	Lg.	Pos.	G	AB	R	H	HR	RBI	SB	BA
1986	Montreal	NL	3B	134	480	50	112	18	71	8	.233
1987	Montreal	NL	3B	153	593	89	177	26	123	9	.298
1988	Montreal	NL	3B	159	592	52	152	12	69	2	.257
1989	Montreal	NL	3B	154	573	76	159	13	77	3	.277
Seasonal Notation					604	72	162	18	91	5	.268

MATT WILLIAMS
Age 24/R   **$30**

Ladies and germs, the next Mike Schmidt! He's got his bat and glove. If he doesn't hit 30 HRs in 1990, we'll shave Harry Stein's head.

Year	Team	Lg.	Pos.	G	AB	R	H	HR	RBI	SB	BA
1987	San Francisco	NL	SS	84	245	28	46	8	21	4	.188
1988	San Francisco	NL	3B	52	156	17	32	8	19	0	.205
1989	San Francisco	NL	3B	84	292	31	59	18	50	1	.202
Seasonal Notation					510	55	100	25	66	3	.198

AMERICAN LEAGUE

Not too long ago, you could rely on your first and third basemen for a power base. Nowadays you'll be lucky to pick up one big bopper. Just remember, you're better off with, say, Pete O'Brien, Kelly Gruber, and Kevin Seitzer than you will be with Fred McGriff, Joey Meyer, and Rick Schu, so spend wisely.

LUIS AGUAYO
Age 31/R   **$1**

If you even think about acquiring him, you're in trouble. And if you actually get him, you should be drummed out of your league.

Year	Team	Lg.	Pos.	G	AB	R	H	HR	RBI	SB	BA
1986	Philadelphia	NL	2B	62	133	17	28	4	13	1	.211
1987	Philadelphia	NL	SS	94	209	25	43	12	21	0	.206
1988	Philadelphia	NL	SS	49	97	9	24	3	5	2	.247
1988	New York	AL	3B	50	140	12	35	3	8	0	.250
1989	Cleveland	AL	3B	47	97	7	17	1	8	0	.175
Seasonal Notation					362	37	78	12	29	1	.217

DAVE BERGMAN   Age 36/L $1

And worth every penny.

Year	Team	Lg.	Pos.	G	AB	R	H	HR	RBI	SB	BA
1986	Detroit	AL	1B	65	130	14	30	1	9	0	.231
1987	Detroit	AL	1B	91	172	25	47	6	22	0	.273
1988	Detroit	AL	1B	116	289	37	85	5	35	0	.294
1989	Detroit	AL	1B	137	385	38	103	7	37	1	.268
Seasonal Notation					386	45	104	7	40	0	.272

WADE BOGGS   Age 31/L $25

While his average didn't suffer from the Margo Affair, his power
did. (No jokes about her sapping his strength. In fact, we found
Wade's behavior so reprehensible, his taste so appalling, and his
interview with Barbara Wawa so insincere that we vowed never to
have him on our team again. Not unless his price dips below **$20**.)
You might also want to consider that Wade could end up in the
other league.

Year	Team	Lg.	Pos.	G	AB	R	H	HR	RBI	SB	BA
1986	Boston	AL	3B	149	580	107	207	8	71	0	.357
1987	Boston	AL	3B	147	551	108	200	24	89	1	.363
1988	Boston	AL	3B	155	584	128	214	5	58	2	.366
1989	Boston	AL	3B	156	621	113	205	3	54	2	.330
Seasonal Notation					623	121	220	10	72	1	.354

GEORGE BRETT   Age 36/L $20

There's fire in the old boy yet—he had a great September. If he
can get his average back above .300 and stay out of the infirmary,
he becomes a **$30** player.

Year	Team	Lg.	Pos.	G	AB	R	H	HR	RBI	SB	BA
1986	Kansas City	AL	3B	124	441	70	128	16	73	1	.290
1987	Kansas City	AL	1B	115	427	71	124	22	78	6	.290
1988	Kansas City	AL	1B	157	589	90	180	24	103	14	.306
1989	Kansas City	AL	1B	124	457	67	129	12	80	14	.282
Seasonal Notation					596	92	174	23	104	10	.293

GREG BROCK   Age 32/L $8

He had a pretty good second half, but he has never lived up to his potential, and he'll be 33 in June.

Year	Team	Lg.	Pos.	G	AB	R	H	HR	RBI	SB	BA
1986	Los Angeles	NL	1B	115	325	33	76	16	52	2	.234
1987	Milwaukee	AL	1B	141	532	81	159	13	85	5	.299
1988	Milwaukee	AL	1B	115	364	53	77	6	50	6	.212
1989	Milwaukee	AL	1B	107	373	40	99	12	52	6	.265
Seasonal Notation					540	70	139	15	81	6	.258

TOM BROOKENS   Age 36/R $1

Jack Morris said that if Kirk Gibson was the heart of the Tigers, then Tom Brookens was the "lungs." That may be true in real life, but in Rotisserie League Baseball, Brookens is the appendix.

Year	Team	Lg.	Pos.	G	AB	R	H	HR	RBI	SB	BA
1986	Detroit	AL	3B	98	281	42	76	3	25	11	.270
1987	Detroit	AL	3B	143	444	59	107	13	59	7	.241
1988	Detroit	AL	3B	136	441	62	107	5	38	4	.243
1989	New York	AL	3B	66	168	14	38	4	14	1	.226
Seasonal Notation					487	64	119	9	49	8	.246

STEVE BUECHELE   Age 28/R $8

His annual stats have become something of a broken record, so at least you know what you're getting. Useful but unspectacular.

Year	Team	Lg.	Pos.	G	AB	R	H	HR	RBI	SB	BA
1986	Texas	AL	3B	153	461	54	112	18	54	5	.243
1987	Texas	AL	3B	136	363	45	86	13	50	2	.237
1988	Texas	AL	3B	155	503	68	126	16	58	2	.250
1989	Texas	AL	3B	155	486	60	114	16	59	1	.235
Seasonal Notation					490	61	118	17	59	2	.242

ALVIN DAVIS   Age 29/L $28

He's wasting his life away in the Pacific Northwest. If this guy played in any kind of media market, he'd be a superstar. And you'd be paying $35 for him.

Year	Team	Lg.	Pos.	G	AB	R	H	HR	RBI	SB	BA
1986	Seattle	AL	1B	135	479	66	130	18	72	0	.271
1987	Seattle	AL	1B	157	580	86	171	29	100	0	.295
1988	Seattle	AL	1B	140	478	67	141	18	69	1	.295
1989	Seattle	AL	1B	142	498	84	152	21	95	0	.305
Seasonal Notation					574	85	167	24	94	0	.292

LUIS DE LOS SANTOS   Age 23/R $1

Or 25 cents a name. Royals scouts say he could be the next
Pete LaCock.

Year	Team	Lg.	Pos.	G	AB	R	H	HR	RBI	SB	BA
1988	Kansas City	AL	1B	11	22	1	2	0	1	0	.091
1989	Kansas City	AL	1B	28	87	6	22	0	6	0	.253
Seasonal Notation					452	29	99	0	29	0	.220

NICK ESASKY   Age 30/R $25

We knew this was going to happen. In fact, we know a man who is
in a Rotisserie League with his wife. He had already filled his first
base slot, so when Esasky came up, he motioned to her to get him,
figuring he could at least keep it in the family. She did get Esasky,
and she ended up winning the league. Not only did Esasky's
season show what a right-handed power hitter can do in Fenway,
but it also showed just how bad a manager Pete Rose was.

Year	Team	Lg.	Pos.	G	AB	R	H	HR	RBI	SB	BA
1986	Cincinnati	NL	1B	102	330	35	76	12	41	0	.230
1987	Cincinnati	NL	1B	100	346	48	94	22	59	0	.272
1988	Cincinnati	NL	1B	122	391	40	95	15	62	7	.243
1989	Boston	AL	1B	154	564	79	156	30	108	1	.277
Seasonal Notation					552	68	142	26	91	2	.258

TERRY FRANCONA   Age 30/L $1

A nice guy, but don't bother.

Year	Team	Lg.	Pos.	G	AB	R	H	HR	RBI	SB	BA
1986	Chicago	NL	OF	86	124	13	31	2	8	0	.250
1987	Cincinnati	NL	1B	102	207	16	47	3	12	2	.227
1988	Cleveland	AL	OF	62	212	24	66	1	12	0	.311
1989	Milwaukee	AL	1B	90	233	26	54	3	23	2	.232
Seasonal Notation					369	37	94	4	26	1	.255

> **Did Whitey Herzog's faith in Todd
> Zeile provoke Pena's envy?**

GARY GAETTI   Age 31/R $25

He found Christ and lost value. In one of the more poignant
quotes of this or any season, his former road roommate Kent
Hrbek said, "Now when I wake up in the morning and fart, there's
nobody there to hear it." Which, of course, brings up the age-old
philosophical question, If you break wind and nobody hears it, is it
still a fart? That aside, Gaetti is still a great player, and thou
wouldst do well to have him on thy team.

Year	Team	Lg.	Pos.	G	AB	R	H	HR	RBI	SB	BA
1986	Minnesota	AL	3B	157	596	91	171	34	108	14	.287
1987	Minnesota	AL	3B	154	584	95	150	31	109	10	.257
1988	Minnesota	AL	3B	133	468	66	141	28	88	7	.301
1989	Minnesota	AL	3B	130	498	63	125	19	75	6	.251
Seasonal Notation					605	88	165	31	107	10	.274

KELLY GRUBER   Age 28/R $20

A good four-category player. And a member of our All-Girl's-Name
Team:

1b-Gail Hopkins	of-Terry Francona
2b-Rene Gonzalez	of-Dale Murphy
ss-Lena Blackburne	of-Cory Snyder
3b-Kelly Gruber	sp-Robin Roberts
c-Jamie Quirk	sp-Ron Darling

Year	Team	Lg.	Pos.	G	AB	R	H	HR	RBI	SB	BA
1986	Toronto	AL	3B	87	143	20	28	5	15	2	.196
1987	Toronto	AL	3B	138	341	50	80	12	36	12	.235
1988	Toronto	AL	3B	158	569	75	158	16	81	23	.278
1989	Toronto	AL	3B	135	545	83	158	18	73	10	.290
Seasonal Notation					499	71	132	15	64	14	.265

JACK HOWELL   Age 28/L $5

Sure he hit a few home runs. But his average was a drag, and the
Angels have a couple of pretty good third base prospects, Billy
Rose and Jeff Manto, ready to take his place.

Year	Team	Lg.	Pos.	G	AB	R	H	HR	RBI	SB	BA
1986	California	AL	3B	63	151	26	41	4	21	2	.272
1987	California	AL	OF	138	449	64	110	23	64	4	.245
1988	California	AL	3B	154	500	59	127	16	63	2	.254
1989	California	AL	3B	144	474	56	108	20	52	0	.228
Seasonal Notation					510	66	125	20	64	2	.245

KENT HRBEK   Age 29/L $25

Give him back the 100 at-bats he lost to injuries, and he would have had his usual season. Maybe what he really needs is a new roommate with earthy tastes.

Year	Team	Lg.	Pos.	G	AB	R	H	HR	RBI	SB	BA
1986	Minnesota	AL	1B	149	550	85	147	29	91	2	.267
1987	Minnesota	AL	1B	143	477	85	136	34	90	5	.285
1988	Minnesota	AL	1B	143	510	75	159	25	76	0	.312
1989	Minnesota	AL	1B	109	375	59	102	25	84	3	.272
Seasonal Notation					569	90	162	33	101	2	.285

BROOK JACOBY   Age 30/R $12

We've lowered our expectations of what he can do, and you'll be happier if you do the same. Say, if he were traded to the Mets and roomed with Randy Myers, they could handle Ron Darling's divorce for a reasonable rate.

Year	Team	Lg.	Pos.	G	AB	R	H	HR	RBI	SB	BA
1986	Cleveland	AL	3B	158	583	83	168	17	80	2	.288
1987	Cleveland	AL	3B	155	540	73	162	32	69	2	.300
1988	Cleveland	AL	3B	152	552	59	133	9	49	2	.241
1989	Cleveland	AL	3B	147	519	49	141	13	64	2	.272
Seasonal Notation					580	69	159	18	69	2	.275

WALLY JOYNER   Age 27/L $20

Wallyworld again offered an A ticket.

Year	Team	Lg.	Pos.	G	AB	R	H	HR	RBI	SB	BA
1986	California	AL	1B	154	593	82	172	22	100	5	.290
1987	California	AL	1B	149	564	100	161	34	117	8	.285
1988	California	AL	1B	158	597	81	176	13	85	8	.295
1989	California	AL	1B	159	593	78	167	16	79	3	.282
Seasonal Notation					613	89	176	22	99	6	.288

CARNEY LANSFORD   Age 33/R $30

That average with those stolen bases made him one of the most coveted properties in Rotisseball. We've always loved him, and we always will, but all those steals may be pounding his 33-year-old body.

Year	Team	Lg.	Pos.	G	AB	R	H	HR	RBI	SB	BA
1986	Oakland	AL	3B	151	591	80	168	19	72	16	.284
1987	Oakland	AL	3B	151	554	89	160	19	76	27	.289
1988	Oakland	AL	3B	150	556	80	155	7	57	29	.279
1989	Oakland	AL	3B	148	551	81	185	2	52	37	.336
Seasonal Notation					608	89	180	12	69	29	.297

EDGAR MARTINEZ   Age 27/R $1

There are two third basemen named Martinez. This is the one you don't want, even though, or perhaps because, he is Carmelo Martinez's cousin.

Year	Team	Lg.	Pos.	G	AB	R	H	HR	RBI	SB	BA
1987	Seattle	AL	3B	13	43	6	16	0	5	0	.372
1988	Seattle	AL	3B	14	32	0	9	0	5	0	.281
1989	Seattle	AL	3B	65	171	20	41	2	20	2	.240
Seasonal Notation					433	45	116	3	52	3	.268

CARLOS MARTINEZ   Age 25/R $5

This is the one you do want. At 6'5", 175 pounds, he can fairly be described as lanky. He is the fruit of one of the Yankees' worst trades in recent years (see two entries below for the worst): Martinez, Bill Lindsay, and Ron Hassey for Ron Kittle, Joel Skinner, and Wayne Tolleson.

Year	Team	Lg.	Pos.	G	AB	R	H	HR	RBI	SB	BA
1988	Chicago	AL	3B	17	55	5	9	0	0	1	.164
1989	Chicago	AL	3B	109	350	44	105	5	32	4	.300
Seasonal Notation					520	63	146	6	41	6	.281

DON MATTINGLY   Age 27/L $30

You've only been kidding us the last two years, right Donnie boy? Right?

Year	Team	Lg.	Pos.	G	AB	R	H	HR	RBI	SB	BA
1986	New York	AL	1B	162	677	117	238	31	113	0	.352
1987	New York	AL	1B	141	569	93	186	30	115	1	.327
1988	New York	AL	1B	144	599	94	186	18	88	1	.311
1989	New York	AL	1B	158	631	79	191	23	113	3	.303
Seasonal Notation					662	102	214	27	114	1	.324

FRED MCGRIFF   Age 26/L $33

We trust the Yankees long ago fired the man who threw McGriff into the deal to get Dale Murray. ("I'm telling you, boss, the guy is a great outfielder. Oh, that's Dale Mur-phy. Never mind.") The only reason we're not assigning McGriff a higher price is because of the next entry . . .

Year	Team	Lg.	Pos.	G	AB	R	H	HR	RBI	SB	BA
1986	Toronto	AL	1B	3	5	1	1	0	0	0	.200
1987	Toronto	AL	1B	107	295	58	73	20	43	3	.247
1988	Toronto	AL	1B	154	536	100	151	34	82	6	.282
1989	Toronto	AL	1B	161	551	98	148	36	92	7	.269
Seasonal Notation					528	97	142	34	82	6	.269

MARK MCGWIRE　　　　　Age 26/R　　　$25

Power hitters are notoriously inconsistent. That's life. That's what all the people say. You're ridin' high in April. Shot down in May. McGwire never got going last year. His batting average could only have been neutralized if you had Nap Lajoie on your team. We're not trying to scare you off McGwire. To the contrary, we think you're better off with him at a deflated price than you are with McGriff at an exorbitant price.

Year	Team	Lg.	Pos.	G	AB	R	H	HR	RBI	SB	BA
1986	Oakland	AL	3B	18	53	10	10	3	9	0	.189
1987	Oakland	AL	1B	151	557	97	161	49	118	1	.289
1988	Oakland	AL	1B	155	550	87	143	32	99	0	.260
1989	Oakland	AL	1B	143	490	74	113	33	95	1	.231
Seasonal Notation					572	92	148	40	111	0	.259

LUIS MEDINA　　　　　Age 27/R　　　$2

The Indians will have to find a place for him because 1) he can hit and 2) he can't field. Talk about playing hard-to-get, Medina has at one time been drafted by the Mets (twice), the Yankees, the Reds, the Athletics, the Astros, and the Indians.

Year	Team	Lg.	Pos.	G	AB	R	H	HR	RBI	SB	BA
1988	Cleveland	AL	1B	16	51	10	13	6	8	0	.255
1989	Cleveland	AL	OF	30	83	8	17	4	8	0	.205
Seasonal Notation					471	63	105	35	56	0	.224

RANDY MILLIGAN　　　　Age 28/R　　　$5

A $35 player in the International League and winter ball, he's strictly a journeyman in the bigs. But you could do worse.

Year	Team	Lg.	Pos.	G	AB	R	H	HR	RBI	SB	BA
1987	New York	NL	3B	3	1	0	0	0	0	0	.000
1988	Pittsburgh	NL	1B	40	82	10	18	3	8	1	.220
1989	Baltimore	AL	1B	124	365	56	98	12	45	9	.268
Seasonal Notation					434	64	112	14	51	9	.259

BASEBALL ANAGRAM #4

Len Dykstra = End starkly

PAUL MOLITOR   Age 33/R $15

On the surface, he seemed to have a decent, slightly off, season. But the Brewers are worried his hard-nosed style and many injuries have taken their toll. It seems like only yesterday that he and Robin Yount were the gold dust twins. We're going to stop now before we start crying.

Year	Team	Lg.	Pos.	G	AB	R	H	HR	RBI	SB	BA
1986	Milwaukee	AL	3B	105	437	62	123	9	55	20	.281
1987	Milwaukee	AL	3B	118	465	114	164	16	75	45	.353
1988	Milwaukee	AL	3B	154	609	115	190	13	60	41	.312
1989	Milwaukee	AL	3B	155	615	84	194	11	56	27	.315
Seasonal Notation					647	114	204	14	74	40	.316

KEITH MORELAND   Age 35/R $3

There must be some reason this guy is now being passed around like a joint at Woodstock. A slower bat would be one guess.

Year	Team	Lg.	Pos.	G	AB	R	H	HR	RBI	SB	BA
1986	Chicago	NL	OF	156	586	72	159	12	79	3	.271
1987	Chicago	NL	3B	153	563	63	150	27	88	3	.266
1988	San Diego	NL	1B	143	511	40	131	5	64	2	.256
1989	Detroit	AL	1B	90	318	34	95	5	35	3	.299
1989	Baltimore	AL	1B	33	107	11	23	1	10	0	.215
Seasonal Notation					587	61	157	14	77	3	.268

PETE O'BRIEN   Age 32/L $8

His 1989 stats were a notch below what he once regularly provided (20 HRs, 90 RBIs). Maybe guys just hate playing in Cleveland. Speaking of the Indians, Whitey Herzog thought *Major League* was one of the funniest movies of all time. We wonder if he's familiar with the *oeuvre* of Preston Sturges. But we digress. . . . O'Brien would be a steady if unspectacular first sacker for you.

Year	Team	Lg.	Pos.	G	AB	R	H	HR	RBI	SB	BA
1986	Texas	AL	1B	156	551	86	160	23	90	4	.290
1987	Texas	AL	1B	159	569	84	163	23	88	0	.286
1988	Texas	AL	1B	156	547	57	149	16	71	1	.272
1989	Cleveland	AL	1B	155	554	75	144	12	55	3	.260
Seasonal Notation					574	78	159	19	78	2	.277

RAFAEL PALMEIRO   Age 25/L $10

We're not sure what happened, but one moment people were touting him for the batting title, and the next moment he was treading water in the .270s. Get him while he's cold—he's a legitimate .300 hitter with a little pop.

Year	Team	Lg.	Pos.	G	AB	R	H	HR	RBI	SB	BA
1986	Chicago	NL	OF	22	73	9	18	3	12	1	.247
1987	Chicago	NL	OF	84	221	32	61	14	30	2	.276
1988	Chicago	NL	OF	152	580	75	178	8	53	12	.307
1989	Texas	AL	1B	156	559	76	154	8	64	4	.275
Seasonal Notation					560	75	160	12	62	7	.287

JIM PRESLEY   Age 28/R $3

In desperate need of a change of scene. In honor of his cousin Elvis, he should be singing, "I'm All Shook Up."

Year	Team	Lg.	Pos.	G	AB	R	H	HR	RBI	SB	BA
1986	Seattle	AL	3B	155	616	83	163	27	107	0	.265
1987	Seattle	AL	3B	152	575	78	142	24	88	2	.247
1988	Seattle	AL	3B	150	544	50	125	14	62	3	.230
1989	Seattle	AL	3B	117	390	42	92	12	41	0	.236
Seasonal Notation					599	71	147	21	84	1	.246

CARLOS QUINTANA   Age 24/R $1

Red Sox scouts say he could be the next Pat Dodson.

Year	Team	Lg.	Pos.	G	AB	R	H	HR	RBI	SB	BA
1988	Boston	AL	OF	5	6	1	2	0	2	0	.333
1989	Boston	AL	OF	34	77	6	16	0	6	0	.208
Seasonal Notation				39	344	29	74	0	33	0	.217

RICK SCHU   28/R $2

We liked him when he was with the Phillies. Now that Schu's on the other foot, i.e., the American League, we wonder what went wrong. He can still hit the occasional homer, and he might just be a sleeper.

Year	Team	Lg.	Pos.	G	AB	R	H	HR	RBI	SB	BA
1986	Philadelphia	NL	3B	92	208	32	57	8	25	2	.274
1987	Philadelphia	NL	3B	92	196	24	46	7	23	0	.235
1988	Baltimore	AL	3B	89	270	22	69	4	20	6	.256
1989	Baltimore	AL	2B	1	0	0	0	0	0	0	.000
1989	Detroit	AL	3B	98	266	25	57	7	21	1	.214
Seasonal Notation					409	44	99	11	38	3	.244

KEVIN SEITZER   Age 28/R $15

A dreadful year, and, we hope, an aberration. He should and will be a four-category player.

Year	Team	Lg.	Pos.	G	AB	R	H	HR	RBI	SB	BA
1986	Kansas City	AL	1B	28	96	16	31	2	11	0	.323
1987	Kansas City	AL	3B	161	641	105	207	15	83	12	.323
1988	Kansas City	AL	3B	149	559	90	170	5	60	10	.304
1989	Kansas City	AL	3B	160	597	78	168	4	48	17	.281
Seasonal Notation					615	94	187	8	65	12	.304

DOUG STRANGE   Age 25/B $1
Tiger scouts say he could be the next Chris Pittaro.

Year	Team	Lg.	Pos.	G	AB	R	H	HR	RBI	SB	BA
1989	Detroit	AL	3B	64	196	16	42	1	14	3	.214
Seasonal Notation					496	40	106	2	35	7	.214

JIM TRABER   Age 28/L $2
Nicknamed "The Whammer" after the Ruthian figure in *The Natural*. Actually, the only thing Ruthian (Babe Ruth, not Ruth Buzzi) about Traber is his girth. He is, however, an accomplished singer and a former Big 8 quarterback—the only man in baseball who has both sung and played Oklahoma—so you're getting a lot more than you bargained for.

Year	Team	Lg.	Pos.	G	AB	R	H	HR	RBI	SB	BA
1986	Baltimore	AL	1B	65	212	28	54	13	44	0	.255
1988	Baltimore	AL	1B	103	352	25	78	10	45	1	.222
1989	Baltimore	AL	1B	86	234	14	49	4	26	4	.209
Seasonal Notation					508	42	115	17	73	3	.227

RANDY VELARDE   Age 27/R $2
Yankee scouts say he could be the next Celerino Sanchez.

Year	Team	Lg.	Pos.	G	AB	R	H	HR	RBI	SB	BA
1987	New York	AL	SS	8	22	1	4	0	1	0	.182
1988	New York	AL	2B	48	115	18	20	5	12	1	.174
1989	New York	AL	3B	33	100	12	34	2	11	0	.340
Seasonal Notation					431	56	105	12	43	1	.245

GREG WALKER   Age 30/L $5
At least he has his health back. We wonder what happened to his swing.

Year	Team	Lg.	Pos.	G	AB	R	H	HR	RBI	SB	BA
1986	Chicago	AL	1B	78	282	37	78	13	51	1	.277
1987	Chicago	AL	1B	157	566	85	145	27	94	2	.256
1988	Chicago	AL	1B	99	377	45	93	8	42	0	.247
1989	Chicago	AL	1B	77	233	25	49	5	26	0	.210
Seasonal Notation					574	75	143	20	83	1	.250

EDDIE WILLIAMS   Age 25/R $1
White Sox scouts think he could be the next Kevin Bell.

Year	Team	Lg.	Pos.	G	AB	R	H	HR	RBI	SB	BA
1986	Cleveland	AL	OF	5	7	2	1	0	1	0	.143
1987	Cleveland	AL	3B	22	64	9	11	1	4	0	.172
1988	Cleveland	AL	3B	10	21	3	4	0	1	0	.190
1989	Chicago	AL	3B	66	201	25	55	3	10	1	.274
Seasonal Notation					460	61	111	6	25	1	.242

CRAIG WORTHINGTON   **Age 24/R**   **$11**

Comedian/actor Robert Wuhl ran into Cal Ripken, Jr. at the All-Star break, and after exchanging mutual compliments (Wuhl was the pitching coach in *Bull Durham*), Wuhl began quizzing Ripken about Worthington. Ripken couldn't figure out why anyone would be so interested in his teammate until it became apparent that Wuhl was in a Rotisserie League. Well, if he picked up Worthington, congratulations, because the Mexican-Hawaiian-Indian third sacker was one of the pleasanter surprises of the season.

Year	Team	Lg.	Pos.	G	AB	R	H	HR	RBI	SB	BA
1988	Baltimore	AL	3B	26	81	5	15	2	4	1	.185
1989	Baltimore	AL	3B	145	497	57	123	15	70	1	.247
Seasonal Notation					547	58	130	16	70	1	.239

UP THE MIDDLE

In the late 19th century, a number of geopoliticians became enamored of a most peculiar theory. Surveying the land mass of the globe like a phrenologist palpating a skull, they came to a rather startling conclusion. According to these pseudo-scientists, world power could be assumed by the nation that controlled the Dzungarian Gate. Located in Sinkiang Province, this mountain pass was regarded as the geographic middle of the world, providing an unobstructed land route between the largest countries on earth, Russia and China. It was, as should be obvious to the enlightened readers of this treatise, the path taken by the Mongols to invade the Russian steppes and the Huns to plunder eastern and central Europe.

What's not so clear is how a geopolitical theory long dismissed as bullspit can be applied to Rotisserie League Baseball. It's simple, of course. The teams which are strongest up the middle should prevail. The middlemen are the heart of a team. The very best hit for both power and average and steal some bases as well. Ripken, Whitaker, Sandberg, Larkin, Alomar, and Trammell help solve problems in several categories at once. You can't afford to be without them.

On the other hand, if you squander all your money on boomers and a few speedy, but punchless outfielders, you'll be left with the likes of José Lind and Marty Barrett to anchor the most critical geopolitical region of the Rotisseworld.

If you have trouble with this concept, just remember the Mongols, the Huns, and Ryne Sandberg.

NATIONAL LEAGUE

ROBERTO ALOMAR   Age 22/B $19

The younger of Papa Alomar's Padre sons, at the tender age of 21, surpassed even the great things expected of him in his sophomore season. Combine his speed and run production with the reasonable assumption that he can only get better and you've got to believe he's one of the premier middle infielders in the game.

Year	Team	Lg.	Pos.	G	AB	R	H	HR	RBI	SB	BA
1988	San Diego	NL	2B	143	545	84	145	9	41	24	.266
1989	San Diego	NL	2B	158	623	82	184	7	56	42	.295
Seasonal Notation					628	89	177	8	52	35	.282

DAVE ANDERSON   Age 29/R $1

This Dodger utilityman has lost most of his utility. Plate appearances, average, and productivity all down. Career average of less than 18 RBI per 100 games is about as bad as it gets.

Year	Team	Lg.	Pos.	G	AB	R	H	HR	RBI	SB	BA
1986	Los Angeles	NL	3B	92	216	31	53	1	15	5	.245
1987	Los Angeles	NL	SS	108	265	32	62	1	13	9	.234
1988	Los Angeles	NL	SS	116	285	31	71	2	20	4	.249
1989	Los Angeles	NL	SS	87	140	15	32	1	14	2	.229
Seasonal Notation					364	43	87	2	24	8	.241

JAY BELL   Age 24/R $2

Although the Pirates gave him every chance to contribute by hitting him in the number two spot, the Bell did not toll for them. He'll probably get another chance to show the offensive punch that's supposed to compensate for his middling D. But if Bell doesn't deliver, look for the Bucs to ring out the old and ring in the new at shortstop.

Year	Team	Lg.	Pos.	G	AB	R	H	HR	RBI	SB	BA
1986	Cleveland	AL	2B	5	14	3	5	1	4	0	.357
1987	Cleveland	AL	SS	38	125	14	27	2	13	2	.216
1988	Cleveland	AL	SS	73	211	23	46	2	21	4	.218
1989	Pittsburgh	NL	SS	78	271	33	70	2	27	5	.258
Seasonal Notation					518	60	123	5	54	9	.238

RAFAEL BELLIARD   Age 28/R $1

Although he was the National League's fielding leader at short
in 1988, the Bucs couldn't live with his stick, so they handed his
job to—you guessed it—Jay Bell.

Year	Team	Lg.	Pos.	G	AB	R	H	HR	RBI	SB	BA
1986	Pittsburgh	NL	SS	117	309	33	72	0	31	12	.233
1987	Pittsburgh	NL	SS	81	203	26	42	1	15	5	.207
1988	Pittsburgh	NL	SS	122	286	28	61	0	11	7	.213
1989	Pittsburgh	NL	SS	67	154	10	33	0	8	5	.214
Seasonal Notation					398	40	87	0	27	12	.218

BILL DORAN   Age 31/B $15

Two years ago he was a legitimate four category man, right up
there with the likes of Ryne Sandberg. Then came his bad back
(among other ailments) and two consecutive seasons in which those
who owned him also ached. No doubt he can still play some, but
he'll be 32 this season, and it's getting harder and harder to
believe that he'll return to his top form.

Year	Team	Lg.	Pos.	G	AB	R	H	HR	RBI	SB	BA
1986	Houston	NL	2B	145	550	92	152	6	37	42	.276
1987	Houston	NL	2B	162	625	82	177	16	79	31	.283
1988	Houston	NL	2B	132	480	66	119	7	53	17	.248
1989	Houston	NL	2B	142	507	65	111	8	58	22	.219
Seasonal Notation					602	85	155	10	63	31	.259

MARIANO DUNCAN   Age 27/B $3

You want to talk about high hopes? Think back to 1985, when a
Dodger rookie name of Duncan had 38 steals and showed some
serious pop at the plate—then hit the skids (and little else). Okay,
so let's talk survival: Duncan resurfaced with the Reds last year
and was useful around the infield when guys were hurt or slump-
ing. But will he get 300 at bats again in 1990? Don't bet on it.

Year	Team	Lg.	Pos.	G	AB	R	H	HR	RBI	SB	BA
1986	Los Angeles	NL	SS	109	407	47	93	8	30	48	.229
1987	Los Angeles	NL	SS	76	261	31	56	6	18	11	.215
1989	Los Angeles	NL	SS	49	84	9	21	0	8	3	.250
1989	Cincinnati	NL	SS	45	174	23	43	3	13	6	.247
Seasonal Notation					537	63	123	9	40	39	.230

SHAWON DUNSTON   Age 27/R $19

Okay, so he still hasn't had that 25 home run season we always thought was in the cards. But he's become more selective at the plate, raising his average without sacrificing power, and he's still got time for that monster year (he'll be 27 this season).

Year	Team	Lg.	Pos.	G	AB	R	H	HR	RBI	SB	BA
1986	Chicago	NL	SS	150	581	66	145	17	68	13	.250
1987	Chicago	NL	SS	95	346	40	85	5	22	12	.246
1988	Chicago	NL	SS	155	575	69	143	9	56	30	.249
1989	Chicago	NL	SS	138	471	52	131	9	60	19	.278
Seasonal Notation					594	68	151	12	62	22	.255

KEVIN ELSTER   Age 25/R $11

He went longer than any shortstop ever had without committing an error. He hit with power and drove in runs and really beefed up his average. And the poor guy could barely keep his job. He'll be 25 years old this season, and if he keeps improving at this rate, he might earn his age some day.

Year	Team	Lg.	Pos.	G	AB	R	H	HR	RBI	SB	BA
1986	New York	NL	SS	19	30	3	5	0	0	0	.167
1987	New York	NL	SS	5	10	1	4	0	1	0	.400
1988	New York	NL	SS	149	406	41	87	9	37	2	.214
1989	New York	NL	SS	151	458	52	106	10	55	4	.231
Seasonal Notation					452	48	101	9	46	3	.223

TOM FOLEY   30/L $3

He ain't glamorous and he's sure not getting any younger, but he hit more homers at the age of 30 than he did at 29, and he probably delivered more dingers per dollar of salary than most second basemen over the last two years.

Year	Team	Lg.	Pos.	G	AB	R	H	HR	RBI	SB	BA
1986	Philadelphia	NL	SS	39	61	8	18	0	5	2	.295
1986	Montreal	NL	SS	64	202	18	52	1	18	8	.257
1987	Montreal	NL	SS	106	280	35	82	5	28	6	.293
1988	Montreal	NL	2B	127	377	33	100	5	43	2	.265
1989	Montreal	NL	2B	122	375	34	86	7	39	2	.229
Seasonal Notation					458	45	119	6	47	7	.261

DAMASO GARCIA   Age 33/R $2

Had to share second base with Foley despite being a couple of years his senior, and showed he could still swing the bat a little. If any of the Expos' excellent second-base prospects pan out, he may be saying au revoir (or is it adios?) to Montreal.

Year	Team	Lg.	Pos.	G	AB	R	H	HR	RBI	SB	BA
1986	Toronto	AL	2B	122	424	57	119	6	46	9	.281
1988	Atlanta	NL	2B	21	60	3	7	1	4	1	.117
1989	Montreal	NL	2B	80	203	26	55	3	18	5	.271
Seasonal Notation					499	62	131	7	49	10	.263

ALFREDO GRIFFIN   Age 33/B $4

He bounced back from his disastrous 1988 season—and he had a
long way to bounce from a year in which he hit .199—but he's
never come close to the stolen base totals he posted in the American League. If you believe he will at age 33, you'll probably be the
high bidder at your draft.

Year	Team	Lg.	Pos.	G	AB	R	H	HR	RBI	SB	BA
1986	Oakland	AL	SS	162	594	74	169	4	51	33	.285
1987	Oakland	AL	SS	144	494	69	130	3	60	26	.263
1988	Los Angeles	NL	SS	95	316	39	63	1	27	7	.199
1989	Los Angeles	NL	SS	136	506	49	125	0	29	10	.247
Seasonal Notation					576	69	146	2	50	22	.255

LENNY HARRIS   Age 25/L $5

He's got speed, he's got youth, he's got some power and he's got
something that made him easy for the Reds to part with. If he's
healthy, he seems well worth a gamble.

Year	Team	Lg.	Pos.	G	AB	R	H	HR	RBI	SB	BA
1988	Cincinnati	NL	3B	16	43	7	16	0	8	4	.372
1989	Cincinnati	NL	2B	61	188	17	42	2	11	10	.223
1989	Los Angeles	NL	OF	54	147	19	37	1	15	4	.252
Seasonal Notation					467	53	117	3	42	22	.251

TOM HERR   Age 33/B $4

Remember the year this guy hit .302 and drove in 110 runs and
stole 31 bases for St. Louis? Okay, just don't get sentimental about
it at draft time. Herr still plugs along like a pro, but he's 33 now,
and he's a Phillie.

Year	Team	Lg.	Pos.	G	AB	R	H	HR	RBI	SB	BA
1986	St. Louis	NL	2B	152	559	48	141	2	61	22	.252
1987	St. Louis	NL	2B	141	510	73	134	2	83	19	.263
1988	St. Louis	NL	2B	15	50	4	13	1	3	3	.260
1988	Minnesota	AL	2B	86	304	42	80	1	21	10	.263
1989	Philadelphia	NL	2B	151	561	65	161	2	37	10	.287
Seasonal Notation					589	68	157	2	60	19	.267

REX HUDLER   Age 29/R $12

When you step up to the big show and promptly steal 19 bases in 19 attempts, it tends to make an impression. Surely, this was the genuine article: keystone speed, good for 50-60 steals, easy, not to mention the occasional home run. An injury put all that on hold, and Rex is no spring chicken. Tough call—he'll probably be worth a lot more or a lot less than you pay for him.

Year	Team	Lg.	Pos.	G	AB	R	H	HR	RBI	SB	BA
1986	Baltimore	AL	2B	14	1	1	0	0	0	1	.000
1988	Montreal	NL	2B	77	216	38	59	4	14	29	.273
1989	Montreal	NL	2B	92	155	21	38	6	13	15	.245
Seasonal Notation					329	53	85	8	23	39	.261

GREGG JEFFERIES   Age 22/B $21

After an early season recall from Cooperstown, where he'd already been installed in the Hall of Fame, this kid somehow survived a three-month slump that could have ruined him forever. But Jefferies flopped in New York and lived to tell about it. The bet here is that he will now take all that talent and some new toughness, and proceed directly to the All-Star team.

Year	Team	Lg.	Pos.	G	AB	R	H	HR	RBI	SB	BA
1987	New York	NL	SS	6	6	0	3	0	2	0	.500
1988	New York	NL	3B	29	109	19	35	6	17	5	.321
1989	New York	NL	2B	141	508	72	131	12	56	21	.258
Seasonal Notation					573	83	155	16	69	23	.271

STEVE JELTZ   Age 30/B $2

His 1989 numbers bring new meaning to "career year." No kidding; that's as good as it gets.

Year	Team	Lg.	Pos.	G	AB	R	H	HR	RBI	SB	BA
1986	Philadelphia	NL	SS	145	439	44	96	0	36	6	.219
1987	Philadelphia	NL	SS	114	293	37	68	0	12	1	.232
1988	Philadelphia	NL	SS	148	379	39	71	0	27	3	.187
1989	Philadelphia	NL	SS	116	263	28	64	4	25	4	.243
Seasonal Notation					425	45	92	1	30	4	.218

BARRY LARKIN   Age 25/R $24

It's really quite simple: If Larkin can stay healthy for a whole season, he will be the most valuable shortstop in the whole wide Rotisseworld. By far. Is his 25-year-old body fully healed? Will this be the big four-category year? You better hope so if you draft him, because he won't come cheap.

Year	Team	Lg.	Pos.	G	AB	R	H	HR	RBI	SB	BA
1986	Cincinnati	NL	SS	41	159	27	45	3	19	8	.283
1987	Cincinnati	NL	SS	125	439	64	107	12	43	21	.244
1988	Cincinnati	NL	SS	151	588	91	174	12	56	40	.296
1989	Cincinnati	NL	SS	97	325	47	111	4	36	10	.342
Seasonal Notation					591	89	171	12	60	30	.289

JOSÉ LIND   Age 25/R $5

In a world full of Orel Hershisers, Lind would be king (he's hitting better than .500 against him lifetime). Alas, lesser hurlers have little trouble keeping José off the bases, where his speed comes into play. His batting average has dropped in each of the last three years. So should his price.

Year	Team	Lg.	Pos.	G	AB	R	H	HR	RBI	SB	BA
1987	Pittsburgh	NL	2B	35	143	21	46	0	11	2	.322
1988	Pittsburgh	NL	2B	154	611	82	160	2	49	15	.262
1989	Pittsburgh	NL	2B	153	578	52	134	2	48	15	.232
Seasonal Notation					630	73	161	1	51	15	.255

JOSÉ OQUENDO   Age 26/B $10

It seems like he's been around forever, but the most versatile man in baseball is only 26—old enough, at last, to have a full-time job. Congratulations, José: you've just blown the lid off your Rotissesalary.

Year	Team	Lg.	Pos.	G	AB	R	H	HR	RBI	SB	BA
1986	St. Louis	NL	SS	76	138	20	41	0	13	2	.297
1987	St. Louis	NL	OF	116	248	43	71	1	24	4	.286
1988	St. Louis	NL	2B	148	451	36	125	7	46	4	.277
1989	St. Louis	NL	2B	163	556	59	162	1	48	3	.291
Seasonal Notation					448	50	128	2	42	4	.286

SPIKE OWEN   Age 28/B $5

Maybe it was his great glove work and his leadership that inspired all that talk about Owen being the Expos' real MVP. At least part of whatever makes him so valuable in Canada is lost in translation.

Year	Team	Lg.	Pos.	G	AB	R	H	HR	RBI	SB	BA
1986	Seattle	AL	SS	112	402	46	99	0	35	1	.246
1986	Boston	AL	SS	42	126	21	23	1	10	3	.183
1987	Boston	AL	SS	132	437	50	113	2	48	11	.259
1988	Boston	AL	SS	89	257	40	64	5	18	0	.249
1989	Montreal	NL	SS	142	437	52	102	6	41	3	.233
Seasonal Notation					519	65	125	4	47	5	.242

LUIS QUINONES   Age 27/B $6

This guy hit enough home runs to make it abundantly clear that it
pays to know your Quinoneses, one from another. You won't have
any trouble spotting Luis at this year's draft: He'll be the expensive one. And he probably won't be worth it. (P.S. He was the
Most Valuable Player Not Owned All Season in 1989. Yep, no
original Rotisserie team drafted him, and none bought him in the
course of the year. Shows how much we know.)

Year	Team	Lg.	Pos.	G	AB	R	H	HR	RBI	SB	BA
1986	San Francisco	NL	SS	71	106	13	19	0	11	3	.179
1987	Chicago	NL	SS	49	101	12	22	0	8	0	.218
1988	Cincinnati	NL	SS	23	52	4	12	1	11	1	.231
1989	Cincinnati	NL	2B	97	340	43	83	12	34	2	.244
Seasonal Notation					404	48	91	8	43	4	.227

RAFAEL RAMIREZ   Age 31/R $6

Who knows—maybe the guy just needed a challenge. But the
move from Atlanta's Launching Pad to the Astrodome (of all places)
brought out the pop in Raffy's bat. (Figure *that* one out!) Which
makes up for the bases he no longer steals.

Year	Team	Lg.	Pos.	G	AB	R	H	HR	RBI	SB	BA
1986	Atlanta	NL	SS	134	496	57	119	8	33	19	.240
1987	Atlanta	NL	SS	56	179	22	47	1	21	6	.263
1988	Houston	NL	SS	155	566	51	156	6	59	3	.276
1989	Houston	NL	SS	151	537	46	132	6	54	3	.246
Seasonal Notation					580	57	148	6	54	10	.255

WILLIE RANDOLPH   Age 36/R $5

Led the league in classiness while demonstrating the salutary
effects of life without Steinbrenner. At 35, Randolph switched
leagues and proved he could still hit. That year of experience
against National League pitching makes him tempting. It also
makes him 36.

Year	Team	Lg.	Pos.	G	AB	R	H	HR	RBI	SB	BA
1986	New York	AL	2B	141	492	76	136	5	50	15	.276
1987	New York	AL	2B	120	449	96	137	7	67	11	.305
1988	New York	AL	2B	110	404	43	93	2	34	8	.230
1989	Los Angeles	NL	2B	145	549	62	155	2	36	7	.282
Seasonal Notation					594	86	163	5	58	12	.275

RYNE SANDBERG   Age 30/R $29

He's the best in the business and he can safely look back, because
there's no one gaining on him. By the time he turned 30 late last

season, he'd already reached a career high in homers that more than offset a slight dip in stolen bases.

Year	Team	Lg.	Pos.	G	AB	R	H	HR	RBI	SB	BA
1986	Chicago	NL	2B	154	627	68	178	14	76	34	.284
1987	Chicago	NL	2B	132	523	81	154	16	59	21	.294
1988	Chicago	NL	2B	155	618	77	163	19	69	25	.264
1989	Chicago	NL	2B	157	606	104	176	30	76	15	.290
Seasonal Notation					643	89	181	21	75	25	.283

OZZIE SMITH   Age 35/B $18

Maybe we shouldn't make too much of last year's big drop in Ozzie's stolen base total. Perhaps it has nothing to do with him being 35, which happens to make him the oldest regular shortstop in the major leagues. Probably doesn't mean a thing.

Year	Team	Lg.	Pos.	G	AB	R	H	HR	RBI	SB	BA
1986	St. Louis	NL	SS	153	514	67	144	0	54	31	.280
1987	St. Louis	NL	SS	158	600	104	182	0	75	43	.303
1988	St. Louis	NL	SS	153	575	80	155	3	51	57	.270
1989	St. Louis	NL	SS	155	593	82	162	2	50	29	.273
Seasonal Notation					597	87	168	1	60	41	.282

GARRY TEMPLETON   Age 34/B $3

Not being the senior shortstop in the senior circuit ought to count for something. But Tempy's bad wheels get no steals, and the odd dinger is about all you can hope for.

Year	Team	Lg.	Pos.	G	AB	R	H	HR	RBI	SB	BA
1986	San Diego	NL	SS	147	510	42	126	2	44	10	.247
1987	San Diego	NL	SS	148	510	42	113	5	48	14	.222
1988	San Diego	NL	SS	110	362	35	90	3	36	8	.249
1989	San Diego	NL	SS	142	506	43	129	6	40	1	.255
Seasonal Notation					559	47	135	4	49	9	.243

TIM TEUFEL   Age 31/R $1

Unless he's traded, there's a lot of pine time dead ahead.

Year	Team	Lg.	Pos.	G	AB	R	H	HR	RBI	SB	BA
1986	New York	NL	2B	93	279	35	69	4	31	1	.247
1987	New York	NL	2B	97	299	55	92	14	61	3	.308
1988	New York	NL	2B	90	273	35	64	4	31	0	.234
1989	New York	NL	2B	83	219	27	56	2	15	1	.256
Seasonal Notation					477	67	125	10	61	2	.263

ANDRES THOMAS   Age 26/R $12

As long as he keeps launching the long ball—and there's nothing to suggest that he's about to stop—RotisseGMs will overlook his egregious shortcomings (his BA, his tending to go into a sound slumber for weeks at a time) and bid a dollar a dinger for him.

Year	Team	Lg.	Pos.	G	AB	R	H	HR	RBI	SB	BA
1986	Atlanta	NL	SS	102	323	26	81	6	32	4	.251
1987	Atlanta	NL	SS	82	324	29	75	5	39	6	.231
1988	Atlanta	NL	SS	153	606	54	153	13	68	7	.252
1989	Atlanta	NL	SS	141	554	41	118	13	57	3	.213
Seasonal Notation					612	50	144	12	66	6	.236

ROBBIE THOMPSON   Age 27/R $13

What you've always seen is what you'll always get. Consistency is his strong suit, never mind last year's slight slip in average (it comes with the slight rise in home runs).

Year	Team	Lg.	Pos.	G	AB	R	H	HR	RBI	SB	BA
1986	San Francisco	NL	2B	149	549	73	149	7	47	12	.271
1987	San Francisco	NL	2B	132	420	62	110	10	44	16	.262
1988	San Francisco	NL	2B	138	477	66	126	7	48	14	.264
1989	San Francisco	NL	2B	148	547	91	132	13	50	12	.241
Seasonal Notation					569	83	147	10	54	15	.259

DICKIE THON   Age 31/R $8

As if he hadn't suffered enough, he ends up a Phillie and makes sure he'll remain one by having his best year since the beaning.

Year	Team	Lg.	Pos.	G	AB	R	H	HR	RBI	SB	BA
1986	Houston	NL	SS	106	278	24	69	3	21	6	.248
1987	Houston	NL	SS	32	66	6	14	1	3	3	.212
1988	San Diego	NL	SS	95	258	36	68	1	18	19	.264
1989	Philadelphia	NL	SS	136	435	45	118	15	60	6	.271
Seasonal Notation					455	48	118	8	44	14	.259

JEFF TREADWAY   Age 27/L $8

Didn't miss Marge Schott, apparently, while winning a regular job.

Year	Team	Lg.	Pos.	G	AB	R	H	HR	RBI	SB	BA
1987	Cincinnati	NL	2B	23	84	9	28	2	4	1	.333
1988	Cincinnati	NL	2B	103	301	30	76	2	23	2	.252
1989	Atlanta	NL	2B	134	473	58	131	8	40	3	.277
Seasonal Notation					534	60	146	7	41	3	.274

JOSÉ URIBE   Age 31/B $3

Had the kind of year that probably makes him wish he could still get lost among the José Gonzalezes.

Year	Team	Lg.	Pos.	G	AB	R	H	HR	RBI	SB	BA
1986	San Francisco	NL	SS	157	453	46	101	3	43	22	.223
1987	San Francisco	NL	SS	95	309	44	90	5	30	12	.291
1988	San Francisco	NL	SS	141	493	47	124	3	35	14	.252
1989	San Francisco	NL	SS	151	453	34	100	1	30	6	.221
Seasonal Notation					508	50	123	3	41	16	.243

AMERICAN LEAGUE

This is a little like going through a flea market, and we don't say that just because most of these guys are small. A lot of flotsam here, but occasionally you run across a Lou Whitaker.

KENT ANDERSON   Age 26/R $1

Saw a lot of playing time due to the injuries to Schofield, and while he filled in nobly, he showed no indication that he could hit.

Year	Team	Lg.	Pos.	G	AB	R	H	HR	RBI	SB	BA
1989	California	AL	SS	86	223	27	51	0	17	1	.229
Seasonal Notation					420	50	96	0	32	1	.229

WALLY BACKMAN   Age 30/B $1

We seem to recall a Mets second baseman of the same name, but that couldn't have been the same one who did so badly for the Twins last year. He made Minnesota pine for Steve Lombardozzi.

Year	Team	Lg.	Pos.	G	AB	R	H	HR	RBI	SB	BA
1986	New York	NL	2B	124	387	67	124	1	27	13	.320
1987	New York	NL	2B	94	300	43	75	1	23	11	.250
1988	New York	NL	2B	99	294	44	89	0	17	9	.303
1989	Minnesota	AL	2B	87	299	33	69	1	26	1	.231
Seasonal Notation					513	74	143	1	37	13	.279

In the San Francisco clubhouse, do Terry Kennedy and Donell Nixon ever debate?

MARTY BARRETT   Age 31/R $4

Coming off a lost season, but even at top form, his value is limited. Red Sox fans, who are legion, will always bid him up, so don't even bother with the heady little second sacker.

Year	Team	Lg.	Pos.	G	AB	R	H	HR	RBI	SB	BA
1986	Boston	AL	2B	158	625	94	179	4	60	15	.286
1987	Boston	AL	2B	137	559	72	164	3	43	15	.293
1988	Boston	AL	2B	150	612	83	173	1	65	7	.283
1989	Boston	AL	2B	86	336	31	86	1	27	4	.256
Seasonal Notation					650	85	183	2	59	12	.282

LANCE BLANKENSHIP   Age 26/R $5

An investment in the future. He'll be stealing bases and playing second base for years to come. And didn't we all go to prep school with a Lance Blankenship?

Year	Team	Lg.	Pos.	G	AB	R	H	HR	RBI	SB	BA
1988	Oakland	AL	2B	10	3	1	0	0	0	0	.000
1989	Oakland	AL	OF	58	125	22	29	1	4	5	.232
Seasonal Notation					304	54	69	2	9	11	.227

JERRY BROWNE   Age 24/B $8

So that's what happened to the former governor of California. Actually, Browne with an E was a very pleasant surprise both for the Indians and those lucky Rotisserians who picked him up for a dollar or two last year. Don't expect the same numbers, though.

Year	Team	Lg.	Pos.	G	AB	R	H	HR	RBI	SB	BA
1986	Texas	AL	2B	12	24	6	10	0	3	0	.417
1987	Texas	AL	2B	132	454	63	123	1	38	27	.271
1988	Texas	AL	2B	73	214	26	49	1	17	7	.229
1989	Cleveland	AL	2B	153	598	83	179	5	45	14	.299
Seasonal Notation					564	77	158	3	45	21	.280

MIKE BRUMLEY   Age 26/B $1

He can't hit, but he can steal a base, and if the Tigers move Trammell to first base, he'll inherit the shortstop position.

Year	Team	Lg.	Pos.	G	AB	R	H	HR	RBI	SB	BA
1987	Chicago	NL	SS	39	104	8	21	1	9	7	.202
1989	Detroit	AL	SS	92	212	33	42	1	11	8	.198
Seasonal Notation					390	50	77	2	24	18	.199

ALVARO ESPINOZA   Age 28/R $2

Yankee fans, if there are any left, will bid him up, but we shy away from guys with no power, no speed and glasses. His nifty glovework is worth nothing to you.

Year	Team	Lg.	Pos.	G	AB	R	H	HR	RBI	SB	BA
1986	Minnesota	AL	2B	37	42	4	9	0	1	0	.214
1988	New York	AL	2B	3	3	0	0	0	0	0	.000
1989	New York	AL	SS	146	503	51	142	0	41	3	.282
Seasonal Notation					477	47	131	0	36	2	.276

FELIX FERMIN   Age 26/R $1

Hey, what's with all these cats named Felix? (Felix Jose, Junior Felix, Felix Fermin, Felix Bloch, Felix Unger.) More errors than RBIs, which tells you something about Fermin's fielding and hitting. One of our biggest regrets is that Felix joined the Indians 10 years too late to room with Oscar Gamble.

Year	Team	Lg.	Pos.	G	AB	R	H	HR	RBI	SB	BA
1987	Pittsburgh	NL	SS	23	68	6	17	0	4	0	.250
1988	Pittsburgh	NL	SS	43	87	9	24	0	2	3	.276
1989	Cleveland	AL	SS	156	484	50	115	0	21	6	.238
Seasonal Notation					466	47	113	0	19	6	.244

TONY FERNANDEZ   Age 27/B $15

Cabeza is beginning to worry us. We thought he'd be a three-category player for years, and while he still drives in runs and steals sacks, his hitting has been a disappointment the last few seasons. Still, he's one of a half-dozen middle infielders who'll make a difference in your offense.

Year	Team	Lg.	Pos.	G	AB	R	H	HR	RBI	SB	BA
1986	Toronto	AL	SS	163	687	91	213	10	65	25	.310
1987	Toronto	AL	SS	146	578	90	186	5	67	32	.322
1988	Toronto	AL	SS	154	648	76	186	5	70	15	.287
1989	Toronto	AL	SS	140	573	64	147	11	64	22	.257
Seasonal Notation					667	86	196	8	71	25	.294

SCOTT FLETCHER   Age 31/R $3

He is reverting to the player who once platooned with Jerry Dybzinski.

Year	Team	Lg.	Pos.	G	AB	R	H	HR	RBI	SB	BA
1986	Texas	AL	SS	147	530	82	159	3	50	12	.300
1987	Texas	AL	SS	156	588	82	169	5	63	13	.287
1988	Texas	AL	SS	140	515	59	142	0	47	8	.276
1989	Texas	AL	SS	83	314	47	75	0	22	1	.239
1989	Chicago	AL	2B	59	232	30	63	1	21	1	.272
Seasonal Notation					603	83	168	2	56	9	.279

JULIO FRANCO Age 28/R $25

Incredibly talented and incredibly infuriating. You can be sure the Rangers will eventually sour on his erratic play at second, but until then, enjoy his daily line. By the way, it's a tribute to baseball scouts and coaches that they knew enough not to change his peculiar batting stance.

Year	Team	Lg.	Pos.	G	AB	R	H	HR	RBI	SB	BA
1986	Cleveland	AL	SS	149	599	80	183	10	74	10	.306
1987	Cleveland	AL	SS	128	495	86	158	8	52	32	.319
1988	Cleveland	AL	2B	152	613	88	186	10	54	25	.303
1989	Texas	AL	2B	150	548	80	173	13	92	21	.316
Seasonal Notation					630	93	195	11	76	24	.310

GREG GAGNE Age 28/R $7

A fine all-around season. The kind of low-priced player who wins Rotisserie League titles for you. Too bad he never roomed with Lee Lacy.

Year	Team	Lg.	Pos.	G	AB	R	H	HR	RBI	SB	BA
1986	Minnesota	AL	SS	156	472	63	118	12	54	12	.250
1987	Minnesota	AL	SS	137	437	68	116	10	40	6	.265
1988	Minnesota	AL	SS	149	461	70	109	14	48	15	.236
1989	Minnesota	AL	SS	149	460	69	125	9	48	11	.272
Seasonal Notation					501	74	128	12	52	12	.256

MIKE GALLEGO Age 29/R $1

The tiny terror stole some bases for the first time. Great glove, which of course means nothing. But you'll feel good about having him on your team.

Year	Team	Lg.	Pos.	G	AB	R	H	HR	RBI	SB	BA
1986	Oakland	AL	2B	20	37	2	10	0	4	0	.270
1987	Oakland	AL	2B	72	124	18	31	2	14	0	.250
1988	Oakland	AL	2B	129	277	38	58	2	20	2	.209
1989	Oakland	AL	SS	133	357	45	90	3	30	7	.252
Seasonal Notation					363	47	86	3	31	4	.238

BASEBALL ANAGRAM #5

Yogi Berra = OY! Big, rare!

JIM GANTNER   Age 36/L $5

Check out his knee first. He was on his way to 30 stolen bases when he wrecked it. A longtime favorite because of his hard-nosed style, it was nice to see him become a valuable Rotisserie player.

Year	Team	Lg.	Pos.	G	AB	R	H	HR	RBI	SB	BA
1986	Milwaukee	AL	2B	139	497	58	136	7	38	13	.274
1987	Milwaukee	AL	2B	81	265	37	72	4	30	6	.272
1988	Milwaukee	AL	2B	155	539	67	149	0	47	20	.276
1989	Milwaukee	AL	2B	116	409	51	112	0	34	20	.274
Seasonal Notation					564	70	154	3	49	19	.274

OZZIE GUILLEN   Age 26/L $15

This Ozzie has become better than Smith. He had career-highs in ribbies and stolen bases, and the mind boggles at the thought of what he could do if he had some support.

Year	Team	Lg.	Pos.	G	AB	R	H	HR	RBI	SB	BA
1986	Chicago	AL	SS	159	547	58	137	2	47	8	.250
1987	Chicago	AL	SS	149	560	64	156	2	51	25	.279
1988	Chicago	AL	SS	156	566	58	148	0	39	25	.261
1989	Chicago	AL	SS	155	597	63	151	1	54	36	.253
Seasonal Notation					594	63	154	1	49	24	.261

JEFF KUNKEL   Age 28/R $3

Versatility and a flash of power are his primary assets. A possible sleeper.

Year	Team	Lg.	Pos.	G	AB	R	H	HR	RBI	SB	BA
1986	Texas	AL	SS	8	13	3	3	1	2	0	.231
1987	Texas	AL	2B	15	32	1	7	1	2	0	.219
1988	Texas	AL	2B	55	154	14	35	2	15	0	.227
1989	Texas	AL	SS	108	293	39	79	8	29	3	.270
Seasonal Notation				186	428	49	108	10	41	2	.252

MANNY LEE   Age 24/B $2

Good enough to start for some teams, but as long as he's a Blue Jay, his contributions will be limited.

Year	Team	Lg.	Pos.	G	AB	R	H	HR	RBI	SB	BA
1986	Toronto	AL	2B	35	78	8	16	1	7	0	.205
1987	Toronto	AL	2B	56	121	14	31	1	11	2	.256
1988	Toronto	AL	2B	116	381	38	111	2	38	3	.291
1989	Toronto	AL	2B	99	300	27	78	3	34	4	.260
Seasonal Notation					465	46	124	3	47	4	.268

NELSON LIRIANO   Age 25/B $5

Progressed by a leap and a bound last year, thus moving Manny Lee into the background. His season was remarkably similar to Tony Fernandez's first full season, and the next year Fernandez broke out. If you pick up Liriano and Guillen, you may feel like naming your next child Ozzie Nelson. Especially if it's a boy.

Year	Team	Lg.	Pos.	G	AB	R	H	HR	RBI	SB	BA
1987	Toronto	AL	2B	37	158	29	38	2	10	13	.241
1988	Toronto	AL	2B	99	276	36	73	3	23	12	.264
1989	Toronto	AL	2B	132	418	51	110	5	53	16	.263
Seasonal Notation					515	70	133	6	51	24	.259

STEVE LYONS   Age 29/L $3

Affectionately called "Psycho." His hell-bent, airhead style of play ticks off opponents and teammates alike. But his numbers are decent, and he is versatile. Just don't take a shower when he's around.

Year	Team	Lg.	Pos.	G	AB	R	H	HR	RBI	SB	BA
1986	Boston	AL	OF	59	124	20	31	1	14	2	.250
1986	Chicago	AL	OF	42	123	10	25	0	6	2	.203
1987	Chicago	AL	3B	76	193	26	54	1	19	3	.280
1988	Chicago	AL	3B	146	472	59	127	5	45	1	.269
1989	Chicago	AL	2B	140	443	51	117	2	50	9	.264
Seasonal Notation					474	58	123	3	46	5	.261

FRED MANRIQUE   Age 28/R $3

He may finally have escaped the shadow of Al Pedrique. For those of you who still might not be able to tell the difference, Manrique is a Venezuelan infielder with very little speed and very little power, and Pedrique is a Venezuelan infielder with very little speed and very little power.

Year	Team	Lg.	Pos.	G	AB	R	H	HR	RBI	SB	BA
1986	St. Louis	NL	3B	13	17	2	3	1	1	1	.176
1987	Chicago	AL	2B	115	298	30	77	4	29	5	.258
1988	Chicago	AL	2B	140	345	43	81	5	37	6	.235
1989	Chicago	AL	2B	65	187	23	56	2	30	0	.299
1989	Texas	AL	SS	54	191	23	55	2	22	4	.288
Seasonal Notation					434	50	113	5	49	6	.262

AL NEWMAN   Age 29/B $6

Al, shame on you for hiding your light under the bushel all this time. If the Twins had known you could steal that many bases, they wouldn't have gone out and traded for Wally Backman. If we had known you could steal that many bases, we wouldn't have laughed at the schmo—we thought—who picked you up in the draft last year.

Year	Team	Lg.	Pos.	G	AB	R	H	HR	RBI	SB	BA
1986	Montreal	NL	2B	95	185	23	37	1	8	11	.200
1987	Minnesota	AL	SS	110	307	44	68	0	29	15	.221
1988	Minnesota	AL	3B	105	260	35	58	0	19	12	.223
1989	Minnesota	AL	2B	141	446	62	113	0	38	25	.253
Seasonal Notation					430	58	99	0	33	22	.230

TONY PHILLIPS　　　　　　　　　Age 30/B　　　　$3

You should have one guy on your team who you can move around a lot to take advantage of openings on your roster, and here's one of the best men for that job.

Year	Team	Lg.	Pos.	G	AB	R	H	HR	RBI	SB	BA
1986	Oakland	AL	2B	118	441	76	113	5	52	15	.256
1987	Oakland	AL	2B	111	379	48	91	10	46	7	.240
1988	Oakland	AL	OF	79	212	32	43	2	17	0	.203
1989	Oakland	AL	2B	143	451	48	118	4	47	3	.262
Seasonal Notation					532	73	131	7	58	8	.246

JOHNNY RAY　　　　　　　　　　Age 33/B　　　　$6

He did what he always does, hit for average and drive in runs. Caveat emptor: He has no range at second and no clue in the outfield, so his teams will always be looking for someone else to play his position.

Year	Team	Lg.	Pos.	G	AB	R	H	HR	RBI	SB	BA
1986	Pittsburgh	NL	2B	155	579	67	174	7	78	6	.301
1987	Pittsburgh	NL	2B	123	472	48	129	5	54	4	.273
1987	California	AL	2B	30	127	16	44	0	15	0	.346
1988	California	AL	2B	153	602	75	184	6	83	4	.306
1989	California	AL	2B	134	530	52	153	5	62	6	.289
Seasonal Notation					628	70	186	6	79	5	.296

JODY REED　　　　　　　　　　　Age 27/R　　　　$4

Marty Barrett, only shorter (Barrett is 5'10"). A couple of summers ago, a dwarf sportswriter was hanging around the Red Sox batting cage, and Rick Cerone came up to him and said, within earshot of Reed, "Jody, get in the cage. It's your turn to hit."

Year	Team	Lg.	Pos.	G	AB	R	H	HR	RBI	SB	BA
1987	Boston	AL	SS	9	30	4	9	0	8	1	.300
1988	Boston	AL	SS	109	338	60	99	1	28	1	.293
1989	Boston	AL	SS	146	524	76	151	3	40	4	.288
Seasonal Notation					547	85	158	2	46	3	.290

HAROLD REYNOLDS   Age 29/B $8

One of baseball's most inefficient base stealers because he gets caught almost as many times as not. Ordinarily, caught stealings shouldn't concern you, but they do real teams, and sooner or later, the Mariners will curtail Reynolds's base-stealing. Still, he has made great strides as a hitter.

Year	Team	Lg.	Pos.	G	AB	R	H	HR	RBI	SB	BA
1986	Seattle	AL	2B	126	445	46	99	1	24	30	.222
1987	Seattle	AL	2B	160	530	73	146	1	35	60	.275
1988	Seattle	AL	2B	158	598	61	169	4	41	35	.283
1989	Seattle	AL	2B	153	613	87	184	0	43	25	.300
Seasonal Notation					593	72	162	1	38	40	.274

BILLY RIPKEN   Age 25/R $3

The only reason to get him is to keep Cal company. If you have Cal, Billy and he can horse around in your imaginary clubhouse. But if you don't have Cal, Billy is about as appealing as Felix Fermin.

Year	Team	Lg.	Pos.	G	AB	R	H	HR	RBI	SB	BA
1987	Baltimore	AL	2B	58	234	27	72	2	20	4	.308
1988	Baltimore	AL	2B	150	512	52	106	2	34	8	.207
1989	Baltimore	AL	2B	115	318	31	76	2	26	1	.239
Seasonal Notation					533	55	127	3	40	6	.239

CAL RIPKEN   Age 29/R $20

The primary advantage of having Cal, Jr. is that you get production out of a position that usually produces very little. The disadvantage, and it's a small one, is that his batting average will anchor your team batting average since he gets so many at-bats. As for his consecutive game streak, well, if we were Lou Gehrig, we'd be worried. (We'd also be dead.)

Year	Team	Lg.	Pos.	G	AB	R	H	HR	RBI	SB	BA
1986	Baltimore	AL	SS	162	627	98	177	25	81	4	.282
1987	Baltimore	AL	SS	162	624	97	157	27	98	3	.252
1988	Baltimore	AL	SS	161	575	87	152	23	81	2	.264
1989	Baltimore	AL	SS	162	646	80	166	21	93	3	.257
Seasonal Notation					618	90	163	24	88	3	.264

LUIS RIVERA   Age 26/R $2

The Expos gave up on him too soon. He's better than Spike Owen, for whom he was traded, and much better than Ed Romero, whom he replaced. He shows a little pop in his bat.

Year	Team	Lg.	Pos.	G	AB	R	H	HR	RBI	SB	BA
1986	Montreal	NL	SS	55	166	20	34	0	13	1	.205
1987	Montreal	NL	SS	18	32	0	5	0	1	0	.156
1988	Montreal	NL	SS	123	371	35	83	4	30	3	.224
1989	Boston	AL	SS	93	323	35	83	5	29	2	.257
Seasonal Notation					500	50	114	5	40	3	.230

STEVE SAX   Age 30/R $25

Like most everybody else, we figured he would crack under the pressure of pinstripes, and we couldn't have been more wrong. Sax's personality leaves something to be desired, as those who saw him in the Dodgers' victorious 1988 clubhouse can attest, but you have to hand it to him. He overcame his throwing disorder, and he turned on the heat of New York and whacked it down the line for extra bases.

Year	Team	Lg.	Pos.	G	AB	R	H	HR	RBI	SB	BA
1986	Los Angeles	NL	2B	157	633	91	210	6	56	40	.332
1987	Los Angeles	NL	2B	157	610	84	171	6	46	37	.280
1988	Los Angeles	NL	2B	160	632	70	175	5	57	42	.277
1989	New York	AL	2B	158	651	88	205	5	63	43	.315
Seasonal Notation					647	85	195	5	56	41	.301

DICK SCHOFIELD   Age 27/R $5

Like the old song says, " So tired, tired of waiting, tired of waiting for you-hoo-hoo." We want a whole season with 15 homers and 20 stolen bases, and we want it now. At least little Ducky is a darn sight better than his Dad, whose entry in *The Baseball Encyclopedia* is one of the more amazing things in there: 20 years with a .220 lifetime average.

Year	Team	Lg.	Pos.	G	AB	R	H	HR	RBI	SB	BA
1986	California	AL	SS	139	458	67	114	13	57	23	.249
1987	California	AL	SS	134	479	52	120	9	46	19	.251
1988	California	AL	SS	155	527	61	126	6	34	20	.239
1989	California	AL	SS	91	302	42	69	4	26	9	.228
Seasonal Notation					551	69	133	9	50	22	.243

GARY SHEFFIELD   Age 21/R $5

There have to be some hard feelings at work here. He accused the Brewers pitchers of not protecting him. Then the club thought he was jaking it, and sent him down to Denver, where it was discovered he had been playing on a broken foot. If everybody can kiss and make up, great, because Sheffield is a very talented package. But if they can't, it may take him a while before he realizes his potential.

Year	Team	Lg.	Pos.	G	AB	R	H	HR	RBI	SB	BA
1988	Milwaukee	AL	SS	24	80	12	19	4	12	3	.237
1989	Milwaukee	AL	SS	95	368	34	91	5	32	10	.247
Seasonal Notation					609	62	149	12	59	17	.246

BILLY SPIERS   Age 23/L $3

Rushed into the breach because of Sheffield's disappointing season, he acquitted himself well. But he still may be a year or two away, even though he's a great athlete.

Year	Team	Lg.	Pos.	G	AB	R	H	HR	RBI	SB	BA
1989	Milwaukee	AL	SS	114	345	44	88	4	33	10	.255
Seasonal Notation					490	62	125	5	46	14	.255

KURT STILLWELL   Age 24/B $5

A very solid performer about whom you won't have to worry and about whom we don't have much to say.

Year	Team	Lg.	Pos.	G	AB	R	H	HR	RBI	SB	BA
1986	Cincinnati	NL	SS	104	279	31	64	0	26	6	.229
1987	Cincinnati	NL	SS	131	395	54	102	4	33	4	.258
1988	Kansas City	AL	SS	128	459	63	115	10	53	6	.251
1989	Kansas City	AL	SS	130	463	52	121	7	54	9	.261
Seasonal Notation					524	65	132	6	54	8	.252

DALE SVEUM   Age 26/B $5

You're going to have to follow the Brewers' shortstop situation the way the National Hurricane Center followed Hugo. Sveum sat out the 1989 season with a broken leg, but if 1987 was any indication, he could be the sleeper of the draft.

Year	Team	Lg.	Pos.	G	AB	R	H	HR	RBI	SB	BA
1986	Milwaukee	AL	SS	91	317	35	78	7	35	4	.246
1987	Milwaukee	AL	SS	153	535	86	135	25	95	2	.252
1988	Milwaukee	AL	SS	129	467	41	113	9	51	1	.242
Seasonal Notation					572	70	141	17	78	3	.247

WAYNE TOLLESON   Age 34/B $1

He can still steal a base, but his injuries have made him stale and unwanted.

Year	Team	Lg.	Pos.	G	AB	R	H	HR	RBI	SB	BA
1986	Chicago	AL	3B	81	260	39	65	3	29	13	.250
1986	New York	AL	SS	60	215	22	61	0	14	4	.284
1987	New York	AL	SS	121	349	48	77	1	22	5	.221
1988	New York	AL	2B	21	59	8	15	0	5	1	.254
1989	New York	AL	3B	79	140	16	23	1	9	5	.164
Seasonal Notation					457	59	107	2	35	12	.236

ALAN TRAMMELL   Age 32/R $15

Don't let last season bother you. He's too good a player. Take advantage of his devaluation, especially since he may not be a shortstop much longer.

Year	Team	Lg.	Pos.	G	AB	R	H	HR	RBI	SB	BA
1986	Detroit	AL	SS	151	574	107	159	21	75	25	.277
1987	Detroit	AL	SS	151	597	109	205	28	105	21	.343
1988	Detroit	AL	SS	128	466	73	145	15	69	7	.311
1989	Detroit	AL	SS	121	449	54	109	5	43	10	.243
Seasonal Notation					613	100	181	20	85	18	.296

OMAR VIZQUEL   Age 22/B $2

One of the four starting shortstops in the AL from Venezuela (Guillen, Espinoza, and Manrique were the others.) FYI, here's the demographic breakdown: U.S.A. 7, Venezuela 4, Dominican Republic 2, Puerto Rico 1. As for Omar, he is too young to judge with any certainty.

Year	Team	Lg.	Pos.	G	AB	R	H	HR	RBI	SB	BA
1989	Seattle	AL	SS	143	387	45	85	1	20	1	.220
Seasonal Notation					438	50	96	1	22	1	.220

WALT WEISS   Age 26/B $3

He fields like he's from San Pedro de Macoris rather than Tuxedo, N.Y. His hitting, however, does not belie his place of origin.

Year	Team	Lg.	Pos.	G	AB	R	H	HR	RBI	SB	BA
1987	Oakland	AL	SS	16	26	3	12	0	1	1	.462
1988	Oakland	AL	SS	147	452	44	113	3	39	4	.250
1989	Oakland	AL	SS	84	236	30	55	3	21	6	.233
Seasonal Notation					468	50	118	3	40	7	.252

BRAD WELLMAN   Age 30/R $1

The best we can say about him is that he's Tom Candiotti's brother-in-law.

Year	Team	Lg.	Pos.	G	AB	R	H	HR	RBI	SB	BA
1986	San Francisco	NL	SS	12	13	0	2	0	1	0	.154
1987	Los Angeles	NL	SS	3	4	1	1	0	1	0	.250
1988	Kansas City	AL	2B	71	107	11	29	1	6	1	.271
1989	Kansas City	AL	2B	103	178	30	41	2	12	5	.230
Seasonal Notation					258	36	62	2	17	5	.242

LOU WHITAKER   Age 32/L $20

For years, he and Trammell were neck-and-neck in statistics. Then Trammell began to pull away. But after last year, in which Lou had career highs in the power figures, he has again taken the lead in home runs and RBIs. Nobody knows the reason for his resurgence, but then Lou has always marched to a different beat. A very hard player to read.

Year	Team	Lg.	Pos.	G	AB	R	H	HR	RBI	SB	BA
1986	Detroit	AL	2B	144	584	95	157	20	73	13	.269
1987	Detroit	AL	2B	149	604	110	160	16	59	13	.265
1988	Detroit	AL	2B	115	403	54	111	12	55	2	.275
1989	Detroit	AL	2B	148	509	77	128	28	85	6	.251
Seasonal Notation					611	97	162	22	79	9	.265

FRANK WHITE   Age 39/R $4

The Great White Way has come to a dead end. No power, no speed, and no way a 40-year-old man (come September) should be playing second base. He was a class act while he lasted, though.

Year	Team	Lg.	Pos.	G	AB	R	H	HR	RBI	SB	BA
1986	Kansas City	AL	2B	151	566	76	154	22	84	4	.272
1987	Kansas City	AL	2B	154	563	67	138	17	78	1	.245
1988	Kansas City	AL	2B	150	537	48	126	8	58	7	.235
1989	Kansas City	AL	2B	135	418	34	107	2	36	3	.256
Seasonal Notation					572	61	144	13	70	4	.252

IN THE OUTFIELD

There was extensive debate in the clubhouse this year as to whether Kevin Mitchell should be included in the player ratings for outfielders or be placed in a separate category for himself.

It's not only that Kevin had his superior year, but that so many guys in the outfield who were supposed to do the job failed us because of injury, ineptitude, or both.

Darryl Strawberry, Eric Davis, Kal Daniels, Kirk Gibson—so many big guns in the National League. Has Tim Raines forgotten how to steal? Was Whitey right after all about Andy Van Slyke? Sure, the young Cubbies were terrific, but Walton and Smith are both capable of pulling a Gant and Sabo on us. And what can you predict this year for Lonnie Smith?

In the American League, the water is no less murky. Mike Greenwell and Kirby Puckett had fine seasons—but tell that to the Rotisserie League owners who spent $40 apiece for them a year ago, and only got 23 home runs between them for their investment. And what about Rickey Henderson—is he sliding downhill faster than he's getting to second base?

There are a *lot* of question marks in the outfield in both leagues, and we don't like it one bit. That's one position where we want constancy—Willie, Mickey, and the Duke, that kind of stuff. We'd even settle for the fabled $100 outfield—Kingman, Bonds (Bobby), and Leflore—that the Fledermice fielded our first championship season.

But that was then, and this is 1990. So get out your dart boards. It's time to play Pick-n-Pay.

NATIONAL LEAGUE

SHAWN ABNER   Age 23/R $1

The Mets wasted a #-1 draft pick on this guy, then passed their mistake on to San Diego for Kevin McReynolds. (Oh, yeah—Kevin Mitchell was part of that deal, wasn't he?)

Year	Team	Lg.	Pos.	G	AB	R	H	HR	RBI	SB	BA
1987	San Diego	NL	OF	16	47	5	13	2	7	1	.277
1988	San Diego	NL	OF	37	83	6	15	2	5	0	.181
1989	San Diego	NL	OF	57	102	13	18	2	14	1	.176
Seasonal Notation					341	35	67	8	38	2	.198

ERIC ANTHONY   Age 22/L $9

He's either the next Fred McGriff or the latest Ralph Bryant. Hope that answers your question.

Year	Team	Lg.	Pos.	G	AB	R	H	HR	RBI	SB	BA
1989	Houston	NL	OF	25	61	7	11	4	7	0	.180
Seasonal Notation					395	45	71	25	45	0	.180

KEVIN BASS   Age 30/B $13

Speaking offhandwise, 1990 will be a pivotal year. Beyond that, we're pledged to secrecy.

Year	Team	Lg.	Pos.	G	AB	R	H	HR	RBI	SB	BA
1986	Houston	NL	OF	157	591	83	184	20	79	22	.311
1987	Houston	NL	OF	157	592	83	168	19	85	21	.284
1988	Houston	NL	OF	157	541	57	138	14	72	31	.255
1989	Houston	NL	OF	87	313	42	94	5	44	11	.300
Seasonal Notation					591	76	169	16	81	24	.287

BARRY BONDS   Age 25/L $24

Probably lost his leadoff spot, so his stolen bases will drop off, but his RBIs should increase. That makes him marginally less valuable to us. AL-bound?

Year	Team	Lg.	Pos.	G	AB	R	H	HR	RBI	SB	BA
1986	Pittsburgh	NL	OF	113	413	72	92	16	48	36	.223
1987	Pittsburgh	NL	OF	150	551	99	144	25	59	32	.261
1988	Pittsburgh	NL	OF	144	538	97	152	24	58	17	.283
1989	Pittsburgh	NL	OF	159	580	96	144	19	58	32	.248
Seasonal Notation					595	104	152	24	63	33	.256

HUBIE BROOKS   Age 33/R $14

Bound to move on to other pastures; insists that he wants no more of the outfield. Getting a bit long in the tooth, and expect no major rejuvenation, wherever he winds up.

Year	Team	Lg.	Pos.	G	AB	R	H	HR	RBI	SB	BA
1986	Montreal	NL	SS	80	306	50	104	14	58	4	.340
1987	Montreal	NL	SS	112	430	57	113	14	72	4	.263
1988	Montreal	NL	OF	151	588	61	164	20	90	7	.279
1989	Montreal	NL	OF	148	542	56	145	14	70	6	.268
Seasonal Notation					615	73	173	20	95	6	.282

TOM BRUNANSKY   Age 29/R $26

Lots of people criticized his 1989 production, but in the end the numbers were nothing to be ashamed of. Part of the problem was Pedro Guerrero's stupendous ability to drive in runs; there were few left for Brunansky. He's horse enough to come back solidly.

Year	Team	Lg.	Pos.	G	AB	R	H	HR	RBI	SB	BA
1986	Minnesota	AL	OF	157	593	69	152	23	75	12	.256
1987	Minnesota	AL	OF	155	532	83	138	32	85	11	.259
1988	Minnesota	AL	OF	14	49	5	9	1	6	1	.184
1988	St. Louis	NL	OF	143	523	69	128	22	79	16	.245
1989	St. Louis	NL	OF	158	556	67	133	20	85	5	.239
Seasonal Notation					582	75	144	25	85	11	.249

BRETT BUTLER   Age 32/L $29

The consummate lead-off man. To coin a phrase.

Year	Team	Lg.	Pos.	G	AB	R	H	HR	RBI	SB	BA
1986	Cleveland	AL	OF	161	587	92	163	4	51	32	.278
1987	Cleveland	AL	OF	137	522	91	154	9	41	33	.295
1988	San Francisco	NL	OF	157	568	109	163	6	43	43	.287
1989	San Francisco	NL	OF	154	594	100	168	4	36	31	.283
Seasonal Notation					604	104	172	6	45	36	.285

MARK CARREON   Age 26/R $4

Has some pop and will bust down a wall for you. If he gets a chance, he'll pleasantly surprise.

Year	Team	Lg.	Pos.	G	AB	R	H	HR	RBI	SB	BA
1987	New York	NL	OF	9	12	0	3	0	1	0	.250
1988	New York	NL	OF	7	9	5	5	1	1	0	.556
1989	New York	NL	OF	68	133	20	41	6	16	2	.308
Seasonal Notation					297	48	94	13	34	3	.318

VINCE COLEMAN   Age 28/B $47

Odds are he'll be playing in the other league. He and Herzog are on the outs, and St. Louis doesn't want him coming back to haunt. Look for Coleman to fetch pitching and more pitching.

Year	Team	Lg.	Pos.	G	AB	R	H	HR	RBI	SB	BA
1986	St. Louis	NL	OF	154	600	94	139	0	29	107	.232
1987	St. Louis	NL	OF	151	623	121	180	3	43	109	.289
1988	St. Louis	NL	OF	153	616	77	160	3	38	81	.260
1989	St. Louis	NL	OF	145	563	94	143	2	28	65	.254
Seasonal Notation					645	103	167	2	37	97	.259

KAL DANIELS   Age 26/L $1

Kalvoski was a total washout in 1989. Look at his 1987 numbers and weep for his bum knees. AL DH may be his only future.

Year	Team	Lg.	Pos.	G	AB	R	H	HR	RBI	SB	BA
1986	Cincinnati	NL	OF	74	181	34	58	6	23	15	.320
1987	Cincinnati	NL	OF	108	368	73	123	26	64	26	.334
1988	Cincinnati	NL	OF	140	495	95	144	18	64	27	.291
1989	Cincinnati	NL	OF	44	133	26	29	2	9	6	.218
1989	Los Angeles	NL	OF	11	38	7	13	2	8	3	.342
Seasonal Notation					522	100	157	23	72	33	.302

ERIC DAVIS   Age 27/R $39

May have been the quietest 34 home runs ever hit. Are we sure
Seymour Siwoff didn't futz around with the computer while the
rest of us were asleep? Davis ran a lot less in 1989 due to leg
injuries. Or was it because he insisted on playing baseball in
boxing shoes? Very uncool, those shoes.

Year	Team	Lg.	Pos.	G	AB	R	H	HR	RBI	SB	BA
1986	Cincinnati	NL	OF	132	415	97	115	27	71	80	.277
1987	Cincinnati	NL	OF	129	474	120	139	37	100	50	.293
1988	Cincinnati	NL	OF	135	472	81	129	26	93	35	.273
1989	Cincinnati	NL	OF	131	462	74	130	34	101	21	.281
Seasonal Notation					560	114	157	38	112	57	.281

ANDRE DAWSON   Age 35/R $24

Showed further signs of creakage. His glorious 1987 season will not
be approached again. The Hawk's career will wind down respect-
ably, and not spectacularly, from here on out.

Year	Team	Lg.	Pos.	G	AB	R	H	HR	RBI	SB	BA
1986	Montreal	NL	OF	130	496	65	141	20	78	18	.284
1987	Chicago	NL	OF	153	621	90	178	49	137	11	.287
1988	Chicago	NL	OF	157	591	78	179	24	79	12	.303
1989	Chicago	NL	OF	118	416	62	105	21	77	8	.252
Seasonal Notation					616	85	175	33	107	14	.284

LENNY DYKSTRA   Age 27/L $28

Davey Johnson was right: he is not an everyday player, nor even a
very good leadoff man. Still, for your purposes, he's certain to be
out there every day, stealing bases.

Year	Team	Lg.	Pos.	G	AB	R	H	HR	RBI	SB	BA
1986	New York	NL	OF	147	431	77	127	8	45	31	.295
1987	New York	NL	OF	132	431	86	123	10	43	27	.285
1988	New York	NL	OF	126	429	57	116	8	33	30	.270
1989	New York	NL	OF	56	159	27	43	3	13	13	.270
1989	Philadelphia	NL	OF	90	352	39	78	4	19	17	.222
Seasonal Notation					529	84	143	9	44	34	.270

RON GANT   Age 25/R $9

Look for him to platoon in center, or even play right if Murphy is
traded.

Year	Team	Lg.	Pos.	G	AB	R	H	HR	RBI	SB	BA
1987	Atlanta	NL	2B	21	83	9	22	2	9	4	.265
1988	Atlanta	NL	2B	146	563	85	146	19	60	19	.259
1989	Atlanta	NL	3B	75	260	26	46	9	25	9	.177
Seasonal Notation					606	80	143	20	62	21	.236

KIRK GIBSON

Age 32/L   **$26**

Go know. And when you do, come back, buy us lunch, and let *us* know.

Year	Team	Lg.	Pos.	G	AB	R	H	HR	RBI	SB	BA
1986	Detroit	AL	OF	119	441	84	118	28	86	34	.268
1987	Detroit	AL	OF	128	487	95	135	24	79	26	.277
1988	Los Angeles	NL	OF	150	542	106	157	25	76	31	.290
1989	Los Angeles	NL	OF	71	253	35	54	9	28	12	.213
Seasonal Notation					596	110	160	29	93	35	.269

JOSÉ GONZALEZ

Age 25/R   **$2**

And he's still only 25 years old! 1989 answered it once and for all: He's no budding superstar, maybe not even an everyday player. But he's better than John Shelby and we say the hell with it.

Year	Team	Lg.	Pos.	G	AB	R	H	HR	RBI	SB	BA
1986	Los Angeles	NL	OF	57	93	15	20	2	6	4	.215
1987	Los Angeles	NL	OF	18	16	2	3	0	1	5	.188
1988	Los Angeles	NL	OF	37	24	7	2	0	0	3	.083
1989	Los Angeles	NL	OF	95	261	31	70	3	18	9	.268
Seasonal Notation					308	43	74	3	19	16	.241

TOMMY GREGG

Age 26/L   **$5**

Could be a sleeper. Has solid offensive skills: could hit for a big average and drive in some runs, though his home run power and speed are decidedly limited. Turns well on the ball. All he cost was Ken Oberkfell. Good goin', Syd.

Year	Team	Lg.	Pos.	G	AB	R	H	HR	RBI	SB	BA
1987	Pittsburgh	NL	OF	10	8	3	2	0	0	0	.250
1988	Pittsburgh	NL	OF	14	15	4	3	1	3	0	.200
1988	Atlanta	NL	OF	11	29	1	10	0	4	0	.345
1989	Atlanta	NL	OF	102	276	24	67	6	23	3	.243
Seasonal Notation					387	37	96	8	35	3	.250

MARQUIS GRISSOM

Age 22/R   **$11**

The first member of the landed gentry to get to the bigs since Duke Snider. Grissom's got loads of promise, though he made some truly dumb baserunning mistakes in September. Rebuilding teams, grab him.

Year	Team	Lg.	Pos.	G	AB	R	H	HR	RBI	SB	BA
1989	Montreal	NL	OF	26	74	16	19	1	2	1	.257
Seasonal Notation					461	99	118	6	12	6	.257

TONY GWYNN   Age 29/L $43

Guys, it doesn't get any better than this.

Year	Team	Lg.	Pos.	G	AB	R	H	HR	RBI	SB	BA
1986	San Diego	NL	OF	160	642	107	211	14	59	37	.329
1987	San Diego	NL	OF	157	589	119	218	7	54	56	.370
1988	San Diego	NL	OF	133	521	64	163	7	70	26	.313
1989	San Diego	NL	OF	158	604	82	203	4	62	40	.336
Seasonal Notation					627	99	211	8	65	42	.337

BILLY HATCHER   Age 29/R $19

A tough call. He stole 53 bases two years ago, hitting just under
.300. If Leyland leads off with him, there's reason to expect
comparable numbers. But will he get on base enough times to
keep himself there?

Year	Team	Lg.	Pos.	G	AB	R	H	HR	RBI	SB	BA
1986	Houston	NL	OF	127	419	55	108	6	36	38	.258
1987	Houston	NL	OF	141	564	96	167	11	63	53	.296
1988	Houston	NL	OF	145	530	79	142	7	52	32	.268
1989	Houston	NL	OF	108	395	49	90	3	44	22	.228
1989	Pittsburgh	NL	OF	27	86	10	21	1	7	2	.244
Seasonal Notation					589	85	156	8	59	43	.265

VON HAYES   Age 31/L $32

He finally took the Iron Horse's advice, closed his ferschlugginer
stance, and was the best hitter in baseball early last spring. Then
he got that Tony Perkins look in his eye. . . .

Year	Team	Lg.	Pos.	G	AB	R	H	HR	RBI	SB	BA
1986	Philadelphia	NL	1B	158	610	107	186	19	98	24	.305
1987	Philadelphia	NL	1B	158	556	84	154	21	84	16	.277
1988	Philadelphia	NL	1B	104	367	43	100	6	45	20	.272
1989	Philadelphia	NL	OF	154	540	93	140	26	78	28	.259
Seasonal Notation					585	92	163	20	86	24	.280

DARRIN JACKSON   Age 26/R $1

Strictly a warm body.

Year	Team	Lg.	Pos.	G	AB	R	H	HR	RBI	SB	BA
1987	Chicago	NL	OF	7	5	2	4	0	0	0	.800
1988	Chicago	NL	OF	100	188	29	50	6	20	4	.266
1989	Chicago	NL	OF	45	83	7	19	1	8	1	.229
1989	San Diego	NL	OF	25	87	10	18	3	12	0	.207
Seasonal Notation					332	43	83	9	36	4	.251

CHRIS JAMES   Age 27/R $16

Kind of an enigma. Came on strong the second half in San Diego.

One of these years he'll hit 20-plus homers, though he's more likely to be Glenn Wilson for the rest of his career.

Year	Team	Lg.	Pos.	G	AB	R	H	HR	RBI	SB	BA
1986	Philadelphia	NL	OF	16	46	5	13	1	5	0	.283
1987	Philadelphia	NL	OF	115	358	48	105	17	54	3	.293
1988	Philadelphia	NL	OF	150	566	57	137	19	66	7	.242
1989	Philadelphia	NL	OF	45	179	14	37	2	19	3	.207
1989	San Diego	NL	OF	87	303	41	80	11	46	2	.264
Seasonal Notation					569	64	145	19	74	5	.256

RON JONES   Age 25/L $1

We really liked this kid before he busted up an already suspect knee.

Year	Team	Lg.	Pos.	G	AB	R	H	HR	RBI	SB	BA
1988	Philadelphia	NL	OF	33	124	15	36	8	26	0	.290
1989	Philadelphia	NL	OF	12	31	7	9	2	4	1	.290
Seasonal Notation					558	79	162	36	108	3	.290

JOHN KRUK   Age 29/L $15

Not just another pretty face. This guy can smoke 'em. He's hitting in a good park, and his physical problems (aside from his hefty gut) seem mended. Look for a big year.

Year	Team	Lg.	Pos.	G	AB	R	H	HR	RBI	SB	BA
1986	San Diego	NL	OF	122	278	33	86	4	38	2	.309
1987	San Diego	NL	1B	138	447	72	140	20	91	18	.313
1988	San Diego	NL	1B	120	378	54	91	9	44	5	.241
1989	San Diego	NL	OF	31	76	7	14	3	6	0	.184
1989	Philadelphia	NL	OF	81	281	46	93	5	38	3	.331
Seasonal Notation					480	69	139	13	71	9	.290

RAY LANKFORD   Age 23/L $5

A rookie Cardinal outfielder who fields like a dream, runs like a whippet, and hits line drives to all fields. So what else is new?

[No major league experience prior to 1990.]

CANDY MALDONADO   Age 29/R $4

See Carmelo Martinez.

Year	Team	Lg.	Pos.	G	AB	R	H	HR	RBI	SB	BA
1986	San Francisco	NL	OF	133	405	49	102	18	85	4	.252
1987	San Francisco	NL	OF	118	442	69	129	20	85	8	.292
1988	San Francisco	NL	OF	142	499	53	127	12	68	6	.255
1989	San Francisco	NL	OF	129	345	39	75	9	41	4	.217
Seasonal Notation					524	65	134	18	86	6	.256

MIKE MARSHALL   Age 30/R $14

A guy his size should hit more than 11 home runs with is feet.
Marshall, you're a sissy! You're a malingerer! You're a wuss face!
C'mon, give us your best shot! Or does your pinkie-winkie have a
boo-boo?

Year	Team	Lg.	Pos.	G	AB	R	H	HR	RBI	SB	BA
1986	Los Angeles	NL	OF	103	330	47	77	19	53	4	.233
1987	Los Angeles	NL	OF	104	402	45	118	16	72	0	.294
1988	Los Angeles	NL	OF	144	542	63	150	20	82	4	.277
1989	Los Angeles	NL	OF	105	377	41	98	11	42	2	.260
Seasonal Notation					586	69	157	23	88	3	.268

CARMELO MARTINEZ   Age 29/R $4

Slipped badly from a strong 1988. Where, how much, and for
whom he'll play this year are questions to be pondered . . . if
you've got nothing better to do. And if you don't, our heart goes
out to you.

Year	Team	Lg.	Pos.	G	AB	R	H	HR	RBI	SB	BA
1986	San Diego	NL	OF	113	244	28	58	9	25	1	.238
1987	San Diego	NL	OF	139	447	59	122	15	70	5	.273
1988	San Diego	NL	OF	121	365	48	86	18	65	1	.236
1989	San Diego	NL	OF	111	267	23	59	6	39	0	.221
Seasonal Notation					442	52	108	16	66	2	.246

DAVE MARTINEZ   Age 25/L $5

Much depends on whether Grissom is ready.

Year	Team	Lg.	Pos.	G	AB	R	H	HR	RBI	SB	BA
1986	Chicago	NL	OF	53	108	13	15	1	7	4	.139
1987	Chicago	NL	OF	142	459	70	134	8	36	16	.292
1988	Chicago	NL	OF	75	256	27	65	4	34	7	.254
1988	Montreal	NL	OF	63	191	24	49	2	12	16	.257
1989	Montreal	NL	OF	126	361	41	99	3	27	23	.274
Seasonal Notation					485	61	127	6	40	23	.263

LLOYD McCLENDON   Age 31/R $1

A good twenty-third player on your roster, but don't look for him
to repeat his solid, part-time numbers of 1989. Wynne and Salazar
will take many of his at-bats.

Year	Team	Lg.	Pos.	G	AB	R	H	HR	RBI	SB	BA
1987	Cincinnati	NL	C	45	72	8	15	2	13	1	.208
1988	Cincinnati	NL	C	72	137	9	30	3	14	4	.219
1989	Chicago	NL	OF	92	259	47	74	12	40	6	.286
Seasonal Notation					362	49	92	13	51	8	.254

ODDIBE MCDOWELL   Age 27/L $19

Keep an orb on him. Remember that he was first brought to the majors after only 31 games in AA, and may be finding himself only now. In the Launching Pad he's capable of a 30-30 season. Dion James for this guy was larceny.

Year	Team	Lg.	Pos.	G	AB	R	H	HR	RBI	SB	BA
1986	Texas	AL	OF	154	572	105	152	18	49	33	.266
1987	Texas	AL	OF	128	407	65	98	14	52	24	.241
1988	Texas	AL	OF	120	437	55	108	6	37	33	.247
1989	Cleveland	AL	OF	69	239	33	53	3	22	12	.222
1989	Atlanta	NL	OF	76	280	56	85	7	24	15	.304
Seasonal Notation					573	92	146	14	54	34	.256

WILLIE MCGEE   Age 31/B $22

Could be a big, big bargain. A winter's rest should get his legs back to normal, but most Rotisserie owners will be gun shy. At anything less than this price he's a steal.

Year	Team	Lg.	Pos.	G	AB	R	H	HR	RBI	SB	BA
1986	St. Louis	NL	OF	124	497	65	127	7	48	19	.256
1987	St. Louis	NL	OF	153	620	76	177	11	105	16	.285
1988	St. Louis	NL	OF	137	562	73	164	3	50	41	.292
1989	St. Louis	NL	OF	58	199	23	47	3	17	8	.236
Seasonal Notation					644	81	176	8	75	28	.274

KEVIN MCREYNOLDS   Age 30/R $26

If he gets any chubbier, he'll be playing leftfield for Nutrisystems.

Year	Team	Lg.	Pos.	G	AB	R	H	HR	RBI	SB	BA
1986	San Diego	NL	OF	158	560	89	161	26	96	8	.287
1987	New York	NL	OF	151	590	86	163	29	95	14	.276
1988	New York	NL	OF	147	552	82	159	27	99	21	.288
1989	New York	NL	OF	148	545	74	148	22	85	15	.272
Seasonal Notation					602	88	169	27	100	15	.281

KEVIN MITCHELL   Age 28/R $38

Hitting between Clark and Williams will keep his power numbers high. But he has two Achilles' heels: one in his knee and the other between his ears. Scheduled to undergo post-season psychiatric counseling. Which can make anybody crazy.

Year	Team	Lg.	Pos.	G	AB	R	H	HR	RBI	SB	BA
1986	New York	NL	OF	108	328	51	91	12	43	3	.277
1987	San Diego	NL	3B	62	196	19	48	7	26	0	.245
1987	San Francisco	NL	3B	69	268	49	82	15	44	9	.306
1988	San Francisco	NL	3B	148	505	60	127	19	80	5	.251
1989	San Francisco	NL	OF	154	543	100	158	47	125	3	.291
Seasonal Notation					550	83	151	29	95	5	.275

JOHN MORRIS   Age 29/L $1
Not a penny more, not a penny less.

Year	Team	Lg.	Pos.	G	AB	R	H	HR	RBI	SB	BA
1986	St. Louis	NL	OF	39	100	8	24	1	14	6	.240
1987	St. Louis	NL	OF	101	157	22	41	3	23	5	.261
1988	St. Louis	NL	OF	20	38	3	11	0	3	0	.289
1989	St. Louis	NL	OF	96	117	8	28	2	14	1	.239
Seasonal Notation					260	25	65	3	34	7	.252

DALE MURPHY   Age 34/R $20
All those times last year he swung at and missed a breaking ball
outside, jeez, you could cool a small house with them. Murf's a sad
case. A change of scene might do him a world of good, but too
many depressing losses in the hot Southern sun have made his bat
as slow as a Georgia dog.

Year	Team	Lg.	Pos.	G	AB	R	H	HR	RBI	SB	BA
1986	Atlanta	NL	OF	160	614	89	163	29	83	7	.265
1987	Atlanta	NL	OF	159	566	115	167	44	105	16	.295
1988	Atlanta	NL	OF	156	592	77	134	24	77	3	.226
1989	Atlanta	NL	OF	154	574	60	131	20	84	3	.228
Seasonal Notation					604	87	153	30	89	7	.254

DWAYNE MURPHY   Age 35/L $1
Put him where you used to put Denny Walling.

Year	Team	Lg.	Pos.	G	AB	R	H	HR	RBI	SB	BA
1986	Oakland	AL	OF	98	329	50	83	9	39	3	.252
1987	Oakland	AL	OF	82	219	39	51	8	35	4	.233
1988	Detroit	AL	OF	49	144	14	36	4	19	1	.250
1989	Philadelphia	NL	OF	98	156	20	34	9	27	0	.218
Seasonal Notation					420	60	101	14	59	3	.241

OTIS NIXON   Age 31/B $20
A one-dimensional player who points out yet another reason why
Rotisserie League Baseball has, in fact, very little to do with Real
Baseball. Like, you're paying him more than the Expos are!

Year	Team	Lg.	Pos.	G	AB	R	H	HR	RBI	SB	BA
1986	Cleveland	AL	OF	105	95	33	25	0	8	23	.263
1987	Cleveland	AL	OF	19	17	2	1	0	1	2	.059
1988	Montreal	NL	OF	90	271	47	66	0	15	46	.244
1989	Montreal	NL	OF	126	258	41	56	0	21	37	.217
Seasonal Notation					305	58	70	0	21	51	.231

PAUL O'NEILL Age 27/L $23

Has become a very solid regular who'll hit 20-plus HRs and drive in 80 or more runs. We like him a lot, though we'd rather have lunch with his sister Molly. She usually pays.

Year	Team	Lg.	Pos.	G	AB	R	H	HR	RBI	SB	BA
1986	Cincinnati	NL	OF	3	2	0	0	0	0	0	.000
1987	Cincinnati	NL	OF	84	160	24	41	7	28	2	.256
1988	Cincinnati	NL	OF	145	485	58	122	16	73	8	.252
1989	Cincinnati	NL	OF	117	428	49	118	15	74	20	.276
Seasonal Notation					498	60	130	17	81	13	.261

TERRY PUHL Age 33/L $1

Classy spare part. The older he gets, the slower he gets, and the more power he loses. Hey, just like you and me!

Year	Team	Lg.	Pos.	G	AB	R	H	HR	RBI	SB	BA
1986	Houston	NL	OF	81	172	17	42	3	14	3	.244
1987	Houston	NL	OF	90	122	9	28	2	15	1	.230
1988	Houston	NL	OF	113	234	42	71	3	19	22	.303
1989	Houston	NL	OF	121	354	41	96	0	27	9	.271
Seasonal Notation					352	43	94	3	30	14	.269

TIM RAINES Age 30/B $32

His stolen base totals have been declining for six years. Two straight years, he's been under .300. The last time he had as many as 70 RBIs was four years ago. And when you remember that he has never hit more than 18 homers in a season, and only 9 last year, you begin to get a more sober sense of his value. $32 may be high.

Year	Team	Lg.	Pos.	G	AB	R	H	HR	RBI	SB	BA
1986	Montreal	NL	OF	151	580	91	194	9	62	70	.334
1987	Montreal	NL	OF	139	530	123	175	18	68	50	.330
1988	Montreal	NL	OF	109	429	66	116	12	48	33	.270
1989	Montreal	NL	OF	145	517	76	148	9	60	41	.286
Seasonal Notation					612	106	188	14	70	57	.308

GARY REDUS Age33/R $7

Even at thirtysomething he has enough speed to justify his existence, even though he doesn't have a regular place to play.

Year	Team	Lg.	Pos.	G	AB	R	H	HR	RBI	SB	BA
1986	Philadelphia	NL	OF	90	340	62	84	11	33	25	.247
1987	Chicago	AL	OF	130	475	78	112	12	48	52	.236
1988	Chicago	AL	OF	77	262	42	69	6	34	26	.263
1988	Pittsburgh	NL	OF	30	71	12	14	2	4	5	.197
1989	Pittsburgh	NL	1B	98	279	42	79	6	33	25	.283
Seasonal Notation					543	89	136	14	57	50	.251

ROLANDO ROOMES   Age 28/R $4

Came from relative obscurity to vague presence when Kal Daniels schlepped his bad legs to L.A. The presence won't last. At best he's a platooner with a little pop.

Year	Team	Lg.	Pos.	G	AB	R	H	HR	RBI	SB	BA
1988	Chicago	NL	OF	17	16	3	3	0	0	0	.188
1989	Cincinnati	NL	OF	107	315	36	83	7	34	12	.263
Seasonal Notation					432	50	112	9	44	15	.260

JUAN SAMUEL   Age 29/R $28

Go on, rip the heart from our chest! It hurts us to say so, but Sammy is never going to be the offensive monster we always thought he'd be. He'll also never make it as a New Yorker: He hates the city so much he refused to come into Manhattan even once all season. So bye-bye. The Mets won't put up with his play in center, or his erratic bat. He's American League bound or off to Cincy in an Eric Davis trade.

Year	Team	Lg.	Pos.	G	AB	R	H	HR	RBI	SB	BA
1986	Philadelphia	NL	2B	145	591	90	157	16	78	42	.266
1987	Philadelphia	NL	2B	160	655	113	178	28	100	35	.272
1988	Philadelphia	NL	2B	157	629	68	153	12	67	33	.243
1989	Philadelphia	NL	OF	51	199	32	49	8	20	11	.246
1989	New York	NL	OF	86	333	37	76	3	28	31	.228
Seasonal Notation					650	91	165	18	79	41	.255

JOHN SHELBY   Age 32/B $1

Don't feel sorry for him. He got more out of very little talent than even Dan Okrent.

Year	Team	Lg.	Pos.	G	AB	R	H	HR	RBI	SB	BA
1986	Baltimore	AL	OF	135	404	54	92	11	49	18	.228
1987	Baltimore	AL	OF	21	32	4	6	1	3	0	.188
1987	Los Angeles	NL	OF	120	476	61	132	21	69	16	.277
1988	Los Angeles	NL	OF	140	494	65	130	10	64	16	.263
1989	Los Angeles	NL	OF	108	345	28	63	1	12	10	.183
Seasonal Notation					541	65	130	13	60	18	.242

PAT SHERIDAN   Age 32/L $2

We're getting drowwwwsy. . . .

Year	Team	Lg.	Pos.	G	AB	R	H	HR	RBI	SB	BA
1986	Detroit	AL	OF	98	236	41	56	6	19	9	.237
1987	Detroit	AL	OF	141	421	57	109	6	49	18	.259
1988	Detroit	AL	OF	127	347	47	88	11	47	8	.254
1989	Detroit	AL	OF	50	120	16	29	3	15	4	.242
1989	San Francisco	NL	OF	70	161	20	33	3	14	4	.205
Seasonal Notation					428	60	105	9	48	14	.245

DWIGHT SMITH   Age 26/L $16

Sings better than Kate, though she might have been a better outfielder. Offensively, though, he's a beaut, capable of 20 dingers, 75 RBIs, and 15-20 steals.

Year	Team	Lg.	Pos.	G	AB	R	H	HR	RBI	SB	BA
1989	Chicago	NL	OF	109	343	52	111	9	52	9	.324
Seasonal Notation					509	77	164	13	77	13	.324

LONNIE SMITH   Age 34/R $20

Who'd 'a thunk it? Just a couple of years ago he spent the summer reading comic books, trying to figure out how such a solid career could fit up his nose. Let him be an inspiration to others. Don't expect a repeat of the glorious year just past. But expect something solid enough.

Year	Team	Lg.	Pos.	G	AB	R	H	HR	RBI	SB	BA
1986	Kansas City	AL	OF	134	508	80	146	8	44	26	.287
1987	Kansas City	AL	OF	48	167	26	42	3	8	9	.251
1988	Atlanta	NL	OF	43	114	14	27	3	9	4	.237
1989	Atlanta	NL	OF	134	482	89	152	21	79	25	.315
Seasonal Notation					573	94	165	15	63	28	.289

DARRYL STRAWBERRY   Age 28/L $45

This is the year, boys and girls. Super-mega-hyper numbers: 40-plus moon shots, 120-plus RBIs, 40-plus stolen bases, .300-plus average. And a real good clubhouse attitude. Remember, you read it here first.

Year	Team	Lg.	Pos.	G	AB	R	H	HR	RBI	SB	BA
1986	New York	NL	OF	136	475	76	123	27	93	28	.259
1987	New York	NL	OF	154	532	108	151	39	104	36	.284
1988	New York	NL	OF	153	543	101	146	39	101	29	.269
1989	New York	NL	OF	134	476	69	107	29	77	11	.225
Seasonal Notation					568	99	147	37	105	29	.260

MILT THOMPSON   Age 31/L $15

At this writing it looks like he will hold down a regular job with the Cardinals in left or in center. He developed into a much steadier player, matching or exceeding Ozzie Smith's offensive numbers in 1989. No reason he shouldn't do it again.

Year	Team	Lg.	Pos.	G	AB	R	H	HR	RBI	SB	BA
1986	Philadelphia	NL	OF	96	299	38	75	6	23	19	.251
1987	Philadelphia	NL	OF	150	527	86	159	7	43	46	.302
1988	Philadelphia	NL	OF	122	378	53	109	2	33	17	.288
1989	St. Louis	NL	OF	155	545	60	158	4	68	27	.290
Seasonal Notation					541	73	155	5	51	33	.286

ANDY VAN SLYKE   Age 29/L $33

Should rebound from an injury-ridden year. Has said, though, that artificial turf does not suit his full-out, diving style of play. Buyers beware.

Year	Team	Lg.	Pos.	G	AB	R	H	HR	RBI	SB	BA
1986	St. Louis	NL	OF	137	418	48	113	13	61	21	.270
1987	Pittsburgh	NL	OF	157	564	93	165	21	82	34	.293
1988	Pittsburgh	NL	OF	154	587	101	169	25	100	30	.288
1989	Pittsburgh	NL	OF	130	476	64	113	9	53	16	.237
Seasonal Notation					573	85	156	19	82	28	.274

JEROME WALTON   Age 24/R $30

His great rookie year was no fluke. In fact, his value will only increase as his base-stealing savvy and confidence go up. In the outfield he's almost as fun to watch as Garry Maddox.

Year	Team	Lg.	Pos.	G	AB	R	H	HR	RBI	SB	BA
1989	Chicago	NL	OF	116	475	64	139	5	46	24	.293
Seasonal Notation					663	89	194	6	64	33	.293

GLENN WILSON   Age 31/R $12

Now here's the really incredible thing about his coming over from Pittsburgh: The Astrodome is only thirty miles from his house.

Year	Team	Lg.	Pos.	G	AB	R	H	HR	RBI	SB	BA
1986	Philadelphia	NL	OF	155	584	70	158	15	84	5	.271
1987	Philadelphia	NL	OF	154	569	55	150	14	54	3	.264
1988	Seattle	AL	OF	78	284	28	71	3	17	1	.250
1988	Pittsburgh	NL	OF	37	126	11	34	2	15	0	.270
1989	Pittsburgh	NL	OF	100	330	42	93	9	49	1	.282
1989	Houston	NL	OF	28	102	8	22	2	15	0	.216
Seasonal Notation					585	62	154	13	68	2	.265

HERM WINNINGHAM   Age 28/L $1

See Marvell Wynne.

Year	Team	Lg.	Pos.	G	AB	R	H	HR	RBI	SB	BA
1986	Montreal	NL	OF	90	185	23	40	4	11	12	.216
1987	Montreal	NL	OF	137	347	34	83	4	41	29	.239
1988	Montreal	NL	OF	47	90	10	21	0	6	4	.233
1988	Cincinnati	NL	OF	53	113	6	26	0	15	8	.230
1989	Cincinnati	NL	OF	115	251	40	63	3	13	14	.251
Seasonal Notation					361	41	85	4	31	24	.236

MARVELL WYNNE   Age 30/L $4

Useful. Boring, but useful.

Year	Team	Lg.	Pos.	G	AB	R	H	HR	RBI	SB	BA
1986	San Diego	NL	OF	137	288	34	76	7	37	11	.264
1987	San Diego	NL	OF	98	188	17	47	2	24	11	.250
1988	San Diego	NL	OF	128	333	37	88	11	42	3	.264
1989	San Diego	NL	OF	105	294	19	74	6	35	4	.252
1989	Chicago	NL	OF	20	48	8	9	1	4	2	.188
Seasonal Notation					382	38	97	8	47	10	.255

GERALD YOUNG   Age 25/B $19

See? Years ago, eons ago, we said this guy was not a major league
hitter. It also turns out he's a lousy base runner (a success rate of
only 58 percent). The poor guy's on a reverse career track; at this
pace he'll turn into Marcus Lawton by June. So why spend $19 on
him? Because if you don't Harry Stein will buy him for $10 and
he'll swipe 90 and the unspeakable Brenners will win another
pennant, that's why.

Year	Team	Lg.	Pos.	G	AB	R	H	HR	RBI	SB	BA
1987	Houston	NL	OF	71	274	44	88	1	15	26	.321
1988	Houston	NL	OF	149	576	79	148	0	37	65	.257
1989	Houston	NL	OF	146	533	71	124	0	38	34	.233
Seasonal Notation					612	85	159	0	39	55	.260

AMERICAN LEAGUE

Pay attention because this is where Rotisserie League titles are
won. Last year, for instance, you could have gotten Jeffrey Leon-
ard, Ruben Sierra, Robin Yount, Jim Eisenreich, and Cecil Espy
for about $50—or what you would have spent on Rickey Hender-
son alone—and gotten the basis of your offense.

BRADY ANDERSON   Age 26/L $3

Then again, don't pay attention because last year we told you that
Brady Anderson would be the next Robin Yount. That was a
typographical error. We meant the next Robin Young. In all seri-
ousness, Brady still may be a good player. But he left the door
open for a better one, Mike Devereaux.

Year	Team	Lg.	Pos.	G	AB	R	H	HR	RBI	SB	BA
1988	Boston	AL	OF	41	148	14	34	0	12	4	.230
1988	Baltimore	AL	OF	53	177	17	35	1	9	6	.198
1989	Baltimore	AL	OF	94	266	44	55	4	16	16	.207
Seasonal Notation					509	64	106	4	31	22	.210

TONY ARMAS   Age 36/R $2

He can still jack the ball out, but to give you some idea of how old the leading citizen of Anzoatequi, Venezuela is, he was traded from the Pirates to the A's in 1977 along with Doc Medich, Mitch Page, and Dave Giusti.

Year	Team	Lg.	Pos.	G	AB	R	H	HR	RBI	SB	BA
1986	Boston	AL	OF	121	425	40	112	11	58	0	.264
1987	California	AL	OF	28	81	8	16	3	9	1	.198
1988	California	AL	OF	120	368	42	100	13	49	1	.272
1989	California	AL	OF	60	202	22	52	11	30	0	.257
Seasonal Notation					529	55	137	18	71	0	.260

JESSE BARFIELD   Age 30/R $11

A spring training headline you're likely to see: BARFIELD OR WINFIELD IN RIGHT FIELD? A few years ago, Barfield would have been our choice. But then he succumbed to the malaise that seemed to affect all Blue Jay outfielders. He showed signs of waking up from his funk, and if he does, you have a **$30** player at a cut-rate price. If only outfield assists were a category.

Year	Team	Lg.	Pos.	G	AB	R	H	HR	RBI	SB	BA
1986	Toronto	AL	OF	158	589	107	170	40	108	8	.289
1987	Toronto	AL	OF	159	590	89	155	28	84	3	.263
1988	Toronto	AL	OF	136	468	62	114	18	56	7	.244
1989	Toronto	AL	OF	21	80	8	16	5	11	0	.200
1989	New York	AL	OF	129	441	71	106	18	56	5	.240
Seasonal Notation					582	90	150	29	84	6	.259

GEORGE BELL   Age 30/R $30

Ask not for whom this Bell tolls, he tolls for thee. In other words, grab him or hang onto him. The big baby carries a big bat, and now that Jimy Williams has gone looking for the other *m* in his first name, George is a happy camper.

Year	Team	Lg.	Pos.	G	AB	R	H	HR	RBI	SB	BA
1986	Toronto	AL	OF	159	641	101	198	31	108	7	.309
1987	Toronto	AL	OF	156	610	111	188	47	134	5	.308
1988	Toronto	AL	OF	156	614	78	165	24	97	4	.269
1989	Toronto	AL	OF	153	613	88	182	18	104	4	.297
Seasonal Notation					643	98	190	31	115	5	.296

JOEY BELLE   Age 23/R $3

Ask not for whom this Belle tolls, he tolls for thee. This guy supposedly would make Jimmy Piersall seem like Dale Murphy. But the angry young man does have talent and power, and if you don't mind having a bad boy on your team, he is a good investment.

Year	Team	Lg.	Pos.	G	AB	R	H	HR	RBI	SB	BA
1989	Cleveland	AL	OF	62	218	22	49	7	37	2	.225
Seasonal Notation					569	57	128	18	96	5	.225

DARYL BOSTON   Age 27/L $2

A decent part-timer, but more importantly, Daryl Boston, Harry Houston, Claudell Washington, and Reggie Cleveland are just some of the major leaguers to have major league cities named after them.

Year	Team	Lg.	Pos.	G	AB	R	H	HR	RBI	SB	BA
1986	Chicago	AL	OF	56	199	29	53	5	22	9	.266
1987	Chicago	AL	OF	103	337	51	87	10	29	12	.258
1988	Chicago	AL	OF	105	281	37	61	15	31	9	.217
1989	Chicago	AL	OF	101	218	34	55	5	23	7	.252
Seasonal Notation					459	67	113	15	46	16	.247

PHIL BRADLEY   Age 31/R $15

Now that the Colts have moved, he is undoubtedly the best quarterback in Baltimore. The three-time All-Big 8 qb (for Missouri) is a nice ballplayer, too, albeit a strange person. It's kind of interesting to note that his father was Al Bumbry's college coach at Virginia Union.

Year	Team	Lg.	Pos.	G	AB	R	H	HR	RBI	SB	BA
1986	Seattle	AL	OF	143	526	88	163	12	50	21	.310
1987	Seattle	AL	OF	158	603	101	179	14	67	40	.297
1988	Philadelphia	NL	OF	154	569	77	150	11	56	11	.264
1989	Baltimore	AL	OF	144	545	83	151	11	55	20	.277
Seasonal Notation					606	94	173	12	61	24	.287

GLENN BRAGGS   Age 27/R $15

He did a vanishing act in the second half, but he has speed, power, and eventually he will hit. There is talk that the Brewers will trade him. Let's hope it's not out of the league.

Year	Team	Lg.	Pos.	G	AB	R	H	HR	RBI	SB	BA
1986	Milwaukee	AL	OF	58	215	19	51	4	18	1	.237
1987	Milwaukee	AL	OF	132	505	67	136	13	77	12	.269
1988	Milwaukee	AL	OF	72	272	30	71	10	42	6	.261
1989	Milwaukee	AL	OF	144	514	77	127	15	66	17	.247
Seasonal Notation					600	77	153	16	81	14	.256

GREG BRILEY   Age 24/L $10

Nicknamed "Pee Wee" for his size, not his taste in clothes. He proves that good things come in small packages. He also made the Mariner fans forget Mickey Brantley.

Year	Team	Lg.	Pos.	G	AB	R	H	HR	RBI	SB	BA
1988	Seattle	AL	OF	13	36	6	9	1	4	0	.250
1989	Seattle	AL	OF	115	394	52	105	13	52	11	.266
Seasonal Notation					544	73	144	17	70	13	.265

JAY BUHNER   Age 25/R $20

Twenty dollars? What, are we crazy? No, the guy will hit 40 homers this year if he stays healthy. Mark our words. Of course, we once felt the same way about Dan Pasqua. Even if Buhner fails to live up to our promise, we still won't feel as foolish as the Yankees, who traded him to the M's for Ken Phelps.

Year	Team	Lg.	Pos.	G	AB	R	H	HR	RBI	SB	BA
1987	New York	AL	OF	7	22	0	5	0	1	0	.227
1988	New York	AL	OF	25	69	8	13	3	13	0	.188
1988	Seattle	AL	OF	60	192	28	43	10	25	1	.224
1989	Seattle	AL	OF	58	204	27	56	9	33	1	.275
Seasonal Notation					525	68	126	23	77	2	.240

ELLIS BURKS   Age 25/R $25

A great player who has the habit of breaking down at the end. Get him, hold him, but trade him at the All-Star break.

Year	Team	Lg.	Pos.	G	AB	R	H	HR	RBI	SB	BA
1987	Boston	AL	OF	133	558	94	152	20	59	27	.272
1988	Boston	AL	OF	144	540	93	159	18	92	25	.294
1989	Boston	AL	OF	97	399	73	121	12	61	21	.303
Seasonal Notation					648	112	187	21	91	31	.289

RANDY BUSH   Age 31/L $6

One of the most underrated hitters in the game. This is the kind of player who comes up at the end of the draft, and the kind of player who goes to a bidder who has spent wisely but well.

Year	Team	Lg.	Pos.	G	AB	R	H	HR	RBI	SB	BA
1986	Minnesota	AL	OF	130	357	50	96	7	45	5	.269
1987	Minnesota	AL	OF	122	293	46	74	11	46	10	.253
1988	Minnesota	AL	OF	136	394	51	103	14	51	8	.261
1989	Minnesota	AL	OF	141	391	60	103	14	54	5	.263
Seasonal Notation					439	63	115	14	60	8	.262

IVAN CALDERON   Age 28/R $10

Do not embarrass us by peeking at last year's entry on Calderon.
We apologize, Ivan. You're not half the dog we thought you were.

Year	Team	Lg.	Pos.	G	AB	R	H	HR	RBI	SB	BA
1986	Seattle	AL	OF	37	131	13	31	2	13	3	.237
1986	Chicago	AL	OF	13	33	3	10	0	2	0	.303
1987	Chicago	AL	OF	144	542	93	159	28	83	10	.293
1988	Chicago	AL	OF	73	264	40	56	14	35	4	.212
1989	Chicago	AL	OF	157	622	83	178	14	87	7	.286
Seasonal Notation					608	88	165	22	84	9	.273

JOSÉ CANSECO   Age 25/R $40

Extrapolating his stats over a whole season, he would have had 45
homers, 132 RBIs and 15 traffic citations. As soon as we heard
about the 900 number set up for José, we just had to dial it, and
we got this recorded message: "Press 1 if you want to hear José
talk about yesterday's game, press 2 if you want to hear José talk
about steroids, his gun possession charge, or his speeding tickets."
Honest, that's what it said. Naturally we pressed 2, but all we got
was some garbled message repeated over and over. What José
meant to say, of course, was "Who cares what I took, what I own,
or how fast I drive? I am still the best player in the land." By the
way, José, you owe us $2 for the call.

Year	Team	Lg.	Pos.	G	AB	R	H	HR	RBI	SB	BA
1986	Oakland	AL	OF	157	600	85	144	33	117	15	.240
1987	Oakland	AL	OF	159	630	81	162	31	113	15	.257
1988	Oakland	AL	OF	158	610	120	187	42	124	40	.307
1989	Oakland	AL	OF	65	227	40	61	17	57	6	.269
Seasonal Notation					621	97	166	36	123	22	.268

JOE CARTER   Age 30/R $35

In Cleveland, they said he couldn't field and couldn't drive in the
big run. As if the Indians have had so many great players over the
years that they could afford to trash one. Carter has hit as high as
.302, bopped as many as 35 home runs, driven in as many as 121
runs and stolen as many as 31 bases in a season. How dare anyone
say anything bad about this quintessential Rotisserie League player?

Year	Team	Lg.	Pos.	G	AB	R	H	HR	RBI	SB	BA
1986	Cleveland	AL	OF	162	663	108	200	29	121	29	.302
1987	Cleveland	AL	1B	149	588	83	155	32	106	31	.264
1988	Cleveland	AL	OF	157	621	85	168	27	98	27	.271
1989	Cleveland	AL	OF	162	651	84	158	35	105	13	.243
Seasonal Notation					648	92	175	31	110	25	.270

HAIL TO THE CHIEFS!

Time out for our All-Presidents Team (25-man roster):

Catchers: Russ Nixon, Scotti Madison, Zack Taylor

Corners: Von Hayes, John Kennedy, Harvard Eddie Grant

Middle Infielders: Dave Johnson, Travis Jackson, Sparky Adams

Outfielders: Joe Carter, Randy Bush, Claudell Washington, Curt Ford, Stanley Jefferson, Hack Wilson

Pitchers: Walter Johnson, Roric Harrison, Babe Adams, Zach Monroe, Lefty Tyler, Rob Buchanan, Billy Pierce, Ezra Lincoln, William Garfield, Rip Reagan

CARMEN CASTILLO   Age 31/R $2

You can almost always count on him for about 10 home runs. We'll spare you our All-Opera Team. (Although who can ever forget the classic, *Il Pagliaroni*?)

Year	Team	Lg.	Pos.	G	AB	R	H	HR	RBI	SB	BA
1986	Cleveland	AL	OF	85	205	34	57	8	32	2	.278
1987	Cleveland	AL	OF	89	220	27	55	11	31	1	.250
1988	Cleveland	AL	OF	66	176	12	48	4	14	6	.273
1989	Minnesota	AL	OF	94	218	23	56	8	33	1	.257
Seasonal Notation					397	46	104	15	53	4	.264

DARNELL COLES   Age 27/R $6

A survivor. His stroke was made for the Kingdome.

Year	Team	Lg.	Pos.	G	AB	R	H	HR	RBI	SB	BA
1986	Detroit	AL	3B	142	521	67	142	20	86	6	.273
1987	Detroit	AL	3B	53	149	14	27	4	15	0	.181
1987	Pittsburgh	NL	OF	40	119	20	27	6	24	1	.227
1988	Pittsburgh	NL	OF	68	211	20	49	5	36	1	.232
1988	Seattle	AL	OF	55	195	32	57	10	34	3	.292
1989	Seattle	AL	OF	146	535	54	135	10	59	5	.252
Seasonal Notation					556	66	140	17	81	5	.253

HENRY COTTO   Age 29/R $4

What do the Mariners do with all their outfielders? Henry is the victim of the most bizarre injury in baseball history. While with the Yankees, he was cleaning out his ears with a Q-Tip, when Ken

Griffey, Sr. accidentally jostled his elbow, pushing the Q-Tip into the ear and puncturing his eardrum. He didn't even do it to get out of the draft.

Year	Team	Lg.	Pos.	G	AB	R	H	HR	RBI	SB	BA
1986	New York	AL	OF	35	80	11	17	1	6	3	.213
1987	New York	AL	OF	68	149	21	35	5	20	4	.235
1988	Seattle	AL	OF	133	386	50	100	8	33	27	.259
1989	Seattle	AL	OF	100	295	44	78	9	33	10	.264
Seasonal Notation					438	60	110	11	44	21	.253

CHILI DAVIS   Age 30/B $12

You will be quite happy to own the Angels' Kingston (Jamaica) Duo, Davis and Devon White.

Year	Team	Lg.	Pos.	G	AB	R	H	HR	RBI	SB	BA
1986	San Francisco	NL	OF	153	526	71	146	13	70	16	.278
1987	San Francisco	NL	OF	149	500	80	125	24	76	16	.250
1988	California	AL	OF	158	600	81	161	21	93	9	.268
1989	California	AL	OF	154	560	81	152	22	90	3	.271
Seasonal Notation					576	82	154	21	86	11	.267

ROB DEER   Age 29/R $9

Dave Kingman minus the psychosis. To neutralize his batting average, you will need Nap Lajoie and Rogers Hornsby.

Year	Team	Lg.	Pos.	G	AB	R	H	HR	RBI	SB	BA
1986	Milwaukee	AL	OF	134	466	75	108	33	86	5	.232
1987	Milwaukee	AL	OF	134	474	71	113	28	80	12	.238
1988	Milwaukee	AL	OF	135	492	71	124	23	85	9	.252
1989	Milwaukee	AL	OF	130	466	72	98	26	65	4	.210
Seasonal Notation					576	87	134	33	96	9	.233

MIKE DEVEREAUX   Age 26/R $8

A great trade for the Orioles, sending Mike Morgan to the Dodgers for this guy. Of course, he's no John Shelby.

Year	Team	Lg.	Pos.	G	AB	R	H	HR	RBI	SB	BA
1987	Los Angeles	NL	OF	19	54	7	12	0	4	3	.222
1988	Los Angeles	NL	OF	30	43	4	5	0	2	0	.116
1989	Baltimore	AL	OF	122	391	55	104	8	46	22	.266
Seasonal Notation					462	62	114	7	49	23	.248

ROB DUCEY   Age 24/L $1

Some pertinent facts: Rob is the third Canadian to play for the
Blue Jays; his wife Yanitza is a former Miss Venezuela; he'll never
be a regular outfielder in the majors.

Year	Team	Lg.	Pos.	G	AB	R	H	HR	RBI	SB	BA
1987	Toronto	AL	OF	34	48	12	9	1	6	2	.188
1988	Toronto	AL	OF	27	54	15	17	0	6	1	.315
1989	Toronto	AL	OF	41	76	5	16	0	7	2	.211
Seasonal Notation					282	50	66	1	30	7	.236

JIM EISENREICH   Age 30/L $15

The Royals deserve all the credit in the world for sticking with this
guy. His story is the stuff of TV movies.

Year	Team	Lg.	Pos.	G	AB	R	H	HR	RBI	SB	BA
1987	Kansas City	AL	OF	44	105	10	25	4	21	1	.238
1988	Kansas City	AL	OF	82	202	26	44	1	19	9	.218
1989	Kansas City	AL	OF	134	475	64	139	9	59	27	.293
Seasonal Notation					487	62	129	8	61	23	.266

CECIL ESPY   Age 27/B $15

The White Sox, Dodgers and Pirates failed to espy his value. (The
Dodgers tried to make a shortstop out of him in the minors, and
Cecil made 50 errors.) Of course, he's no John Shelby.

Year	Team	Lg.	Pos.	G	AB	R	H	HR	RBI	SB	BA
1987	Texas	AL	OF	14	8	1	0	0	0	2	.000
1988	Texas	AL	OF	123	347	46	86	2	39	33	.248
1989	Texas	AL	OF	142	475	65	122	3	31	45	.257
Seasonal Notation					481	65	120	2	40	46	.251

DWIGHT EVANS   Age 38/R $15

He has hit at least 10 home runs 16 years in a row, but you always
wonder if and when this son of Donald Duck will play his age.

Year	Team	Lg.	Pos.	G	AB	R	H	HR	RBI	SB	BA
1986	Boston	AL	OF	152	529	86	137	26	97	3	.259
1987	Boston	AL	1B	154	541	109	165	34	123	4	.305
1988	Boston	AL	OF	149	559	96	164	21	111	5	.293
1989	Boston	AL	OF	146	520	82	148	20	100	3	.285
Seasonal Notation					579	100	165	27	116	4	.286

MIKE FELDER   Age 27/B $5

A good fifth outfielder for you or the Brewers.

Year	Team	Lg.	Pos.	G	AB	R	H	HR	RBI	SB	BA
1986	Milwaukee	AL	OF	44	155	24	37	1	13	16	.239
1987	Milwaukee	AL	OF	108	289	48	77	2	31	34	.266
1988	Milwaukee	AL	OF	50	81	14	14	0	5	8	.173
1989	Milwaukee	AL	OF	117	315	50	76	3	23	26	.241
Seasonal Notation					426	69	103	3	36	42	.243

JUNIOR FELIX   Age 22/B $10

A good talent but a bad actor. Take your chances.

Year	Team	Lg.	Pos.	G	AB	R	H	HR	RBI	SB	BA
1989	Toronto	AL	OF	110	415	62	107	9	46	18	.258
Seasonal Notation					611	91	157	13	67	26	.258

STEVE FINLEY   Age 24/L $6

This is the player we thought Brady Anderson was going to be. His full name is Steven Allen Finley. He is no relation to either Charlie Finley or Jayne Meadows.

Year	Team	Lg.	Pos.	G	AB	R	H	HR	RBI	SB	BA
1989	Baltimore	AL	OF	81	217	35	54	2	25	17	.249
Seasonal Notation					434	70	108	4	50	34	.249

DAVE GALLAGHER   Age 29/R $3

Responsible for one of the better lines of the year: Upon seeing a helicopter hover over Comiskey Park, Gallagher said, "Look, a high chopper over the mound." A splendid outfielder and the inventor of a hitting device, this career minor leaguer had a Cinderella batting average of over .300 the first few months. But then midnight came. Worse yet, the glass sneakers in center field now seem to fit Lance Johnson.

Year	Team	Lg.	Pos.	G	AB	R	H	HR	RBI	SB	BA
1987	Cleveland	AL	OF	15	36	2	4	0	1	2	.111
1988	Chicago	AL	OF	101	347	59	105	5	31	5	.303
1989	Chicago	AL	OF	161	601	74	160	1	46	5	.266
Seasonal Notation					575	78	157	3	45	7	.273

DAN GLADDEN   Age 32/R $15

He helps you in every category AND he is one of the three transitive verbs now playing outfield in the American League. (The others are Espy and Rick Leach.)

Year	Team	Lg.	Pos.	G	AB	R	H	HR	RBI	SB	BA
1986	San Francisco	NL	OF	102	351	55	97	4	29	27	.276
1987	Minnesota	AL	OF	121	438	69	109	8	38	25	.249
1988	Minnesota	AL	OF	141	576	91	155	11	62	28	.269
1989	Minnesota	AL	OF	121	461	69	136	8	46	23	.295
Seasonal Notation					609	94	166	10	58	34	.272

MIKE GREENWELL   Age 26/L $30

Another damn good season, especially since he missed a month. Since 1939 the Red Sox have had just four left fielders: Ted Williams, Carl Yastrzemski, Jim Rice and Greenwell. All of them will be in the Hall of Fame someday.

Year	Team	Lg.	Pos.	G	AB	R	H	HR	RBI	SB	BA
1986	Boston	AL	OF	31	35	4	11	0	4	0	.314
1987	Boston	AL	OF	125	412	71	135	19	89	5	.328
1988	Boston	AL	OF	158	590	86	192	22	119	16	.325
1989	Boston	AL	OF	145	578	87	178	14	95	13	.308
Seasonal Notation					570	87	182	19	108	12	.320

KEN GRIFFEY, THE YOUNGER   Age 20/L $25

The only thing he can't do is shave.

Year	Team	Lg.	Pos.	G	AB	R	H	HR	RBI	SB	BA
1989	Seattle	AL	OF	127	455	61	120	16	61	16	.264
Seasonal Notation					580	77	153	20	77	20	.264

MEL HALL   Age 29/L $8

An odd man. And the odd man out when Winfield returns.

Year	Team	Lg.	Pos.	G	AB	R	H	HR	RBI	SB	BA
1986	Cleveland	AL	OF	140	442	68	131	18	77	6	.296
1987	Cleveland	AL	OF	142	485	57	136	18	76	5	.280
1988	Cleveland	AL	OF	150	515	69	144	6	71	7	.280
1989	New York	AL	OF	113	361	54	94	17	58	0	.260
Seasonal Notation					535	73	150	17	83	5	.280

DANNY HEEP   Age 32/L $2

He did a nice job filling in for the Red Sox. Maybe he likes the American League. At least it affords him the chance of DHing.

Year	Team	Lg.	Pos.	G	AB	R	H	HR	RBI	SB	BA
1986	New York	NL	OF	86	195	24	55	5	33	1	.282
1987	Los Angeles	NL	OF	60	98	7	16	0	9	1	.163
1988	Los Angeles	NL	OF	95	149	14	36	0	11	2	.242
1989	Boston	AL	OF	113	320	36	96	5	49	0	.300
Seasonal Notation					348	37	92	4	46	1	.266

DAVE HENDERSON   Age 31/R $12

We give up. We never have a clue as to what kind of season he
will have, and this uncertainty dates back to 1982.

Year	Team	Lg.	Pos.	G	AB	R	H	HR	RBI	SB	BA
1986	Seattle	AL	OF	103	337	51	93	14	44	1	.276
1986	Boston	AL	OF	36	51	8	10	1	3	1	.196
1987	Boston	AL	OF	75	184	30	43	8	25	1	.234
1987	San Francisco	NL	OF	15	21	2	5	0	1	2	.238
1988	Oakland	AL	OF	146	507	100	154	24	94	2	.304
1989	Oakland	AL	OF	152	579	77	145	15	80	8	.250
Seasonal Notation					516	82	138	19	75	4	.268

RICKEY HENDERSON   Age 31/R $49

He has enlivened more drafts that anyone in the history of the
Rotisserie League. His name usually comes up right away. "Rickey
Henderson, $1." "Rickey Henderson, $2." And so it goes, until
someone cuts to the chase and says, "Rickey Henderson, $45."
The bidding always comes down to a mano a mano test of valor.
And you know what? The winner of Rickey Henderson is rarely
the winner of the league. Maybe he ties up too much money. But
we suspect that the responsibility of owning him, and wondering
just when Mr. Hamstring will act up, reduces his masters to blobs
of Tofutti.

Year	Team	Lg.	Pos.	G	AB	R	H	HR	RBI	SB	BA
1986	New York	AL	OF	153	608	130	160	28	74	87	.263
1987	New York	AL	OF	95	358	78	104	17	37	41	.291
1988	New York	AL	OF	140	554	118	169	6	50	93	.305
1989	New York	AL	OF	65	235	41	58	3	22	25	.247
1989	Oakland	AL	OF	85	306	72	90	9	35	52	.294
Seasonal Notation					620	132	174	18	65	89	.282

BASEBALL ANAGRAM #6

Randy Bush = Dry bash, nu?

PETE INCAVIGLIA   Age 26/R $15

Inky's dinky batting average is too much to bear. We like to think of him as a watered-down version of Gorman Thomas.

Year	Team	Lg.	Pos.	G	AB	R	H	HR	RBI	SB	BA
1986	Texas	AL	OF	153	540	82	135	30	88	3	.250
1987	Texas	AL	OF	139	509	85	138	27	80	9	.271
1988	Texas	AL	OF	116	418	59	104	22	54	6	.249
1989	Texas	AL	OF	133	453	48	107	21	81	5	.236
Seasonal Notation					574	82	144	29	90	6	.252

BO JACKSON   Age 27/R $35

Give up this football thing, Vincent. Baseball needs you. Specifically, Rotisserie League baseball needs you. Even more specifically, our team needs you. We can't bear to watch any Raiders game for fear that some steroid-crazed linebacker will chop down on those wonderful legs or rattle those wonderful eyes or twist those wonderful wrists. Pro football can have Deion Sanders. They can't have you.

Year	Team	Lg.	Pos.	G	AB	R	H	HR	RBI	SB	BA
1986	Kansas City	AL	OF	25	82	9	17	2	9	3	.207
1987	Kansas City	AL	OF	116	396	46	93	22	53	10	.235
1988	Kansas City	AL	OF	124	439	63	108	25	68	27	.246
1989	Kansas City	AL	OF	135	515	86	132	32	105	26	.256
Seasonal Notation					579	82	141	32	95	26	.244

DION JAMES   Age 27/L $6

Above average average, below average everything else. But he's a lot less worrisome than the man he was traded for, Oddibe McDowell.

Year	Team	Lg.	Pos.	G	AB	R	H	HR	RBI	SB	BA
1987	Atlanta	NL	OF	134	494	80	154	10	61	10	.312
1988	Atlanta	NL	OF	132	386	46	99	3	30	9	.256
1989	Atlanta	NL	OF	63	170	15	44	1	11	1	.259
1989	Cleveland	AL	OF	71	245	26	75	4	29	1	.306
Seasonal Notation					524	67	150	7	53	8	.287

STAN JAVIER   Age 25/B $3

The Athletics are holding him hostage. We still have a feeling there's a **$10** player lurking inside Stan.

Year	Team	Lg.	Pos.	G	AB	R	H	HR	RBI	SB	BA
1986	Oakland	AL	OF	59	114	13	23	0	8	8	.202
1987	Oakland	AL	OF	81	151	22	28	2	9	3	.185
1988	Oakland	AL	OF	125	397	49	102	2	35	20	.257
1989	Oakland	AL	OF	112	310	42	77	1	28	12	.248
Seasonal Notation					417	54	98	2	34	18	.237

LANCE JOHNSON   Age 26/L $15

He failed his first audition in 1988, but in August and September
last year, he electrified the White Sox offense. We think this junior
college teammate of Kirby Puckett is next year's version of Cecil
Espy.

Year	Team	Lg.	Pos.	G	AB	R	H	HR	RBI	SB	BA
1987	St. Louis	NL	OF	33	59	4	13	0	7	6	.220
1988	Chicago	AL	OF	33	124	11	23	0	6	6	.185
1989	Chicago	AL	OF	50	180	28	54	0	16	16	.300
Seasonal Notation					506	60	125	0	40	39	.248

TRACY JONES   Age 29/R $3

Tracy, do you want to talk about it? Do you want to tell us why
you went from a $20 player two years ago to Gary Pettis's caddy?
Did something terrible happen to you? Did you see Rick Reuschel
naked? Please tell us. We're your friends.

Year	Team	Lg.	Pos.	G	AB	R	H	HR	RBI	SB	BA
1986	Cincinnati	NL	OF	46	86	16	30	2	10	7	.349
1987	Cincinnati	NL	OF	117	359	53	104	10	44	31	.290
1988	Cincinnati	NL	OF	37	83	9	19	1	9	9	.229
1988	Montreal	NL	OF	53	141	20	47	2	15	9	.333
1989	San Francisco	NL	OF	40	97	5	18	0	12	2	.186
1989	Detroit	AL	OF	46	158	17	41	3	26	1	.259
Seasonal Notation					441	57	123	8	55	28	.280

ROBERTO KELLY   Age 25/R $20

The biggest single source of joy for Yankee fans last year. As good
as Roberto is, you have to feel sorry for someone who grew up in
Panama under Manuel Noriega and now plays for another dictator.
At least George's face has cleared up.

Year	Team	Lg.	Pos.	G	AB	R	H	HR	RBI	SB	BA
1987	New York	AL	OF	23	52	12	14	1	7	9	.269
1988	New York	AL	OF	38	77	9	19	1	7	5	.247
1989	New York	AL	OF	137	441	65	133	9	48	35	.302
Seasonal Notation					466	70	135	9	50	40	.291

BRAD KOMMINSK   Age 29/R $3
This cat is on his ninth life.

Year	Team	Lg.	Pos.	G	AB	R	H	HR	RBI	SB	BA
1986	Atlanta	NL	OF	5	5	1	2	0	1	0	.400
1987	Milwaukee	AL	OF	7	15	0	1	0	0	1	.067
1989	Cleveland	AL	OF	71	198	27	47	8	33	8	.237
Seasonal Notation					425	54	97	15	66	17	.229

RICK LEACH   Age 32/L $1
Only if you're desperate. He always seems to be going AWOL for
mysterious personal reasons, but the biggest mystery of all is why
clubs take him back.

Year	Team	Lg.	Pos.	G	AB	R	H	HR	RBI	SB	BA
1986	Toronto	AL	OF	110	246	35	76	5	39	0	.309
1987	Toronto	AL	OF	98	195	26	55	3	25	0	.282
1988	Toronto	AL	OF	87	199	21	55	0	23	0	.276
1989	Texas	AL	OF	110	239	32	65	1	23	2	.272
Seasonal Notation					351	45	100	3	44	0	.286

CHET LEMON   Age 35/R $7
His worst season since his rookie year, way back in 1976. (He was
once traded, along with Dave Hamilton, from Oakland to Chicago
for Stan Bahnsen and Skip Pitlock.) We've written Chet off before
and been surprised, but he is moving into a new demographic
group (35-50).

Year	Team	Lg.	Pos.	G	AB	R	H	HR	RBI	SB	BA
1986	Detroit	AL	OF	126	403	45	101	12	53	2	.251
1987	Detroit	AL	OF	146	470	75	130	20	75	0	.277
1988	Detroit	AL	OF	144	512	67	135	17	64	1	.264
1989	Detroit	AL	OF	127	414	45	98	7	47	1	.237
Seasonal Notation					536	69	138	16	71	1	.258

JEFFREY LEONARD   Age 34/R $12
Old Correctional Facility Face has been paroled. Flaps up, flaps
down, who cares? He had the most productive power season of his
career just when we thought it was ending.

Year	Team	Lg.	Pos.	G	AB	R	H	HR	RBI	SB	BA
1986	San Francisco	NL	OF	89	341	48	95	6	42	16	.279
1987	San Francisco	NL	OF	131	503	70	141	19	63	16	.280
1988	San Francisco	NL	OF	44	160	12	41	2	20	7	.256
1988	Milwaukee	AL	OF	94	374	45	88	8	44	10	.235
1989	Seattle	AL	OF	150	566	69	144	24	93	6	.254
Seasonal Notation					619	77	162	18	83	17	.262

FRED LYNN
Age 38/L   **$6**

The Tigers must be as tired of him as we are. He hasn't been able to drive in runs in years, but at least in the past you could rely on him for 23 homers. In fact, his home run totals from 1982 to 1988 were 21, 22, 23, 23, 23, 23, and 25. He coulda been a contender for Cooperstown.

Year	Team	Lg.	Pos.	G	AB	R	H	HR	RBI	SB	BA
1986	Baltimore	AL	OF	112	397	67	114	23	67	2	.287
1987	Baltimore	AL	OF	111	396	49	100	23	60	3	.253
1988	Baltimore	AL	OF	87	301	37	76	18	37	2	.252
1988	Detroit	AL	OF	27	90	9	20	7	19	0	.222
1989	Detroit	AL	OF	117	353	44	85	11	46	1	.241
Seasonal Notation					548	73	140	29	81	2	.257

LLOYD MOSEBY
Age 30/L   **$6**

We actually think more of him than the Blue Jays do, but then we don't have to put up with his fielding. He can still pilfer, but Mookie has reduced his status to trade bait.

Year	Team	Lg.	Pos.	G	AB	R	H	HR	RBI	SB	BA
1986	Toronto	AL	OF	152	589	89	149	21	86	32	.253
1987	Toronto	AL	OF	155	592	106	167	26	96	39	.282
1988	Toronto	AL	OF	128	472	77	113	10	42	31	.239
1989	Toronto	AL	OF	135	502	72	111	11	43	24	.221
Seasonal Notation					612	97	153	19	75	35	.251

JOHN MOSES
Age 32/B   **$2**

The kind of player you want when you have **$10** left to spend on five guys. He brings us to the All-Biblical team:

1b-Rico Joseph   c-Mike Simon
2b-James Hymie Solomon   of-John Moses
  (aka Jimmie Reese)   of-Hank Aaron
 ss-Ivan DeJesus   of-Andre David
3b-Frank Thomas   sp-Tommy John

Year	Team	Lg.	Pos.	G	AB	R	H	HR	RBI	SB	BA
1986	Seattle	AL	OF	103	399	56	102	3	34	25	.256
1987	Seattle	AL	OF	116	390	58	96	3	38	23	.246
1988	Minnesota	AL	OF	105	206	33	65	2	12	11	.316
1989	Minnesota	AL	OF	129	242	33	68	1	31	14	.281
Seasonal Notation					442	64	118	3	41	26	.268

JOE ORSULAK   Age 27/L $5

When Hank Peters was canned as the Orioles' GM in 1987, farm
director Doug Melvin took over his duties on an interim basis, and
he actually made the deal that brought Orsulak over from the
Pirates for two minor leaguers. It was the one and only deal
Melvin, now the assistant GM, made, and it was a small gem.
Those are a lot of RBIs per at bat. Another good fifth outfielder for
your team.

Year	Team	Lg.	Pos.	G	AB	R	H	HR	RBI	SB	BA
1986	Pittsburgh	NL	OF	138	401	60	100	2	19	24	.249
1988	Baltimore	AL	OF	125	379	48	109	8	27	9	.288
1989	Baltimore	AL	OF	123	390	59	111	7	55	5	.285
Seasonal Notation					491	70	134	7	42	15	.274

DAN PASQUA   Age 28/L $5

There is still some home run potential in this man, whom *Sports
Illustrated* once predicted would win the AL homer title.

Year	Team	Lg.	Pos.	G	AB	R	H	HR	RBI	SB	BA
1986	New York	AL	OF	102	280	44	82	16	45	2	.293
1987	New York	AL	OF	113	318	42	74	17	42	0	.233
1988	Chicago	AL	OF	129	422	48	96	20	50	1	.227
1989	Chicago	AL	OF	73	246	26	61	11	47	1	.248
Seasonal Notation					491	62	121	24	71	1	.247

GARY PETTIS   Age 32/B $7

Only if you need speed. The following players had more RBIs than
Pettis last year: Omar Vizquel, Kent Anderson, Brady Anderson,
Stanley Jefferson, Kevin Romine, Randy Kutcher, and Mike Mac-
farlane. And all had far fewer at-bats than Pettis.

Year	Team	Lg.	Pos.	G	AB	R	H	HR	RBI	SB	BA
1986	California	AL	OF	154	539	93	139	5	58	50	.258
1987	California	AL	OF	133	394	49	82	1	17	24	.208
1988	Detroit	AL	OF	129	458	65	96	3	36	44	.210
1989	Detroit	AL	OF	119	444	77	114	1	18	43	.257
Seasonal Notation					555	85	130	3	39	48	.235

Does Kevin Bass fish?

228

LUIS POLONIA   Age 25/B $8

Works closely with Milwaukee youth. If you can remain blind to his peccadillos, he's a keeper.

Year	Team	Lg.	Pos.	G	AB	R	H	HR	RBI	SB	BA
1987	Oakland	AL	OF	125	435	78	125	4	49	29	.287
1988	Oakland	AL	OF	84	288	51	84	2	27	24	.292
1989	Oakland	AL	OF	59	206	31	59	1	17	13	.286
1989	New York	AL	OF	66	227	39	71	2	29	9	.313
Seasonal Notation					560	96	164	4	59	36	.293

KIRBY PUCKETT   Age 29/R $30

Just a wonderful player, but he doesn't steal or homer like he used to. His Hall of Fame induction will come in the year 2004.

Year	Team	Lg.	Pos.	G	AB	R	H	HR	RBI	SB	BA
1986	Minnesota	AL	OF	161	680	119	223	31	96	20	.328
1987	Minnesota	AL	OF	157	624	96	207	28	99	12	.332
1988	Minnesota	AL	OF	158	657	109	234	24	121	6	.356
1989	Minnesota	AL	OF	159	635	75	215	9	85	11	.339
Seasonal Notation					662	101	224	23	102	12	.339

KEVIN ROMINE   Age 28/R $1

Inconsequential to Rotisserie baseball, essential to a Caesar salad.

Year	Team	Lg.	Pos.	G	AB	R	H	HR	RBI	SB	BA
1986	Boston	AL	OF	35	35	6	9	0	2	2	.257
1987	Boston	AL	OF	9	24	5	7	0	2	0	.292
1988	Boston	AL	OF	57	78	17	15	1	6	2	.192
1989	Boston	AL	OF	92	274	30	75	1	23	1	.274
Seasonal Notation					344	48	88	1	27	4	.258

DEION SANDERS   Age 22/L $3

Neon Deion is loads of talent and loads of trouble. As one Yankee beat writer put it, "Deion made Rickey Henderson look like Archbishop Desmond Tutu."

Year	Team	Lg.	Pos.	G	AB	R	H	HR	RBI	SB	BA
1989	New York	AL	OF	14	47	7	11	2	7	1	.234
Seasonal Notation					543	81	127	23	81	11	.234

RUBEN SIERRA   Age 24/B $33

Congratulations to those of you who stayed with Ruben. All that business about him being "the next Clemente" seems a lot more reasonable now. By the way, how can a team with Sierra, Franco, Baines, Palmeiro, Buechele, Espy, and a pretty good pitching staff finish a distant fourth? Oh, that's right. The Rangers have Incaviglia.

Year	Team	Lg.	Pos.	G	AB	R	H	HR	RBI	SB	BA
1986	Texas	AL	OF	113	382	50	101	16	55	7	.264
1987	Texas	AL	OF	158	643	97	169	30	109	16	.263
1988	Texas	AL	OF	156	615	77	156	23	91	18	.254
1989	Texas	AL	OF	162	634	101	194	29	119	8	306
Seasonal Notation					625	89	170	26	102	13	.273

CORY SNYDER   Age 27/R $15

He can do a lot better. Take advantage of the devaluation.

Year	Team	Lg.	Pos.	G	AB	R	H	HR	RBI	SB	BA
1986	Cleveland	AL	OF	103	416	58	113	24	69	2	.272
1987	Cleveland	AL	OF	157	577	74	136	33	82	5	.236
1988	Cleveland	AL	OF	142	511	71	139	26	75	5	.272
1989	Cleveland	AL	OF	132	489	49	105	18	59	6	.215
Seasonal Notation					604	76	149	30	86	5	.247

SAMMY SOSA   Age 21/R $7

He won't yield an immediate return because he's so young, but the White Sox didn't trade Harold Baines for nothing (and Scott Fletcher).

Year	Team	Lg.	Pos.	G	AB	R	H	HR	RBI	SB	BA
1989	Texas	AL	OF	25	84	8	20	1	3	0	.238
1989	Chicago	AL	OF	33	99	19	27	3	10	7	.273
Seasonal Notation					511	75	131	11	36	19	.257

DANNY TARTABULL   Age 27/R $20

An extremely disappointing season from someone capable of .300, 30 homers, and 100 RBIs. If a good player has a bad year, you can generally count on a return to form.

Year	Team	Lg.	Pos.	G	AB	R	H	HR	RBI	SB	BA
1986	Seattle	AL	OF	137	511	76	138	25	96	4	.270
1987	Kansas City	AL	OF	158	582	95	180	34	101	9	.309
1988	Kansas City	AL	OF	146	507	80	139	26	102	8	.274
1989	Kansas City	AL	OF	133	441	54	118	18	62	4	.268
Seasonal Notation					576	86	162	29	101	7	.282

GARY THURMAN   Age 25/R $1

A mini-Gary Pettis.

Year	Team	Lg.	Pos.	G	AB	R	H	HR	RBI	SB	BA
1987	Kansas City	AL	OF	27	81	12	24	0	5	7	.296
1988	Kansas City	AL	OF	35	66	6	11	0	2	5	.167
1989	Kansas City	AL	OF	71	87	24	17	0	5	16	.195
Seasonal Notation					285	51	63	0	14	34	.222

GREG VAUGHN   Age 24/R $12

Some outfielder in Milwaukee is out of a job. If you're in a
neophyte Rotisserie League, this guy may come cheap. But if
you're in a league in which they do their homework, prepare to
spend $20 on him. Don't worry. He's worth it.

Year	Team	Lg.	Pos.	G	AB	R	H	HR	RBI	SB	BA
1989	Milwaukee	AL	OF	38	113	18	30	5	23	4	.265
Seasonal Notation					481	76	127	21	98	17	.265

CLAUDELL WASHINGTON   Age 35/L $6

Mention the name, and we think immediately of Audrey Hepburn.
Both Claudell and Audrey have incredibly long necks and both are
beginning to show their age.

Year	Team	Lg.	Pos.	G	AB	R	H	HR	RBI	SB	BA
1986	Atlanta	NL	OF	40	137	17	37	5	14	4	.270
1986	New York	AL	OF	54	135	19	32	6	16	6	.237
1987	New York	AL	OF	102	312	42	87	9	44	10	.279
1988	New York	AL	OF	126	455	62	140	11	64	15	.308
1989	California	AL	OF	110	418	53	114	13	42	13	.273
Seasonal Notation					546	72	153	16	67	18	.281

DEVON WHITE   Age 27/B $28

Some baseball people assert that White may never be all that he
was cracked up to be, but we'll still take a flyer on the flyer.

Year	Team	Lg.	Pos.	G	AB	R	H	HR	RBI	SB	BA
1986	California	AL	OF	29	51	8	12	1	3	6	.235
1987	California	AL	OF	159	639	103	168	24	87	32	.263
1988	California	AL	OF	122	455	76	118	11	51	17	.259
1989	California	AL	OF	156	636	86	156	12	56	44	.245
Seasonal Notation					619	94	157	16	68	34	.255

KEN WILLIAMS   Age 25/R $2

The Tigers are still paying for the disastrous White Sox experiment of moving him to third. He hasn't been the same since.

Year	Team	Lg.	Pos.	G	AB	R	H	HR	RBI	SB	BA
1986	Chicago	AL	OF	15	31	2	4	1	1	1	.129
1987	Chicago	AL	OF	116	391	48	110	11	50	21	.281
1988	Chicago	AL	OF	73	220	18	35	8	28	6	.159
1989	Detroit	AL	OF	94	258	29	53	6	23	9	.205
Seasonal Notation					489	52	109	14	55	20	.224

MOOKIE WILSON   Age 34/B $10

The Mookman cometh, and the Blue Jays took off. He does a lot of things to help a team, on and off the field, but he has rarely been a sensational Rotisserie player. Doesn't make much contact, doesn't have much home run power, and doesn't steal like he once did. And we bet his value will be inflated by his late-season heroics.

Year	Team	Lg.	Pos.	G	AB	R	H	HR	RBI	SB	BA
1986	New York	NL	OF	123	381	61	110	9	45	25	.289
1987	New York	NL	OF	124	385	58	115	9	34	21	.299
1988	New York	NL	OF	112	378	61	112	8	41	15	.296
1989	New York	NL	OF	80	249	22	51	3	18	7	.205
1989	Toronto	AL	OF	54	238	32	71	2	17	12	.298
Seasonal Notation					535	76	150	10	50	26	.281

WILLIE WILSON   Age 34/B $10

For the first time in his long career, he failed to reach 30 stolen bases. But he did have a strong second half. One more time, Willie.

Year	Team	Lg.	Pos.	G	AB	R	H	HR	RBI	SB	BA
1986	Kansas City	AL	OF	156	631	77	170	9	44	34	.269
1987	Kansas City	AL	OF	146	610	97	170	4	30	59	.279
1988	Kansas City	AL	OF	147	591	81	155	1	37	35	.262
1989	Kansas City	AL	OF	112	383	58	97	3	43	24	.253
Seasonal Notation					639	90	170	4	44	43	.267

DAVE WINFIELD   Age 38/R $25

We missed you, big guy. After a year in which he underwent a back operation, a paternity suit, and the smearing of the Winfield Foundation, we have a feeling he'll be so happy to be playing baseball that he'll have a very big year. If you were shrewd, you picked him up cheap at last year's draft and reserved him.

Year	Team	Lg.	Pos.	G	AB	R	H	HR	RBI	SB	BA
1986	New York	AL	OF	154	565	90	148	24	104	6	.262
1987	New York	AL	OF	156	575	83	158	27	97	5	.275
1988	New York	AL	OF	149	559	96	180	25	107	9	.322
Seasonal Notation					599	94	171	26	108	7	.286

ROBIN YOUNT   Age 34/R $25

Year in, year out he does it, and year in, year out he's undervalued
in the draft. Why that is we don't know, although we suspect it's
because his home run and stolen base totals aren't sexy enough. If
you resolve to get one player in the draft, this is the guy.

Year	Team	Lg.	Pos.	G	AB	R	H	HR	RBI	SB	BA
1986	Milwaukee	AL	OF	140	522	82	163	9	46	14	.312
1987	Milwaukee	AL	OF	158	635	99	198	21	103	19	.312
1988	Milwaukee	AL	OF	162	621	92	190	13	91	22	.306
1989	Milwaukee	AL	OF	160	614	101	195	21	103	19	.318
Seasonal Notation					625	97	194	16	89	19	312

DESIGNATED HITTERS

This section is dedicated to Ron Blomberg, the first man to come
to the plate in a regular season major league game as a DH. Jewish
ballplayers are often trend-setters in baseball. Lipman Pike was
the game's very first professional. Sandy Koufax threw four no-
hitters in his career, a record until Nolan Ryan came along. Hank
Greenberg, Al Rosen, Moe Berg, Larry Sherry, Bo Belinsky,
Steve Stone . . . the list goes on and on. And let us not forget
Richie Scheinblum, the only man to be waved to first base on an
intentional walk—it was a short-lived experiment some 20 spring
trainings ago. (By the way, none of the current DHs are Jewish.
Larry Sheets, however, is Mennonite.)

HAROLD BAINES   Age 31/L $20

The Rangers really caught fire when he came aboard, huh? Actually, it wasn't his fault; he hit pretty good. But the soft-spoken
Baines is hardly a take-charge guy. His stats are kind of soft-
spoken, too.

Year	Team	Lg.	Pos.	G	AB	R	H	HR	RBI	SB	BA
1986	Chicago	AL	OF	145	570	72	169	21	88	2	.296
1987	Chicago	AL	OF	132	505	59	148	20	93	0	.293
1988	Chicago	AL	OF	158	599	55	166	13	81	0	.277
1989	Chicago	AL	OF	96	333	55	107	13	56	0	.321
1989	Texas	AL	OF	50	172	18	49	3	16	0	.285
Seasonal Notation					607	72	178	19	93	0	.293

STEVE BALBONI   Age 33/R $4

A one-dimensional hitter who may be no-dimensional before long.

Year	Team	Lg.	Pos.	G	AB	R	H	HR	RBI	SB	BA
1986	Kansas City	AL	1B	138	512	54	117	29	88	0	.229
1987	Kansas City	AL	1B	121	386	44	80	24	60	0	.207
1988	Kansas City	AL	1B	21	63	2	9	2	5	0	.143
1988	Seattle	AL	1B	97	350	44	88	21	61	0	.251
1989	New York	AL	1B	110	300	33	71	17	59	0	.237
Seasonal Notation					535	58	121	30	90	0	.227

BILL BUCKNER   Age 40/L $1

In the 10th inning of the sixth game of the 1986 Series, we asked, "What's Buckner doing out there?" In 1989 we were asking the same thing. Still a good question.

Year	Team	Lg.	Pos.	G	AB	R	H	HR	RBI	SB	BA
1986	Boston	AL	1B	153	629	73	168	18	102	6	.267
1987	Boston	AL	1B	75	286	23	78	2	42	1	.273
1987	California	AL	1B	57	183	16	56	3	32	1	.306
1988	California	AL	1B	19	43	1	9	0	9	2	.209
1988	Kansas City	AL	1B	89	242	18	62	3	34	3	.256
1989	Kansas City	AL	1B	79	176	7	38	1	16	1	.216
Seasonal Notation					535	47	141	9	80	4	.264

DAVE CLARK   Age 27/L $2

Admit it. Every time you hear the name, you start to sing, "I'm in pieces, bits and pieces." Do you remember when people seriously debated who was better, the Dave Clark Five or the Beatles? Those who favored the Dave Clark Five are now partial to this guy.

Year	Team	Lg.	Pos.	G	AB	R	H	HR	RBI	SB	BA
1986	Cleveland	AL	OF	18	58	10	16	3	9	1	.276
1987	Cleveland	AL	OF	29	87	11	18	3	12	1	.207
1988	Cleveland	AL	OF	63	156	11	41	3	18	0	.263
1989	Cleveland	AL	OF	102	253	21	60	8	29	0	.237
Seasonal Notation					423	40	103	12	51	1	.244

BRIAN DOWNING   Age 39/R $8

If there were Rotisserie body-building (now there's a concept!), Downing would be $40. With a physique like his, he should be hitting 30 homers a year.

Year	Team	Lg.	Pos.	G	AB	R	H	HR	RBI	SB	BA
1986	California	AL	OF	152	513	90	137	20	95	4	.267
1987	California	AL	OF	155	567	110	154	29	77	5	.272
1988	California	AL	OF	135	484	80	117	25	64	3	.242
1989	California	AL	OF	142	544	59	154	14	59	0	.283
Seasonal Notation					584	94	155	24	81	3	.267

SAM HORN   Age 26/L $1

Asked once what it would take to turn Horn into a decent first baseman, his minor league manager, Ed Nottle, said, "A million ground balls. And I've already hit him my million." It would take a similar program to get Horn to hit the curve ball.

Year	Team	Lg.	Pos.	G	AB	R	H	HR	RBI	SB	BA
1987	Boston	AL	C	46	158	31	44	14	34	0	.278
1988	Boston	AL	C	24	61	4	9	2	8	0	.148
1989	Boston	AL	1B	33	54	1	8	0	4	0	.148
Seasonal Notation					429	56	95	25	72	0	.223

RON KITTLE   Age 32/R $7

Not bad for a third of the season. Rarely has he had a full season.

Year	Team	Lg.	Pos.	G	AB	R	H	HR	RBI	SB	BA
1986	Chicago	AL	OF	86	296	34	63	17	48	2	.213
1986	New York	AL	OF	30	80	8	19	4	12	2	.237
1987	New York	AL	OF	59	159	21	44	12	28	0	.277
1988	Cleveland	AL	OF	75	225	31	58	18	43	0	.258
1989	Chicago	AL	1B	51	169	26	51	11	37	0	.302
Seasonal Notation					499	64	126	33	90	2	.253

GENE LARKIN   Age 27/B $5

Wewewe wouldwouldwould considersidersider ourselvesselvesselves thethethe luckiestuckiestuckiest menmenmen ononon thethethe facefaceface ofofof thethethe earthearthearth ifififif GeneGeneGene werewerewere halfhalfhalf asasas goodgoodgood asasas anotherotherother formerormerormer Columbiaumbiaumbia firstfirstfirst baseman-asemanaseman.

Year	Team	Lg.	Pos.	G	AB	R	H	HR	RBI	SB	BA
1987	Minnesota	AL	1B	85	233	23	62	4	28	1	.266
1988	Minnesota	AL	1B	149	505	56	135	8	70	3	.267
1989	Minnesota	AL	1B	136	446	61	119	6	46	5	.267
Seasonal Notation					518	61	138	7	63	3	.267

LEE MAZZILLI   Age 35/B $1
He played well for the Blue Jays, but that was a last gasp.

Year	Team	Lg.	Pos.	G	AB	R	H	HR	RBI	SB	BA
1986	Pittsburgh	NL	OF	61	93	18	21	1	8	3	.226
1986	New York	NL	OF	39	58	10	16	2	7	1	.276
1987	New York	NL	OF	88	124	26	38	3	24	5	.306
1988	New York	NL	OF	68	116	9	17	0	12	4	.147
1989	New York	NL	OF	48	60	10	11	2	7	3	.183
1989	Toronto	AL	OF	28	66	12	15	4	11	2	.227
Seasonal Notation					252	41	57	5	33	8	.228

JOEY MEYER   Age 27/R $2
The Big Kahuna, a 6'5", 260-pound Hawaiian, has been an even bigger disappointment. Sayonara, Joey.

Year	Team	Lg.	Pos.	G	AB	R	H	HR	RBI	SB	BA
1988	Milwaukee	AL	1B	103	327	22	86	11	45	0	.263
1989	Milwaukee	AL	1B	53	147	13	33	7	29	1	.224
Seasonal Notation					492	36	123	18	76	1	.251

RANCE MULLINIKS   Age 34/L $2
Long an unsung Rotisserie hero, Rance had his first disappointing season since 1982 last year. Let's hope the Jays stick with him and not succumb to the Mazzilli temptation.

Year	Team	Lg.	Pos.	G	AB	R	H	HR	RBI	SB	BA
1986	Toronto	AL	3B	117	348	50	90	11	45	1	.259
1987	Toronto	AL	3B	124	332	37	103	11	44	1	.310
1988	Toronto	AL	3B	119	337	49	101	12	48	1	.300
1989	Toronto	AL	3B	103	273	25	65	3	29	0	.238
Seasonal Notation					451	56	125	12	58	1	.278

DAVE PARKER   Age 38/L $10
After watching him flail away in the 1988 World Series like a beached whale, we figured he was indeed washed up. Obviously, he wasn't. But one theory has it that he just wanted to stick around long enough to enjoy Pete Rose's torment. For years, Parker kept telling people what a bad guy Rose was, but nobody would listen.

Year	Team	Lg.	Pos.	G	AB	R	H	HR	RBI	SB	BA
1986	Cincinnati	NL	OF	162	637	89	174	31	116	1	.273
1987	Cincinnati	NL	OF	153	589	77	149	26	97	7	.253
1988	Oakland	AL	OF	101	377	43	97	12	55	0	.257
1989	Oakland	AL	OF	144	553	56	146	22	97	0	.264
Seasonal Notation					623	76	163	26	105	2	.263

KEN PHELPS   Age 35/L $1

Just when is he going to come to bat on a team that already has Parker? Here's some of that inside stuff you've come to expect from our ratings: Phelps looks like Dan Quisenberry's older, bigger brother.

Year	Team	Lg.	Pos.	G	AB	R	H	HR	RBI	SB	BA
1986	Seattle	AL	1B	125	344	69	85	24	64	2	.247
1987	Seattle	AL	1B	120	332	68	86	27	68	1	.259
1988	Seattle	AL	1B	72	190	37	54	14	32	1	.284
1988	New York	AL	1B	45	107	17	24	10	22	0	.224
1989	New York	AL	1B	86	185	26	46	7	29	0	.249
1989	Oakland	AL	1B	11	9	0	1	0	0	0	.111
Seasonal Notation					411	76	104	28	75	1	.254

JIM RICE   Age 37/R $5

He's sticking around to 1) boost his career totals for the Hall of Fame and 2) try to play in the same outfield with Billy Bean and Billy Beane—Bean(e)s and Rice, get it? If you're an old softie for moody has-beens who hit into lots of double plays, then Jim is your kind of player. But not Bostons.

Year	Team	Lg.	Pos.	G	AB	R	H	HR	RBI	SB	BA
1986	Boston	AL	OF	157	618	98	200	20	110	0	.324
1987	Boston	AL	OF	108	404	66	112	13	62	1	.277
1988	Boston	AL	OF	135	485	57	128	15	72	1	.264
1989	Boston	AL	OF	56	209	22	49	3	28	1	.234
Seasonal Notation					609	86	173	18	96	1	.285

LARRY SHEETS   Age 30/L $5

Last year we devoted 14 lines to Sheets. We wasted our time and yours.

Year	Team	Lg.	Pos.	G	AB	R	H	HR	RBI	SB	BA
1986	Baltimore	AL	OF	112	338	42	92	18	60	2	.272
1987	Baltimore	AL	OF	135	469	74	148	31	94	1	.316
1988	Baltimore	AL	OF	136	452	38	104	10	47	1	.230
1989	Baltimore	AL	OF	102	304	33	74	7	33	1	.243
Seasonal Notation					522	62	139	22	78	1	.267

BASEBALL ANAGRAM #7

Harold Baines = Able, or Danish?

PAT TABLER   Age 32/R $5

We all know about Tabler's incredible stats when the bases are loaded. That means that when the bases aren't loaded, he hits about .129.

Year	Team	Lg.	Pos.	G	AB	R	H	HR	RBI	SB	BA
1986	Cleveland	AL	1B	130	473	61	154	6	48	3	.326
1987	Cleveland	AL	1B	151	553	66	170	11	86	5	.307
1988	Cleveland	AL	1B	41	143	16	32	1	17	1	.224
1988	Kansas City	AL	OF	89	301	37	93	1	49	2	.309
1989	Kansas City	AL	OF	123	390	36	101	2	42	0	.259
Seasonal Notation					564	65	166	6	73	3	.296

GARY WARD   Age 36/R $2

A suggestion for ESPN's Chris Berman: Call him Gary (Back) Ward, because that's the direction in which he's headed.

Year	Team	Lg.	Pos.	G	AB	R	H	HR	RBI	SB	BA
1986	Texas	AL	OF	105	380	54	120	5	51	12	.316
1987	New York	AL	OF	146	529	65	131	16	78	9	.248
1988	New York	AL	OF	91	231	26	52	4	24	0	.225
1989	New York	AL	OF	8	17	3	5	0	1	0	.294
1989	Detroit	AL	OF	105	275	24	69	9	29	1	.251
Seasonal Notation					509	61	134	12	65	7	.263

900-226-STAT

Introducing the Official
Rotisserie League Stat Phone!
No more waiting for
tomorrow's box scores!
All the stats you want—NOW!

That's right. Just dial 900-226-STAT and get all the numbers you need for a good night's sleep—or, as the case may be, some particularly vivid nightmares. (Sorry, we can promise up-to-the-minute Rotissestats—how good they are is up to your players.)

Home Runs! RBI! Stolen Bases! Wins! Saves!
Earned Runs! Walks! Hits! Innings Pitched!
Also:
Injury Report, Game Results, and Daily Rotisserie
Analysis featuring the Old Iron Horse,
Glen Waggoner!
Only 95 cents a minute!

900-226-STAT

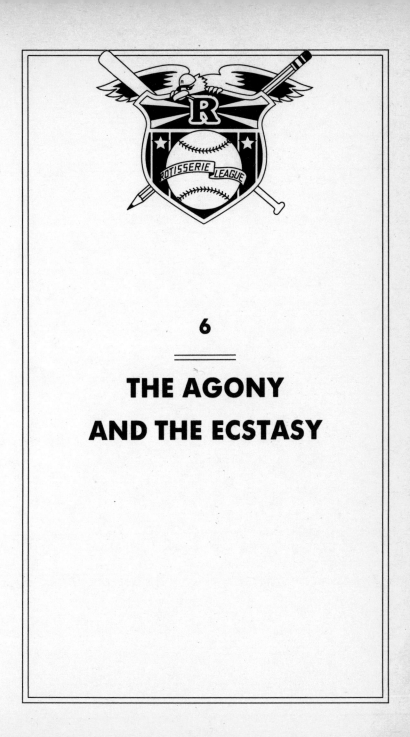

6

THE AGONY
AND THE ECSTASY

Two from the Heart

The Rotisserecipe calls for a heaping cup of fun and a soupcon of necessity. A league secretary might tell you that his (or her) drudgery comes in a 50-gallon pot, but secretaries get to go to spring training, too—somebody has to record all those trades down there—so what are they complaining about? Herewith, tales of woe and joy: groans of distress from Cary Schneider on behalf of League Secretaries everywhere, groans of pleasure from Peter Gethers extolling Florida springtime and some famous smoked fish. —The Editors

The Thankless Job of the League Secretary

A Personal Lament by Cary Schneider, Owner of the Cary Nations

It must have been close to 2 A.M. when the call came. Maybe nearer 3. Whatever, it was the bizarre blend of anxiety and contrition in the voice on the phone that made the moment memorable: "I hope it's not too late, but did I get Oddibe McDowell at $24?"

"Yes, it is. No, you didn't," I replied as brusquely as anyone can from the fringes of REM sleep. "Anyway, you're nearly 12 hours past the deadline." Click.

There it was in a flash: The agony and the ecstasy of a Rotisserie League Secretary. It's a world of post-midnight calls from club executives who ignore both the rules of the game and common civility, balanced by the unquestioned authority to utterly dash a competitor's hopes for the first division.

No one seeks the League Secretariat willingly. It's a responsibility thrust upon us by those for whom the careful, accurate recording of every trade, waiver, and fee looks suspiciously like work. They don't know what they're missing.

A League Secretary understands that he's more than a mere clerk of the game. A League Secretary is, preeminently, the clearinghouse of information. And therein lies his power.

As the first to learn of a trade, he's also the first to perceive a team's newly acquired strengths or weaknesses, recognize a strategic blunder or an inspired masterstroke. He's in a perfect position to provide counsel to the perplexed and sow doubt among the arrogant. Often a Switzerland among warring nations, the Secretary sometimes even wears the aura of integrity.

So why is the Secretary also the league kvetch? Mainly because of everyone else. Let's begin with rules.

Okay, first of all no one knows the rules, or more appropriately, people find a convenient time to forget them. The Chairman of the League Rules Committee is most often the first to have mislaid what he never wrote down in the first place. Given the volume of common law amassed over the last decade, the League Secretary is usually the one asked to settle a rules dispute.

In such instances, the credo of the Secretary is that it's more important to be consistent than correct. This perverse form of justice is most artfully expressed in the dissenting opinions of Eisenberg v. Stein (1984) and Plessy v. Ferguson (1892).

But, given a chance, Rotisserians will do everything in their power to get away with murder.

Take the simplest of all statutes—the transaction deadline. The excuses for calling in after our league's "absolute" 2 P.M. Tuesday deadline usually fall into the 'dog ate my homework' level of wile. How about this one: "I was at Wrigley Field and couldn't get to a phone." At a night game, no less.

But beyond the flaunting of the rulebook is an even more vexing problem for a beleaguered scrivener.

Rotisserians are fond of phoning in complex multi-player deals and letting the Secretary figure out what roster positions to put them in. And when dutifully called back to inquire of their intentions, you receive an annoyed reply: "Just stick DiStefano in the outfield; he's played a couple of games there." Well, he hadn't. Trouble is, it took you a few weeks to find out you'd been duped again, and more paper shuffling to get the offending numbers deleted from the standings report.

Such oversights are compounded when a league enters the mind-expanding world of Rotisserie Ultra.

Remember: Ultra is the game within the game. Playing Ultra means the Secretary has to keep two sets of books—one reporting deals with **Rotisserie League Stats** (see p. 281) involving players who appear or previously appeared on an active roster, and another for recording deals involving active players as well as those on the reserve roster, whose very existence is unknown to the stats service.

This means that should one team send several active players to another in return for minor leaguers and reserves, the transaction sheet would record only the names of the active players. As far as the stats service knows, someone received something for nothing. In the past, such trades usually involved Lee Eisenberg and Michael Pollet.

Another new twist introduced by Ultra is the free-agent auction. This ingenious Ultra concept allows teams to acquire free-agents—players not on active or reserve rosters—through a sealed-bid auction process. Each team is permitted to throw away up to $100 during the season to purchase the likes of Frank Viola or Jeff King. There's a catch, of course. For every free agent acquired, a team must release a player from its active roster.

Now, the conduct of this auction is in the capable hands of the League Secretary, who needs more work like you need Kevin Romine in your outfield. He must receive secret bids from callers, keep them confidential, declare the winners and maintain ongoing financial accounts of the purchases. But unlike the auctioneer at Sothebys, the Secretary has the right to bid along with his competitors.

In the spirit of trust that infuses all league activities, there is a supplementary procedure used just to keep the Secretary honest. The Secretary must submit his bid to a non-bidding team owner prior to the receipt of all other bids. Makes sense. But it does put this paragon of virtue in the position of making up his mind to participate in this foolishness a little sooner than anyone else.

All of which brings us back to Oddibe McDowell. That early morning caller didn't bid enough to win the much coveted Brave in the open market. Instead, he finally picked him up in a trade, in which he probably gave up too much. But at least that was one deadline he managed to meet.

Le Sacre du Printemps de Choo-Choo*
*(The Rite of Spring Training)

A *Cri De Coeur*** from Sudden Pete Gethers, Owner of Pete's Famous Smoked Fish
**(Primordial Screech)

Consider the following. It may be the most important warning you have received since *Caution: Cigarette smoking is hazardous to your health* . . .

YOU CANNOT EVER BE A SERIOUS ROTISSERIE LEAGUE PLAYER UNTIL YOU MAKE YOUR FIRST SPRING TRAINING TRIP!

There. It's out in the open. Most of you should, at this point, drop this book in the trash, burn it, and forget you've ever heard the words "ratio of hits and walks per inning pitched." Sure, you go out and get a subscription to *Baseball America*. Yes, yes, of course you read *Mazeroski* and know Ramon Martinez's recipe for refried beans and Robin Ventura's social security number. Big deal. *Everyone* knows that. Eight-year-old kids who've never even dreamed of owning Tommy Gregg for way too much money could draft a team with that kind of knowledge. Sorry, Charlie. If you want to play with the big boys, you've got to buy a pair of loud pants, get on a plane, and head for a place where, for six weeks in February and March, you can hire Luis Polonia to babysit your kids. Cheap.

Arizona is nice. In fact, it's highly recommended. But Florida is the state to get your baseball blood boiling. You got your Vero Beach. You got your Port St. Lucie. You got your plethora of stadiums, all within a couple of hours drive of each other, all of which allow you to see major league players in settings as cozy as high school parks.

Florida is where all true Rotisserians want to own two-bedroom condominiums. Florida in February and March is Rotisserie League heaven.

And here are the best ways to open those heavenly gates . . .

1. *Hotel Accommodations:* What is this, a travel guide? You're already getting plenty for your money. Cough up the additional bucks for a *Fodor's* and check out a few hotels and motels. Clean sheets and a working air conditioner; beyond

that is unnecessary luxury. The key is to be centrally located, so it's not out of the question to go see the first three innings of the Blue Jays, the next three of the Phillies, and the final three of the Cardinals. It can be done. If you're like me, the first thing you'll do is a buy a map. Then, if you're also like me, the next thing you'll do is hire some 18-year-old blonde girl to read it for you, since who can make sense of all those little lines? *You* try to figure out what's a river and what's a major thoroughfare.

There are plenty of motels around. But remember, you're a Rotisserian and you represent an important segment of society. The Official Spring Training Hotel of the Rotisserie League is a special, secret place revealed only to members of the Rotisserie League Baseball Association, plus a few of my own dearest friends. The rooms are comfortable, the help is nice (some of them even wear tanktops), and there are several bars where, in the evenings, you can sit and discuss the day's observations on whose swing looks good and who looks over-matched. All the drinks, even water, are served with little umbrellas. Class all the way.

2. *Golf:* With age and maturity come a certain desire to broaden one's scope. In years past, it was enough to go to a game, eat a hot dog, go to a disco, strike out trying to pick up a *shiksa*, then go to bed. It still sounds pretty good, doesn't it? But, if you want some *real* fun, stay at a place that has a good golf course and get up a couple of hours earlier. That way you can make yourself suicidally depressed before noon, *then* go to a game, eat a hot dog, etc. etc.

Golf and spring training just seem to go together, like pretzels and beer, like George and Billy, like Harry Stein and body odor.

3. *Food:* This is an absolute necessity. Don't be a hero and try to spend your whole spring training trip without eating. For one thing, you won't have the strength to play golf. For another, the food is pretty good down there.

Avoid fancy places. In fact, don't even bring a tie on this trip, just in case you get tempted to go to a fancy place. There are no good fancy restaurants in Florida. Barbecue is a safe bet. A couple of the older ballparks are located in what are now predominantly black neighborhoods. By those parks, there are some great barbecue stands. There are usually signs, often accompanied by some very helpful directional arrows.

If you can find it, make a bee-line for Peter's Famous Smoked Fish in St. Pete Beach. You won't be disappointed—unless you hate smoked fish. If you *do* hate smoked fish and you go there anyway after reading this, please call me at home. My number's listed. I have some land to sell you in Jersey.

I'm prejudiced, but most of the fish places are good, especially the ones with long wooden tables and signs that say "cold beer." For some reason, the burger/singles bar kind of places are also okay. Look for restaurants with names like Corky's and Hasta La Vista. If they have bouncers who look like they could rip your head off your body and throw it down an alley for a strike, go on in. Order the cheeseburger with raw onion and fries. It'll be fine.

4. *Entertainment:* Once you've seen 18 innings in one day, played a round of bogey golf and fueled up with a few margaritas, what else is left in life? Why, getting your own personal dancer, of course. This seems to be big in this neck of the woods, for some reason, and the Rotisserie League recommends it highly. For a modest fee, you can have a topless woman dance just for you. Somehow, looking at this in the cold glare of black and white print, it doesn't sound nearly as appealing as it is. Trust us. There's a particularly nice joint near the Sarasota airport. You can't miss. Nobody wears any clothes. Mention the name Michael Pollet. But don't tell his wife or little 18-year-old son, who would be heartbroken if they heard or read about this.

5. *Baseball:* This is why you came down here, or have you already forgotten? Don't overdo it, that's our suggestion. Try to limit yourself to one game a day (except once—one day, go to two different parks; you'll feel good about yourself). Get there early. Spring games have got a real following. There are a lot of regulars and tickets are scarce. In fact, if you're able to get tickets before you head down, do so. You'll be happy with that tip. Even if you wind up missing a game or two, the tickets aren't very expensive. So be a sport and save yourself a lot of aggravation.

It doesn't really matter where you sit. The parks are small and intimate for the most part.

As far as judging talent is concerned, your biggest worry is that you're going to know too much. Yes, that's right. We original Rotisserians have learned this the hard way. I remember, quite distinctly, the first time I ever laid eyes on Andy

Van Slyke. Did this boy look like a ballplayer. He was a can't miss. I decided he was going to be worth whatever I had to pay for him. And I paid a lot. Twenty-five smackers, if I recall correctly. As it turned out, he *was* one of those can't-miss players. Unfortunately, he did nothing *but* miss his first two years in the league. Sure, he was good. And sure, a whole bunch of us could pick out his talent. But he was still a rookie. And you're not seeing major league curve balls in spring training games. You're seeing professional pitchers trying to get in shape, trying to throw strikes, trying to loosen up their arms. They're not trying to get guys like a young Andy Van Slyke out. Remember to keep things in perspective. If you spot a hot talent down there, good for you. But don't go overboard on draft day. And don't forget about his talent, either. If he's a bust his rookie year, he'll go for a lot less his second year. You'll look like a genius.

The Five Greatest Moments in Rotisserie Spring Training History

1. *The First (and last) Annual Softball Game:* Great fun and highly, highly recommended if you come down with a bunch of people. There are plenty of public parks and high school fields where you can play. Ask at your hotel; they'll probably be helpful here. Our softball game was particularly memorable for several reasons. First of all, *People* Magazine was doing a story on us and was covering the game. Which means that we all sucked in our guts and tried to play as if we weren't all terrified that we were going to break our noses on the first high pop fly that came our way. The game was a hard-fought battle, memorable for its exciting ending. Unfortunately, no one in the Rotisserie League actually remembers being around for the end. We were all either passed out from exhaustion or visiting the local hospital.

2. *Lee Eisenberg Goes to a Disco:* Unfortunately, the First Furrier's disco days seem to be over now. He is now married and has a new-born son. But there was one night . . . well, let it suffice to say that Lee picked up a girl in tight jeans who turned out to be Larry Bowa's ex-babysitter. If ever there was a combination born to send a Rotisserian's helmeted love soldier a marching. . . .

3. *The Rotisserie League Meets Pete Rose:* Poor Pete. He's certainly got enough troubles, and I certainly don't intend to add to them. But this is a chance to show the man's true gracious and sophisticated character . . .

Through a bit of luck and sleazy influence-peddling, the Rotisserians were given press passes for our first spring training outing. This meant we could actually go on the field during batting practice, which, of course, we did, trying our best to look cool.

This was during Rose's Phillies days and, at a Phils' game, a couple of us wandered over in Rose's direction. He nodded at us. We nodded back. We asked him how it was goin'. He grunted that it was goin' okay. He asked us where we were stayin'. We told him. He asked us if the beef was any good there. We looked at each other, a tad confused. The beef? It was fine, we told him. Though we thought the flounder was probably the best thing on the menu. Pistol Pete shook his head sadly and said the immortal words: "Beef, man! Beef! I'm talkin' about [women]!"

We went back to our rooms, locked the doors, and stayed there until it was time to go back to New York.

4. *The First Official Rotisserie Banquet:* More fun than Margo Adams! It was only the original members, all good friends, and a few valued, invited guests. We had Dave LaPoint as our after dinner speaker (he's gone for at least seven dollars over his actual value every year since), drank cognac on the porch 'til midnight and high fived ourselves silly. Since that rather naive and unsophisticated evening, the banquet has turned into a convention. We now attract over a hundred sycophantic Rotisserians from around the country who come to worship at our feet. Don't worry. We much prefer it that way. After all, new friends can always be gotten . . . check out LaPoint's ERA this past year . . . and cognac gives us all headaches now. Besides, we all get free T-shirts at the convention.

5. *Wait 'til next year* . . . Just like real baseball players and owners, as soon as the World Series ends, Rotisserie Spring Training sojourners begin counting the days, hours and minutes until pitchers and catchers report. Past highlights are forgotten (except for that one trick Glen Waggoner does with the lampshade and his boxer shorts). It's time to turn ahead to the future. To the new discovery . . . to the certainty that you've finally licked the game and have a sure-fire system this

year . . . to seeing the next Bo Jackson knock one out of the stadium and play his way onto a major league roster . . . to the hope that, sometime in the near future, there may actually *be* a fifth highlight so we won't have to cheat you anymore with cheap sentimentalism like this.

WHAT ROTISSERIE LEAGUE BASEBALL HAS BROUGHT TOGETHER, LET NO MAN CAST ASUNDER

(Here, in its romantic entirety, is a letter we received from Mitchell Rosenthal, a team owner in Connie Mack's White Elephant Baseball Federation & Sport Fishing League in New York. We think you'll get just as choked up as we did.)

"At the conclusion of last season I took on a partner for life and Rotisserie. Following the World Series I proposed marriage and co-ownership of my Rotisserie team in the first base dugout of Doubleday Field in Cooperstown, New York.

Despite losing my season-long hold on first place in the second-to-last week of the season (due to a month-long batting slump that lowered my team average five points and relegated me to a second-place finish), she said Yes [*Editor's Note:* What a woman!]

To commemorate our partnership, we donned a new and fitting team name for our seasons ahead. My bride is Barbara Mazza. Henceforth, our team will be known as the Mazza Roskies. Hopefully our team will share the magic Bill Mazeroski's did in 1960 and finish on top. We're certain our marriage will!"

(What a sweet couple of crazy kids! To get them started in Rotisselife together, we're sending along TWO T-shirts and a copy of Dr. Spock!)

7

YEE GADS!
(AND OTHER
GREAT MONICKERS)

How to Play the Name Game

Every so often we get an application for membership in the Rotisserie League Baseball Association from a league with no name. Boy, does that make us sad! Think about it. There's something so doggone low and lonely about a League With No Name, you could almost write a country-western song about it. Makes the whole front office go all whimpery every time we have to send something to a League With No Name.

Nomenclature has been a critical element of Rotisserie League Baseball since way back in 1980, when we named a brand-new game after a quasi-French bistro on Manhattan's fashionable East Side. (And so it is in baseball. Can you imagine how different the game would be if Tinker, Evers, and Chance had been named Smith, Brown, and Jones?)

Okay, so maybe "Rotisserie" wasn't the most intelligent of choices. (Half of America thinks the game was founded at a backyard barbecue; the other half can't even spell it.) And yes, if we had it to do all over again, we might try to think up something that made a little more sense. But you gotta admit it's better than nothing. Can you imagine getting all worked up about something called "No-Name League Baseball," even if it was purported to be "The Greatest Game for Baseball Fans Since Baseball?" Our case rests.

But even more important than a good league name is a great team name. Before you even begin to think about how much you're willing to pay for Kirby Puckett, you should spend quality time coming up with a monicker for his new ballclub. To do less is to shortchange the only bowling ball in the world capable of hitting .340. Birds gotta fly, fish gotta swim, and baseball teams gotta have nicknames.

Not that everyone has gotten the message. There once was a league in Colorado whose teams were named Team One, Team Two, Team Three, and so forth. Real imagination there. The league folded, needless to say, and the last we heard its members had formed a Morton Downey, Jr. study group.

Almost as bad are team owners who don't go further than the major leagues for inspiration. That's like going to the local Pick-n-Pay for pâté de foie gras. Don't look away sheepishly; you know who you are. Tom's Cubs. Dick's White Sox. Harry's Yankees. Ho's Hum.

You can do better than that.

From Day One we followed simple guidelines: The more tortured the pun, the more twisted the link, the more outrageous the reference . . . the better the team name. Starting with your last name as the "city," the idea is to create the most absurd, ridiculous sobriquet you can conceive. If the Commissioner of Major League Baseball had a Rotisserie League team, for instance, it would be the Pealers or the Van Go-Go's. If Michael Jordan had a team, it would be the Errors. (And if Peter Gethers had a team, it would be a miracle.)

Finally, remember this: Bad taste is good in Rotissenomenclature, but be sure to stop just a little this side of obscene. Unless, of course, you think of something dirty that's really, *really* funny.

THE 1990 ROTISSERIE LEAGUE BASEBALL TEAM NAME CONTEST

Each finalist in the 1990 Team Name Contest wins a beautiful, limited edition, designer T-shirt, featuring the fabulous Rotisserie League Baseball logo silkscreened in four bedazzling colors. Impeccably tailored in durable, 100% cotton hand-picked by Harry Stein in them old cotton fields back home. This shirt can be worn proudly anywhere, from bedroom to board room. Virtually indestructible, it will never shrink, stretch, or wrinkle (at least until you unfold it). What's more, this shirt can't be bought in any store (more's the pity)—although we still have a few left for sale by mail: write to **RLBA SHIRTS**, 41 Union Square West, Suite 936, New York, NY 10003 for an order form.

The Grand Prize Winner was selected this year by a distinguished panel of judges with some great names in their own right—Ned Eisenberg, Bo Wulf, Jackson Fleder, Sam Schneider, and Charlie Brenner. You'll learn the lucky winner's name in just a few pages, but first read what he or she will win:

- An Official Rotisserie League T-shirt for every owner in his or her league!
- An official National or American League Baseball autographed by every member of the original Rotisserie League!
- Frozen strawberry daiquiris for two and a double order of fried grouper at a Rotisserie League Baseball Association's Annual Spring Training Scouting Trip!
- An autographed copy of *Baseball by the Rules* (by Glen Waggoner, Kathleen Moloney, and Hugh Howard)!
- A one-year subscription to *Baseball America*, the Rotisserie League owner's best friend!
- An unsigned photograph (suitable for framing) of Willie, the Rotisserie League's Official Dog!
- One hour of free calls to 900-226-STAT, the Official Rotisserie League Stat Phone!
- And more! (Or less, should you decide you don't want any of this stuff!)

THE NOMINEES

1. **ROSEN SPANISH HARLEMS**
   Owner: Mark Rosen
   I Wish Haywood Sullivan Were Red Auerbach League (Massachusetts)
   Future contest participants, take note. If it's got anything remotely to do with Lady Soul, it's a winner in our book.

2. **MURDTER'S ROW**
   Owner: Charlie Murdter
   Samurai League of Washington (District of Columbia)
   You don't want to go into this team's clubhouse after a close loss.

3. **KEITH STONE COPS**
   Owner: Keith Bart
   Louviers League (Delaware)
   For them, a routine double play goes 6-4-7-2-3-9.

4. DELOSH NESS DEMONSTERS
Owner: Jeff DeLosh
Wolverine Baseball League (Michigan)
*It didn't exactly hurt this entry's chances that the wolverine is
BFFCL Dan Okrent's alma mater's mascot. Or that the Starman
and the Iron Horse, editors of the volume you hold in your
hands, used to mold young minds at the University of Michi-
gan, a.k.a. Harvard of the Midwest. Go Blue!*

5. MCDANIEL MCBOONES
Owner: Chip McDaniel
Dallas On-Tap Players Circuit League (Texas)
Not exactly the name he submitted; this one is better.

6. P C COMPATIBLES
Owner: Paul Chandler
Penny Ante League (Vermont)
*Not a "great" name. Not even a very good name. (The CHAN-
DLER HAPPIES at least have a baseball subplot.) But in
submitting his league's nominations, Commissioner Chandler
caught our eye with his observations about his colleagues'
teams. Of CHARLIE'S ANGELS (Owner: Charlie Sargent):
"Could have been SARGENT'S FLEA COLLARS, but we
didn't want to tick him off." Of BIG BO'S BOMBERS (Owner:
Mike Boulerice): "We wanted him to be BOULERICE PUD-
DING, but would he listen?" Having won our heart, he gets a
T-shirt.*

7. RUFOLESS PEOPLE
Owner: Paul Rufo
ORMU Baseball League (Massachusetts)
*They play their home games in the House that Rufo Built.
(Actually, we're even more interested in what ORMU means.
We figured if we gave one of them a prize, they would tell us.
We're waiting.)*

8. BARRYMORES
Owners: Barry Blum and Barry Haft
Miami Downtown League (Florida)
*These guys are lawyers, as are all the other members of this
league. Which explains the relative lack of . . . what do you
call it? Imagination? Creativity? Life?*

9. HANDY WIPES
Owner: Paul Handy
A-Major League (Virginia)
Commissioner Dean A. Hess describes the A-Majors—probably without authority, and we'd sure hate to see him get thrown in the brig for this, so keep it quiet—as "the official Rotisserie League of the United States Army Band." The WIPES make sure all the right brass gets polished.

10. ADAMS SMASHERS
Owner: Frank Adams
A-Major League (Virginia)
You think the Oakland A's have a lot of power?

11. PALER MOWERS
Owner: Adam Palermo
Ten Cities League (California)
Problem is, they play on Astro-Turf.

12. DOUGHTY THOMASES
Owner: Chris Doughty
dataBase Ball League (California)
Tough team to trade with. Very negative.

13. FRENCH TICKLERS
Owner: Doug French
Farrah Fawcett Major League (LA—where else?)
They play Safe Rotisserie, but with a certain joie de vivre. *Games with their arch-rivals, the FUCHS EWES (owned by Ken and Fred Fuchs), can only be seen on local cable after 11:00 P.M.; parental discretion is advised.*

14. TINKER TAYLORS
Owner: Glenn Taylor
Great Lakes Basteballers League (Michigan)
Some guys know how to punch the right buttons: This is our all-time numero-uno favorite TV dramatic series. There's even a move afoot to name Alec Guinness to the Rotisserie League Hall of Fame.

15. MITCH DEMEANORS*
Owner: Mitch Teemley
Pacific Bro's League (California)
Perennial league leaders in stolen bases. They get an asterisk because they're no longer in the league. Which means they get the honor but no shirt. (Sorry, Mitch, wherever you are. You know what they say: No Shirt, No Shoes, No Service.)

THANKS—WE NEEDED THAT!

Remember on *Hollywood Squares* when Peter Marshall, in need of a ruling, would look off-camera and ask, "Jay?" Well, *we* do, which is why we're giving a special Emmy . . . uhh, T-shirt, to Jay Redack, the honest-to-goodness creator of *Hollywood Squares*. Yep, the *creator*. (Imagine! Up until now, we thought that show sprang, fully formed, from the brow of God!)

Jay owns a team in the Farrah Fawcett Major League in LA called *Jay Fred Muggs*. The *Fred* is a pal of his named Fred Rosenberg, but Jay is obviously the brains of the outfit. Not exactly a super team name, but both get T-shirts because of Jay's off-the-field contributions to the game. (Hey, Fred—it pays to hang around with famous guys, right?)

Just one question, Jaybird, baby. What is Phyllis Diller really like?

16. **YEE GADS!**
Owner: Preston Yee
Pacific Bro's League (California)
Also owns a farm team in PETER'S FAMOUS SMOKED FISH minor league system. You guessed it: the PRESTON STURGEONS.

17. **BROWN BAGGERS**
Owner: Tyler Brown
Pacific Bro's League (California)
Simple, strong, what-you-see-is-what-you-get kind of team. Post-game spread? Tuna on white, slice of pickle, apple, and Twinkies.

18. **DAVID'S COPPER FIELDERS**
Owner: David Ginzl
River City American League (Florida)
Worst post-game spread in baseball.

19. **WHITNEY HOUSTONS**
Owner: Shawn Whitney
Desperado League (Michigan)
Players take turns warbling the Star Spangled Banner before gigs.

20. ANDREAS FAULTS
Owner: Andreas Michael Fruhner
Durhamerican League (Ontario)
Will relocate team in a California league as soon as there's an opening.

21. FOREN CORRESPONDENTS
Owner: Keith Foren
Diamond Truckers League (Michigan)
Actually, their real name is FOREIGNER, but we never have liked the band. This name is more grown up. (Hey, nobody ever said we weren't arrogant. It comes with the T-shirt.)

22. DWIRE STRAITS
Owner: Conrad Dwire
Mesquite Rotisserie League (Connecticut)
Now that band, we like.

23. BAILEY'S COMETS
Owner: Dean Bailey
Gaylen's Barbecue League (Texas)
Originally, the IRISH CREAMS before they went on the wagon, the COMETS win a pennant every 76 seasons.

24. CLIFF'S NOTES
Owner: Cliff Holcomb
Ron Hodges Memorial League (Connecticut)
Easiest signs to learn of any team in baseball.

25. HESS STATIONS
Owner: Gary Hess
Delaware Valley Rotisserie Baseball League (New Jersey)
Multi-zillionaire Leon Hess owns, among other things, the New York Jets, an oil company or two, and a string of fillerups on the Eastern Seaboard. Gary Hess is his first-born son and likely heir who, as soon as he comes into his inheritance, has hinted that he will make a sizeable gift to the Rotisserie League Baseball Retirement Home in Clearwater, Florida. That's why we're giving him a T-shirt. It's certainly not for the cleverness of the name.

26. ST. LUCIE BROWNS
Owner: Jeff Brown
Coot Veal League (Florida)
Jeff lives in St. Lucie county about three Strawberry homers from where the Mets spring train. Normally, we don't care

all that much for team names that aren't completely self-explanatory. But for anything evoking Ned Garver's old team, we make an exception.

27. BOSS SOX
Owner: Jim Boss
Green Mountain League (Vermont)
You gotta hand it to Jim. He passed up a lot of opportunities for better names (e.g., BOSS TWEEDS, BOSS SPRING-STEENS, BOSS RULES). But what's a guy to do if he drafts Boggs, Esasky, Burks, and Lee Arthur Smith?

28. DIOIRIO COOKIES
Owner: Ray DiOirio
No Brains—No Pain League (Rhode Island)
Only beverage sold at Cookie Park is milk.

29. EVAN DEADLY SINS
Owner: Evan Smith
Carpetbaggers League (Tennessee)
In constant trouble with the Commissioner's Office, but they seem to have a lot more fun than most teams.

30. GOET ZMARTS
Owner: Carl Goetz
Budville 10 Microleague (Missouri)
In his nominating letter, Carl had the Z where it belongs. But we think it looks more exotic this way. Besides, he wasn't all that sure himself, offering GOETZ LONG LITTLE DOGIES and CARL'S BAD CAVERNS as alternatives if we didn't go all dewy-eyed over GOETZ MARTS/GOET ZMARTS. Pathetic, isn't it—a man who would prostitute his team's name, its most precious possession (next to Pedro Guerrero at $21), for a damned T-shirt. We hope it shrinks three sizes the first time he washes it! (Most of them do.)

31. LEMMEN CHIFFONS
Owner: Murray Lemmen
The General William Dole Eckert Memorial Rotisserie Base-ball League (Michigan)
We added the "S" to honor one of the greatest girl-groups of all-time. Either way, it's a great name. (By the way—and stop us if you've read this in one of our earlier books—we have a very special award in our league that goes each year to the team that finishes dead last. So far, not one single last-place

finisher has deigned to take the Spike Eckert Trophy home from the awards banquet.)

32. BRAUN SCHWEIGERS
Owner: Bill Braun
Rendezvous League (California)
Baloney!

33. HEDLEY LAMARS
Owner: Dick Hedley
Rendezvous League (California)
Hubba!

34. FITZ OF FURY
Owner: Brian Fitzgerald
Mass Pikers League (Massachusetts)
Eeeeeyaaaaa!

35. GOLDEN GERLS
Owners: Hal Goldstein and Mark Gerling
Greater Albany Rotisserie League (New York)
Usually joint ownership does not produce good team nomenclature. This is no exception.

36. KREBS CYCLE
Owners: Steven and Evie Krebs
Bronx River National League (New York)
Remember your biochemistry? Steven and Evie hint—a little smugly, if you want the truth of it—that if you do, you'll know what their name means. We don't. But we're easily intimidated by Science.

37. TOULOUSE JOCKS
Owner: Ted Toulouse
Des Moines Media League (Iowa)
From the nominating letter: "The logo features a skinny, pimply type wearing a baseball cap and nothing else but a huge jock strap around his ankles. Ted is always saying things like, 'my team is going to snap back and go streaking up the standings.' The rest of us just think his team is a bunch of flashers in the pan."

38. CLEFF DWILLERS
Owner: Mike Cleff
Des Moines Media League (Iowa)
Commissioner Randy Speer submitted it as DWELLERS, which

*is not funny; we've changed it to DWILLERS, which is—
barely.*

39. LYNCH MOB
Owner: Andy Lynch
Green Bay Metro Area Rotisserie League (Wisconsin)
*League Commissioner William J. "King Kong" Keller says that
the MOB leader did not make a single move all last season.
We say, string him up!*

40. KINGFISCHERS
Owner: Karl Fischer
Valley League (California)
*Here only because Sudden Pete Gethers (Holy Mackerel of the
SMOKED FISH) insisted. Team logo: "Trade to Live/Live to
Trade." In first place through the All-Star break last season,
the KINGFISCHERS traded their entire pitching staff for a
school of "good young arms." Net result: a 6th place finish.
Another reason why Sudden Pete took such a liking to this
outfit!*

41. HOERR BESIDES
Owner: Robb Hoerr
Labatt's & Balls Rotisserie League (Pennsylvania)
*Worst ground crew in the league—they have to play on artifi-
cial turf (Don't mind our tinkering with the spelling of your
name a little, do you Rob, old podnah? Could have been
worse. We could have changed your name to MONGERS or
something.)*

AND THE WINNER IS . . .

It was a tough call. Our panel of judges labored long and hard. But
finally, just before deadline, they arrived at their decision. The
Evan Deadly Sins took an early lead in the race through bribery
and threats, and the *Lemmen Chiffons* held on to the very end.
But in the end, it was back to a basic food group: The grand-prize
winner in the 1990 Rotisserie League Baseball Team Name Contest
is . . . the *Dioirio Cookies!*

Let's hear it for owner Ray DiOirio! According to Commissioner Jude Plante of the No Brains-No Pain League in Rhode
Island, this is the only good news Ray's had since last year's
auction draft, when he spent $25 for Jack Morris and plummeted
straight to the cellar. He stayed there the whole season.

Congratulations, Ray—your prizes are in the mail! (Just don't hold your breath: 1989 winner Joe Cucci of the *Cucci Coups* is still waiting.) And don't be too upset by your team's performance last year.

Hey, that's the way the *Cookies* crumble.

YER OUT!

"The explanation to this one is more complicated than the others," understated Mike Fenger, secretary of the dataBase Ball League in Oakland, when submitting his own *Humpback Liners* as one of his league's *Team Name Contest* nominations.

"Does it help to know that my nickname is 'Frampton,' that Peter Frampton once had a band called 'Frampton's Camel,' and that the name permitted me to call my newsletter 'Liner Notes,' with a logo including a Humpback Whale? I was afraid that it wouldn't, but it does have some relevance to baseball, especially to a team that has never been in the top five in homers or RBIs."

Sure, Mike . . . uhh, Frampton. Right. Go ahead, take a shirt and leave quietly. And you might want to think about giving somebody a call. You know, get a little help with your problem?

8

KEEPING SCORE

Why You Should Let Us Keep Score

In the RL's rookie season, our Beloved Founder took on the task of compiling official standings. He also wrote the Constitution, called meetings, prepared news releases, made up new rules, met with the press, established a League archive, and finished eighth. That last fact, as Former Commissioner-for-Life Okrent admits, had a direct impact on the first. In the early weeks of the season, when the Fenokees were still in the race, we got stat reports . . . well, if not regularly, at least often enough to know where we stood, what strengths we could trade from, what weaknesses needed shoring up. As his team sank into the swamp, Bogmaster Okrent lost interest in quantifying the decline. From early July until the end of the season, the League had no official standings to guide us— only the "Okrent Unofficials" to monitor our first pennant drive. (Perversely, the Beloved Founder continued to tabulate, as he still does, unofficial standings *each day* from newspaper box scores.)

At the Rotisserie League's winter meetings, team owners voted unanimously to relieve the Beloved Founder of scorekeeping responsibilities the next season. (The vote was 6–4 to terminate with extreme prejudice, but league bylaws require a two-thirds majority.) Sharing the task was briefly considered, but passing the records around is cumbersome, and it still meant that someone would have to devote seven to ten hours per reporting period to get the stats out. So we took the smart way out: we hired someone reliable to do it for us.

Enter Sandra Krempasky, the unsung heroine of the Rotisserie League. A music producer in her other job, Sandra was named Director of Statistical Services of the Rotisserie League (and of the Junior League, whose appreciative owners named their championship trophy after her). Armed only with a calculator and a penchant for perfection, she provided the RL with accurate, neatly organized standings on a regular schedule for three seasons. She did such a terrific job, it's a criminal shame that we fired her.

Rotisserie League Baseball Enters the Computer Age

You may think that you can get by with monthly standings reports, or every other week, or occasionally. You can't. Trust us. The minute you get your first standings report, however you get it, and see your team in third place, but just a couple of homers and one win out of first, you won't be able to sleep until you get your hands on the *next* standings report.

What's really needed are weekly stats, and that's why the Rotisserie League replaced the estimable Sandra and her accurate but unavoidably slow way of keeping score with a computerized method. (Sentimentalists need not fret: Sandra Krempasky was recently voted into the Rotisserie League Hall of Fame, the very first year she was on the ballot.)

As you form your own league and address the issue of keeping score, you will have four options (ranked here from "Worst" to "Best"):

1. Do it yourself.

2. Hire someone to do it for you.

3. Develop your own computer program and put the family computer to a better use than prepping for the SATs or solving math problems.

4. Subscribe to the **Rotisserie League Stats**, the official, authorized stats service of the Rotisserie League Baseball Association. (*Yes, we'll do it for you!*—See box, page 281, for full details.)

The Abacus Method

In an era of pocket calculators and microcomputers, people don't do long division any more. Engineering students don't walk around with slide rules strapped to their hips. Ask a third-grader recently to recite his multiplication tables? Might as well ask him to parse a little Greek verse.

Well, the next ten pages of this chapter are a lesson in long division. We offer it as a public service for two reasons.

First, there may be some kids out there whose allowances won't stretch far enough to cover a stats service *and* baseball cards. Should they be deprived of the glories of Rotisserie League Baseball until they've finished their MBA and knocked back that first mil? No way. With a calculator, a couple of hours of concentration, and these instructions, they can keep their own stats. Be good for them, too: like math homework, only with a point.

The second reason is a bit more arcane. It just seems that it's important, in some obscure philosophical sense, to understand and appreciate the old ways as well as the new. Otherwise, why have Cooperstown?

So, here we go.

STEP 1 is to prepare work sheets for the players and pitchers on your team. (See **EXHIBITS A-1** and **A-2**, pp. 273–274 for model you can use.)

STEP 2: It's late April, and *USA Today* has finally decided that the batters have enough at-bats and the pitchers enough innings pitched to give us their first round of cumulative stats. You take a deep breath, gird your loins, throw back a neat shot the way Randolph Scott always did before a gunfight—and discover that entering the numbers on the work sheets is a snap. (See **EXHIBITS B-1** and **B-2**, pp. 275 and 276).

So, what's the big deal? A few hours of adding, multiplying, and dividing—where's the problem?

Easy does it, rookie. The first reporting period is so easy because there haven't been any player changes to give the scorekeeper grief yet. The players on a team's work sheet are the players a team started with on Auction Draft Day. Any trades, call-ups, or other transactions made in the intervening weeks *do not take effect until the day after the first reporting period ends*. The first reporting period *is* a piece of cake by comparison to what follows.

NOTE: Careful readers of the charts on pp. 275–280, will note that some of the players on the Fenokees have been out of baseball for a while. The same can be said for the team's front office, of course, but in fact the players listed in the next few pages are from the 1983 Fenokees, exactly as listed in our first book. Call us lazy, but Fenokee teams have a certain sameness from year to dreary year. The idea here is to show you how to keep score, not keep you up to date on the Fenokees' sad performances.

STEP 3: Take a look at the difference between the Fenokees' work sheets for Period 1 and Period 7. It's late June, and the picture has become a little more complicated. (See **EXHIBITS C-1** and **C-2**, pp. 277–278). What's happened is that the Swampmen, like any big-league team, have had injuries, call-ups from the free agent pool to replace disabled players, and one activation from their farm system. And, like any good GM who wants to improve his team's chances, Okrent has acquired some new players in trades. This means that he has *pieces* of certain players' years. And this means that whoever keeps score for the league has to keep tabs of those pieces and take them into account when compiling the standings. Attached to each work sheet, then, will be a "Tabulation Sheet of Partial Stats" (**EXHIBITS D-1** and **D-2**, pp. 279–280) that contains the names of players and pitchers who have been with the Fenokees only part of the season, and the numbers for each of them that must be deducted from the cumulative stats carried each week in *USA Today*, or simply carried as part of the Fenokees' total statistics, as with Rick Monday, for example, who was traded away.

Not as tricky as $e = mc^2$, but you will need someone who's careful with numbers.

STEP 4: If you do not prepare a standings report weekly, and if you allow trading, call-ups, waiver moves, and farm-system activity between reporting periods—and you should—it is imperative that scoring records be updated routinely. One reporting period might end July 14 and the next one August 4, but there could be transactions that are effective July 21 and July 28. Appropriate notations (along with numbers to be deducted at the next reporting period) must be made on the backup work sheet.

STEP 5: You've figured or totaled BA, HR, RBI, SB, ERA, Ratio, W, and S for every team, so now you rank the teams in each category from first to last. Assign points accordingly (10 down to 1 for ten-team leagues, 12 down to 1 for those with twelve teams), add up the points each team accumulates in all the categories, and tote up the period's standings.

EXHIBIT A-1

WORK SHEET: PERIOD_____

TEAM:___Okrent Fenokees_____ OWNER:__Dan Okrent___

GAMES THROUGH:_____   *USA TODAY* DATED:_____

PLAYERS

Name	NL Team	AB	H	HR	RBI	SB	Trade/Reserve Status
Totals							BA:

EXHIBIT A-2

TEAM: Okrent Fenokees   OWNER: Dan Okrent

GAMES THROUGH:_____   *USA TODAY* DATED:_____

PITCHERS

Name	NL Team	IP	H	BB	ER	W	S	Trade/Reserve Status
Totals								Ratio: ERA:

EXHIBIT B-1

TEAM: __Okrent Fenokees__   OWNER: __Dan Okrent__

GAMES THROUGH:_____   USA TODAY DATED:_____

PLAYERS

Name	NL Team	AB	H	HR	RBI	SB	Trade/Reserve Status
Foster	NY	50	11	2	4	0	
Monday	LA	4	0	0	0	0	
Horner	ATL	61	14	5	10	0	
Clark	SF	63	12	0	4	1	
Lacy	PITT	64	20	1	3	12	
Sax	LA	69	19	1	7	9	
Virgil	PHIL	5	1	0	0	0	
Scioscia	LA	18	4	0	0	0	
Bergman	SF	14	2	0	0	0	
O'Malley	SF	44	12	0	4	0	
O. Smith	ST L	55	16	0	2	2	
Bowa	CHI	60	15	0	2	0	
Cedeno	CIN	53	19	1	10	2	
Youngblood	SF	24	5	0	2	0	
Totals		584	150	10	48	26	BA: .257

EXHIBIT B-2

TEAM: __Okrent Fenokees_____ OWNER: __Dan Okrent__

GAMES THROUGH:_____   USA TODAY DATED:_____

PITCHERS

Name	NL Team	IP	H	BB	ER	W	S	Trade/Reserve Status
Minton	SF	9	9	9	8	1	3	
Show	SD	29^1	29	10	11	3	0	
Swan	NY	14^2	17	13	11	1	0	
Forsch	ST L	28^2	25	11	11	1	0	
Monge	PHIL	7^1	13	4	3	2	0	
Denny	PHIL	31	27	6	10	2	0	
Ruhle	HOUS	18^1	16	6	5	0	1	
Ownbey	NY	10^2	7	10	6	0	0	
McGraw	PHIL	5	7	0	0	0	0	
Totals		151	150	69	65	10	4	Ratio: 1.45 ERA: 3.87

EXHIBIT C-1

WORK SHEET: PERIOD 7

TEAM: __Okrent Fenokees__   OWNER: __Dan Okrent__

GAMES THROUGH:_____   USA TODAY DATED:_____

PLAYERS

Name	NL Team	AB	H	HR	RBI	SB	Trade/Reserve Status
Foster	NY	305	76	15	45	0	
Monday *	LA	52	11	3	7	0	Trade 6/17
Horner	ATL	271	82	15	51	4	
Clark	SF	311	77	14	45	2	
Lacy	PITT	192	58	4	11	20	
Sax	LA	313	87	4	22	31	
Virgil	PHIL	84	18	3	12	0	
Scioscia *	LA	35	11	1	7	0	Reserve 5/20
Bergman	SF	57	10	1	5	0	
O'Malley *	SF	189	56	2	17	1	Trade 6/17
O. Smith	ST L	292	63	0	24	16	
Bowa	CHI	295	76	2	28	2	
Cedeno *	CIN	134	32	4	17	5	Trade 6/17
Youngblood	SF	157	43	8	20	5	
Strawberry*	NY	69	17	6	20	3	Acquire 6/17
Maldonado*	LA	0	0	0	0	0	Acquire 6/17
Ashford *	NY	0	0	0	0	0	Acquire 6/17; Release 6/24
Roenicke *	LA	48	11	2	7	1	Acquire 6/17
Esasky *	CIN	65	17	4	9	1	Call up 6/24
Bilardello *	CIN	88	22	1	8	0	Call up 5/20
Totals		2957	767	89	355	91	BA: .259

EXHIBIT C-2

WORK SHEET: PERIOD 7

TEAM: __Okrent Fenokees__   OWNER: __Dan Okrent__

GAMES THROUGH:_____   *USA TODAY* DATED:_____

PITCHERS

Name	NL Team	IP	H	BB	ER	W	S	Trade/Reserve Status
Minton	SF	53	59	30	25	2	8	
Show *	SD	86²	80	27	26	7	0	Trade 6/17
Swan	NY	64¹	72	28	36	1	1	
Forsch *	ST L	81	76	26	36	4	0	Trade 6/17
Monge	SD	36²	42	11	13	3	4	
Denny	PHIL	124²	110	36	30	7	0	
Ruhle	HOUS	64	75	24	35	2	1	
Ownbey *	NY	29²	28	20	18	0	0	Release 6/17
McGraw *	PHIL	6	7	0	0	0	0	Trade 5/13
Diaz *	NY	26	19	15	7	1	0	Acquire 5/13
Welsh *	MONT	14	14	8	8	0	0	Acquire 6/17
Reed *	PHIL	16¹	17	4	7	0	0	Acquire 6/17
Hernandez*	PHIL	22	18	6	7	2	3	Acquire 6/17
Totals		621¹	617	235	248	29	17	Ratio: 1.372 ERA: 3.59

EXHIBIT D-1

TABULATION SHEET
FOR PARTIAL STATS

TEAM: __Okrent Fenokees__   OWNER: __Dan Okrent__

PLAYERS

Trans-action date(s)	Name CARRY or DEDUCT	NL Team	Stats apply from – to				
			AB	H	HR	RBI	SB
5/20	Scioscia CARRY	LA	Opening Day–5/19				
			35	11	1	7	0
5/20	Bilardello DEDUCT	Cin	5/20–current				
			–59	–12	–1	–4	–1
6/17	Monday CARRY	LA	Opening Day–6/16				
			52	11	3	7	0
6/17	O'Malley CARRY	SF	Opening Day–6/16				
			189	56	2	17	1
6/17	Cedeno CARRY	Cin	Opening Day–6/16				
			134	32	4	17	5
6/17	Strawberry DEDUCT	NY	6/17–current				
			–118	–22	–3	–12	–6
6/17	Maldonado DEDUCT	LA	6/17–current				
			–20	–3	–0	–1	–0
6/17 & 6/24	Ashford CARRY	NY	6/17–6/23				
			0	0	0	0	0
6/17	Roenicke DEDUCT	LA	6/17–current				
			–95	–21	–0	–5	–2
6/24	Esasky DEDUCT	Cin	6/24–current				
			–19	–7	–0	–1	–1

279

EXHIBIT D-2

TABULATION SHEET
FOR PARTIAL STATS

TEAM: __Okrent Fenokees__   OWNER: __Dan Okrent__

PITCHERS

Trans-action date(s)	Name CARRY or DEDUCT	NL Team	Stats apply from – to IP		H	BB	ER	W	S
5/13	McGraw CARRY	Phil	Opening Day–5/12 6		7	0	0	0	0
5/13	Diaz DEDUCT	NY	5/13–current −16		−19	−5	−6	−1	−0
6/17	Show CARRY	SD	Opening Day–6/16 86^2		80	27	26	7	0
6/17	Forsch CARRY	St L	Opening Day–6/16 81		76	26	36	4	0
6/17	Ownbey CARRY	NY	Opening Day–6/16 29^2		28	20	18	0	0
6/17	Welsh DEDUCT	Mont	6/17–current −14		−14	−8	−8	−0	−0
6/17	Reed DEDUCT	Phil	6/17–current $−16^1$		−17	−4	−7	−0	−0
6/17	Hernandez DEDUCT	Phil	6/17–current −22		−18	−6	−7	−2	−3

LAST STEP: All that's left to do is double check everything, type up the results, prepare a list of transactions since the last period so teams can keep tabs on each other's rosters, make copies of everything, and mail a set of standings and transactions to each owner.

Are we having fun yet?

So there you have it: the old way of keeping score in Rotisserie League Baseball. Still works, too. Just not as well as the new way.

See p. 281 for the *best* way.

Official Rotisserie League Stats Service

The best way to be sure that you get accurate standings reports every week of the season is to subscribe to the official **Rotisserie League Stats**. We compile stats, record transactions, compute standings, and mail a report to your league *the same day* the numbers appear in *USA Today* (Tuesdays for American League teams, Wednesdays for National League). FAX service, too.

For more information about the RLBA Stats Service, including current price, a sample standings report, and an application form: **Rotisserie League Stats**, 41 Union Square West, Suite 936, New York, NY 10003. Telephone: 212-691-7846.

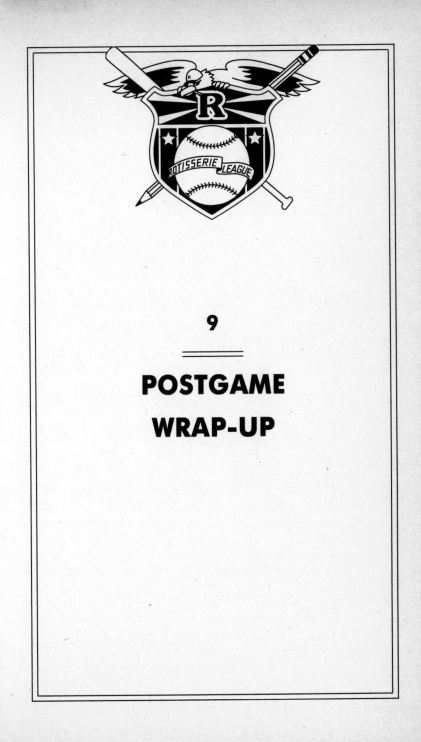

9

POSTGAME
WRAP-UP

The Rotisserie League
Baseball Association

You've collared nine other fanatics, memorized this book, sub-scribed to *Baseball America* and *USA Today*, bought every base-ball mag on the racks, and appointed someone else to work on the logistics of your first Auction Draft Day. What's next? Membership in the Rotisserie League Baseball Association. Join now and beat the Christmas rush. Here's what your new league gets with RLBA membership:

1. A complete, up-to-date, attractively presented Position Eligi-bility List (American or National League).

2. Official Opening-Day rosters (American or National League), compiled by the RLBA's crack research department and mailed to you within forty-eight hours after Opening Day. Includes last-minute disabled-list moves.

3. The right to pay outrageous prices for a complete line of official Rotisserie League products (caps, patches, T-shirts, cars, vacation homes, etc.), all bearing the famous RL logo.

4. Four annual updates, with information on rule changes, new wrinkles, variations on the game, news from other leagues, and other happenings around the RLBA world.

5. A certificate, signed by Beloved Founder and Former Com-missioner-for-Life Okrent, awarded to your league's pennant winner.

6. Commissioner's services, wherein we adjudicate disputes, in-terpret rules, and otherwise maintain law and order.

Here's how to join. Send the name and mailing address of your new league, along with $50 (check or money order only, please; no cash), to: **Rotisserie League Baseball Association**, 41 Union Square West, Suite 936, New York, NY 10003. Or call **212-691-7846** and we'll send you information and an application.

A Yoo-Hoo to Arms

Wrigley Field has Harry Caray singing "Take Me Out to the Ball Game" at the seventh-inning stretch. Fenway Park has the Green Monster. Candlestick has the wind. (And the fog. And the cold.) Not to be outdone, Rotisserie League Baseball has Yoo-Hoo.

The payoff for outsmarting and outlucking your fellow GMs in the Greatest Game for Baseball Fans Since Baseball is a Yoo-Hoo shower, duly administered by the preceding year's champion. Without it, the pennant-winner's check is not negotiable, the victory not official, the season not over.

But what if you live outside the Yoo-Hoo Belt? What are you supposed to do? Rip the kiddos out of school and move to the East Coast?

Don't despair. The game's Founding Fathers, wise and generous to a fault (scored E-FF), got together on Mount Olympus a few months ago for their annual winter meetings and ruled that substitutions are permissible, "so long as they are chosen in the spirit of Yoo-Hoo."

To untangle the legal mumbo jumbo, this means "a regionally indigenous potable—that is, a local brew." Examples: in Detroit and its environs, a bottle of Vernor's . . . in the Lone Star State, a cold Lone Star beer . . . in Maine, a filthy tasting soft drink called Moxie . . . in northern California, a perky little Chardonnay . . . in St. Louis, a Miller Lite (just kidding, Mr. Busch, JUST KID-DING!). Get the pitcher? Sure you do, although a six-ounce bottle will suffice.

Whatever you pour, think of it as Yoo-Hoo—and do your doggone best to be under it!

The following dispatch from Maestro Steve Wulf of the Wulfgang is the way we ended our first three books. It's how we're ending this book. And it's the way we'll end our next book. That's because tradition is everything in Rotisserie League Baseball . . . provided you have cheap relief and plenty of speed to go with it.

Unseen hands hold you, force your head down and pour water, dairy whey, corn sweetener, non-fat milk, sugar, coconut oil, cocoa, sodium caseinate, salt, sodium bicarbonate, dipotassium phosphates, calcium phosphates, guar gum, natural flavors, xanthan gum, vanillin (an artificial flavor), sodium ascorbate, ferric ortho- phosphate, palmitate, niacinamide, vitamin D, and, yes, *riboflavin* all over your hair. The bizarre ritual is a Yoo-Hoo shampoo, and it is what you get for winning the Rotisserie League pennant.

The chocolate-flavored rinse will not leave your locks radiant and soft to the touch, and squirrels will probably follow you around for a day or two. All and all, the ritual is pretty distasteful. But there's not a member of the Rotisserie League who wouldn't gladly suffer the rite so long as it came at the end of a championship season.

Since we traditionally end each Rotisseseason with an out- pouring of the chocolate drink of our youth, we figured we may as well end the book the same way. Besides, as the beverage compa- ny's former executive vice-president for promotions, Lawrence Peter Berra, once noted, or at least we think he noted, "Yoo-Hoo tastes good. And it's good for you, too."

Yoo-Hoo does taste good if your taste buds also happen to be impressed with the nose on strawberry fizzies. To sophisticated palates, Yoo-Hoo tastes a little like the runoff in the gutter outside a Carvel store.

As for Yoo-Hoo being good for you, well, Yogi says he let his kids drink it, and one of them grew up to be the .255-hitting shortstop for the Pittsburgh Pirates. But then, maybe if Dale *hadn't* touched the stuff, he might actually be worth more than the $7 the Fleder Mice paid for him in 1983.

Yoo-Hoo is not unlike the Rotisserie League. Both of them taste good, and both of them are good for you. Just don't tell anybody that. Whenever one of us tries to explain just what the Rotisserie League is, we all get the same kind of look. It's the look one might get from a bartender if one ordered, say, a Kahlua and Yoo-Hoo. The look says, "Aren't you a little too old to be partaking of that stuff?" Our look invariably replies, "But it tastes good, and it's good for you."

Yoo-Hoo's current slogan is, "Yoo-Hoo's Got Life." Catchy, isn't it? But then, Yogi Berra used to be a catchy. The Rotisserie League's got life, too. It enlivens not only box scores, but Kiner's

Korner, as well. Why, the game adds color to every fiber of your being, it gives you a sense of purpose in this crazy, cock-eyed world, it puts a spring in your step and a song in your heart, and it makes you care, deeply care, for your fellow man, especially if your fellow man's name is Biff Pocoroba. So the Rotisserie League is childish, is it? Yoo-Hoo and a bottle of rum, barkeep.

In case you're wondering where Yoo-Hoo comes from, we thought we'd tell you. It comes from Carlstadt, N.J. Yoo-Hoo also goes back to the days of Ruth and Gehrig. It first arrived on the American scene as a fruit drink named after a popular greeting of that day. Founder Natale Olivieri was obsessed with making a stable chocolate drink, and after years of experimentation, he hit upon the idea of heating the chocolate. The rest is soft-drink history.

In the fifties, Yoo-Hoo's Golden Age, the product came to be associated with Yogi. A billboard of Yogi and a bottle of Yoo-Hoo greeted fans in Yankee Stadium. And Yogi wasn't the only Yankee who endorsed Yoo-Hoo—Whitey, Mickey, and the Moose could all be seen on the insides of Yoo-Hoo bottle caps. Nowadays, nobody inhabits the inside of the bottle cap. However, if you turn the cap upside down, it reads, "ooh-ooy," which is Yiddish for Rod Scurry's ERA.

Yoo-Hoo is also like baseball: you don't want to know too much about it. In the interests of this chapter, we sent an envoy out to Yankee Stadium to talk to Yogi. Yes, you've read all those funny Berra quotes over the years, about how it's not over until it's over, and about how nobody goes to that restaurant any more because it's too crowded. To tell you the truth, Yogi is not the man that people suppose him to be. He is actually two different people, depending on his mood. When he is on guard, he is full of monosyllables, and when he is relaxed, he can be genuinely engaging. But the star of "The Hathaways" he is not.

We—actually, it was only one of us, who shall remain nameless, and if *The New Yorker* can do it, why can't we—asked Yogi if he would mind talking about Yoo-Hoo. He said, "Sorry, I can't." This caught us by surprise, but being quick on our tongue, we asked, "You can't?" Yogi said, "Nope. Ask Cerone."

At which point, we approached Rick Cerone, the catcher who took Yogi's place as executive vice-president for promotions. For all their sterling qualities, Berra and Cerone do not strike us as being pillars of the corporate structure, but Yoo-Hoo obviously saw through to their executive talents. We asked Cerone if he would mind talking about Yoo-Hoo. He said, "I can't." This time, we asked, "Why?" and Cerone said, "Because I'm suing them, that's why."

As it turns out, the company has changed hands, and Cerone claims that Yoo-Hoo never paid him for certain appearances. Yogi ran into similar problems, but he settled out of court. So that's why Yoo-Hoo is just like baseball: if you look too closely, it can get ugly on you.

We went back to Yogi and pleaded with him. All we cared about, we said, were the old days of Yoo-Hoo. He warmed to the subject in much the same way Natale Olivieri warmed Yoo-Hoo—slowly. Through his grunts and moans, we determined that Yogi thought Yoo-Hoo tasted good, that his kids drank it, that he wishes he had some money invested in it, and that people still link him with Yoo-Hoo, and vice versa. Then he said, "What's this for, anyway?"

We explained to him about the Rotisserie League and the book. When we said, "Then, at the end of the year, we pour Yoo-Hoo over the head of the winner," Yogi—dripping tobacco juice out of the left side of his mouth—gave us a look of partial disgust and said something like "ooh-ooy."

So, if you decide to take up baseball as played by the Rotisserie League, be warned. People will look at you funny. Pay them no mind. Just pay the treasurer.

We hate long good-byes. When we meet again, perhaps at a theater near you showing "The Rotisserie League Goes to Japan," let's just say, "Yoo-Hoo."

Appendix

SCOUTING
WORKSHEETS

Use the following pages to rank the top
players and pitchers in each category.

PLAYERS

BATTING AVERAGE

1. _____
2. _____
3. _____
4. _____
5. _____
6. _____
7. _____
8. _____
9. _____
10. _____

11. _____
12. _____
13. _____
14. _____
15. _____
16. _____
17. _____
18. _____
19. _____
20. _____

HOME RUNS

1. _____
2. _____
3. _____
4. _____
5. _____
6. _____
7. _____
8. _____
9. _____
10. _____

11. _____
12. _____
13. _____
14. _____
15. _____
16. _____
17. _____
18. _____
19. _____
20. _____

RBI

1. _____
2. _____
3. _____
4. _____
5. _____
6. _____
7. _____
8. _____
9. _____
10. _____

11. _____
12. _____
13. _____
14. _____
15. _____
16. _____
17. _____
18. _____
19. _____
20. _____

STOLEN BASES

1. _____
2. _____
3. _____
4. _____
5. _____
6. _____
7. _____
8. _____
9. _____
10. _____

11. _____
12. _____
13. _____
14. _____
15. _____
16. _____
17. _____
18. _____
19. _____
20. _____

PITCHERS

WINS

1. _____
2. _____
3. _____
4. _____
5. _____
6. _____
7. _____
8. _____
9. _____
10. _____

11. _____
12. _____
13. _____
14. _____
15. _____
16. _____
17. _____
18. _____
19. _____
20. _____

ERA

1. _____
2. _____
3. _____
4. _____
5. _____
6. _____
7. _____
8. _____
9. _____
10. _____

11. _____
12. _____
13. _____
14. _____
15. _____
16. _____
17. _____
18. _____
19. _____
20. _____

RATIO

1. _____	11. _____
2. _____	12. _____
3. _____	13. _____
4. _____	14. _____
5. _____	15. _____
6. _____	16. _____
7. _____	17. _____
8. _____	18. _____
9. _____	19. _____
10. _____	20. _____

SAVES

1. _____	11. _____
2. _____	12. _____
3. _____	13. _____
4. _____	14. _____
5. _____	15. _____
6. _____	16. _____
7. _____	17. _____
8. _____	18. _____
9. _____	19. _____
10. _____	20. _____